THE
BOLEYNS

ABOUT THE AUTHOR

Amanda Harvey Purse is the author of half a dozen books and a historical researcher for London-based museums. She is a member of The Royal Historical Society. Amanda studied the Tudors at the University of Roehampton and is the founder of *Tudor Secrets and Myths*.

PRAISE FOR *THE BOLEYNS*

'*The Boleyns* provides a fascinating summary of the lives of some of the Boleyns' descendants. With adulteresses, soldiers, statesmen, and queens numbered amongst their progeny, it provides a great overview of the later history of a family usually overshadowed by their most famous member.'

ELIZABETH NORTON

'In taking the long view of the Boleyns, this wonderful book offers a genuinely fresh perspective on one of the most famous families in British history. The executioner's sword might have brought Anne's story to a brutal close, but her bloodline would endure far beyond that of Henry VIII and is still part of the royal family today.'

TRACY BORMAN

THE
BOLEYNS
FROM THE TUDORS
TO THE WINDSORS

AMANDA HARVEY PURSE

AMBERLEY

This edition published 2024

Amberley Publishing
The Hill, Stroud
Gloucestershire, GL5 4EP

www.amberley-books.com

Copyright © Amanda Harvey Purse, 2022, 2024

The right of Amanda Harvey Purse to be
identified as the Author of this work has been
asserted in accordance with the Copyright,
Designs and Patents Act 1988.

ISBN 978 1 3981 1961 1 (paperback)
ISBN 978 1 3981 0023 7 (ebook)

British Library Cataloguing in Publication Data.
A catalogue record for this book is available
from the British Library.

1 2 3 4 5 6 7 8 9 10

Typesetting by SJmagic DESIGN SERVICES, India.
Printed in India.

CONTENTS

ACKNOWLEDGEMENTS

This book was a long time in the making. I have been entranced by all things Boleyn ever since visiting Hever Castle as a six-year-old. Although the story of Anne Boleyn has intrigued me for many years, and no doubt many others, it was Mary Boleyn who captured my imagination the most. I would not have been able to complete this task without the help of some very kind people I would like to thank here.

Firstly, I would like to thank Connor Strait and all at Amberley Publishing for allowing me to complete a childhood dream, for your patience, understanding, care, knowledge and time. I am indebted to Dr Owen Emmerson, the Historian and Assistant Curator (but I like to think of as the keeper) of Hever Castle, the childhood home of Anne, George and of course Mary Boleyn. His love for all things Anne Boleyn shines through, so to have him write the foreword means the world to me and I really can't thank him enough. My thanks also go to Elizabeth Griffiths, Natalie Grueninger and Sarah Morris for the use of their family tree, which originally appeared in Grueninger and Morris's excellent *In the Footsteps of Anne Boleyn* (Amberley, 2013).

I would like to thank Roger Evernden for his time and knowledge of the area surrounding St Thomas's church in Kent, and for introducing me to Fiona Woodfield, a local historian. I thank Alison Weir for allowing me to quote her on the subject of the 2020 findings concerning Mary Boleyn's portrait. Thanks to Justin Davis for his time and details of the findings on said portrait. Thank you to all of the staff of St Mary's Church in Warwick for their time, knowledge and care they take over of the tomb of Lettice Knollys, Robert Dudley and their son. Special acknowledgement needs to be given to Mary Adams, the Operations Manager of the church for permitting me to use photographs I took of the tombs and to Tim Clark, a volunteer guide at the church for his very useful input. I would also like to thank Graham Bathe, the author of 'The Seymour Legacy' chapter in the *Book of Bedwyn*, for his detailed information about the will of Frances Seymour. I would also like to thank him and Sue Challen from Great Bedwyn Church for their insights into the last days of Frances Seymour's life, and for permission to include photographs.

I would like to thank Coral De Anne for her opinions on the manuscript and my husband for listening to me go on and on about the Tudors. Finally, I thank my parents; without their love of history, which they have both passed on to me – and their petrol to get me to places in my childhood – I would probably not have found the Boleyns at all.

FOREWORD

Like the accomplished author of this impressive and enlightening book, I, too, became enchanted by the story of the Boleyn family at a young age. That enduring interest was solidified by a trip to Hever Castle in Kent, the place I like to call the Boleyn family 'headquarters'. It is now my privilege to be Castle Historian and Assistant Curator of that magical moated manor, where so much of the Boleyns' story played out. Some of the most significant annals of our history happened between the crenelated walls of Hever when King Henry VIII moved heaven and earth to marry Anne Boleyn. That story, of course, ended with terrible brutality when Anne and her beloved brother George were slaughtered in 1536. The cannons which fired from the Tower of London to signal the untimely end of Henry VIII's second queen consort sounded the death knell of that vibrant and divisive family's time at Hever Castle. And yet, this was far from being the end of the story of the Boleyns. This engaging and edifying book completes the untold and captivating saga of the Boleyns. In most of the histories written about the family, their story ends with the accession of the Boleyn heir, Anne Boleyn's daughter Queen Elizabeth I. The story of Gloriana, the 'Virgin Queen', provides a triumphant encore to her mother's horrific demise, and her reign is held up as the pinnacle of the Boleyns' achievements. With the odds stacked against her, it is not hard to see why this narrative is so dominant: there is more than a feeling of schadenfreude to be found in the reality that Henry's delegitimised daughter triumphed in a way that his much-desired male heir could not. And yet, centuries later, the crown of England would be placed again upon the head of another queen with Boleyn blood flowing through her veins: Queen Elizabeth II.

This timely study allows us to see the Boleyn family's successes and failures through a new lens; one that is not restricted to the triumphs and tragedy of Anne Boleyn, but which recognises the longevity of the heirs of the 'other' Boleyn daughter: Mary Boleyn. Mary is a somewhat mercurial character, often barely visible in the fringes of the source materials which illuminate the lives of her dazzling siblings. However, it was Mary's place in the shadow of the crown that proved to be the most fertile for her family to thrive. This fascinating woman, who defied her family and chose to live in relative obscurity so that she could marry for love, should be recognised – as this study so brilliantly does – as a key player in the ever-fascinating Boleyn saga. By liberating the Boleyns' story from the traditional confines we typically view them in, we can fully understand the impressive trajectory of their accomplishments. In doing so, this study also challenges how we should measure the successes of a family over generations, and on what terms we should do so. It has been an honour to watch this project blossom into such an innovative and revealing book and it has significantly challenged my own perceptions of the Boleyns. It is sure to educate and delight you, too.

Dr Owen Emmerson

The Boleyn Family Tree

Courtesy of Elizabeth Griffiths and adapted by N. Grueninger & S. Morris

Geoffrey Boleyn Gt. of Salle, m. Alice, dau. of Sir John Bracton, descendant of jurist, Henry Bracton
d. 1440

Sir Geoffrey Boleyn, of Blickling, Hever and London m. Anne, dau. Lord Hoo and Hastings of Bedfordshire
1406–63   d. 1484

Children of Sir Geoffrey Boleyn:
- Thomas d. 1471
- Sir William 1451–1505 m. Margaret Butler, dau. 7th Earl of Ormond d. 1540
- Elizabeth m. Henry Heydon of Baconsthorpe
- Alice m. Sir John Fortescue s. & h. Lord Chief Justice
- Isabel m. Sir John Cheyney of Kent
- Cecily d. young
- Simon d. young

Children of Sir William Boleyn:
- Sir Thomas 1477–1539 m. Elizabeth Howard, dau. of 2nd Duke of Norfolk d. 1538
- John Anthony both d. young
- William d. 1552
- Sir James 1493–1561 m. Elizabeth Wood of East Barsham d.s.p.
- Sir Edward m. Anne, dau. Sir Robert Tempest — daughters
- Anne — Anne m. Sir Jo. Shelton of Shelton — issue
- Jane m. Sir Ph. Calthorpe of Norwich — daughters
- Alice 1487–1538 m. Sir Robert Clere of Ornesby
- Margaret m. Sir John Sackville of Sussex — Earls of Dorset

Children of Sir Thomas Boleyn:
- Mary c.1500–43 m. William Carey — issue
- George c.1504–36 m. Jane, dau. Sir Henry Parker d.s.p.
- Anne c.1501–36 m. HENRY VIII 1509–47 — ELIZABETH I 1558–1603

Descendants of Alice Boleyn / Sir Robert Clere:
- Sir John Clere, d. 1529 m. Anne, dau. of Sir Thomas Tirrells of Gipping
- Sir Edward Clere m. Frances, dau. of Sir Richard Fulmerston
- Sir Edward Clere, d. 1606 m. 1. Margaret, dau. of Wm. Yaxley of Suffolk m. 2. Agnes, widow of Sir Christopher Heydon
- Sir Henry Clere, d. 1622

Introduction

THE EARLY BOLEYNS

It has been suggested that the surname 'Boleyn' was originally pronounced as Boulogne, owing to the idea of a French origin for the family.[1] However, it seems this French connection may not be true, or at least had been forgotten by the late 1200s. This was when John Boleyn of Salle in Norfolk first appears on the register of Walsingham Abbey.[2] There is a possibility that this John Boleyn had a father called 'Simon de Boleyne' who bought lands in the same village of Salle in Norfolk in 1252, and that he had a brother called William Boleyn of Thurning.[3]

In 1318, another Boleyn appears in the village of Salle, his name was Nicholas and things do not seem to have gone well for him. In 1318 he was accused of theft and accused of it again in 1333.[4] In the same year, he was ordered to repair the banks between his and the Lord of Salle's fields by the county court after he had damaged them, as well as pastures and trees, while farming.

In the Court Rolls documents, a register of land holdings, we find an Emma Boleyn in 1337. It has been suggested that this Boleyn might be the widow of a second John Boleyn, who had passed away in 1369.[5] This is perhaps the first recorded Boleyn lady, so it is sad that nothing more is known of her to date.

There was a Thomas Boleyn who married Agnes in 1398.[6] Sadly, Agnes was also impossible to find in other records, however, we come across Thomas her husband almost fifteen years earlier in 1386, when he was mentioned in Richard Anabille of Salle's will.[7] Agnes and Thomas seem to have had one son, Geoffrey Boleyn.

Thomas was a wealthy man by 1399 as he was able to pass on some of his lands in Salle to his son by then. This we know because this action saw Thomas summoned to court as he did not ask permission to pass his lands over before doing so; a transgression that Mary Boleyn would repeat.[8]

A visitor came to the village of Salle in the Georgian period and when they entered the local church they made a note of an inscription they found there. One of the church's windows was dedicated to a 'Thomas Boleyn'.[9] Perhaps this was the same Thomas Boleyn, as the church was built around the time that this particular Thomas lived in the village and he may well have had enough money to donate to the church's window. This Thomas Boleyn passed away in 1411 and knowing this date, we can be fairly sure that it was his son, Geoffrey, who made the family name of Boleyn known in Norfolk.

Geoffrey Boleyn: Great-Great-Grandfather of Mary, Anne and George

Geoffrey seems to have been a builder of some sort, as in 1408 he and six other men were brought before the court for entering a lord's manor and taking timber to be used on the same church that may have had a window dedicated to his father.[10] Four years later, Geoffrey was up in front of the court again. This time it was for ploughing over a border line to extend his own lands.[11] Geoffrey claimed a lot of land in the village of Salle and in the neighbouring area which he farmed. He did not always pay for his lands up front, often leaving it until the last possible moment to hand over the money.[12] Ultimately, by the time of his death in 1440, Geoffrey Boleyn was a very wealthy man, eclipsing his father's prosperity. Although Geoffrey owned much land, he still did not quite make it to being a lord. While he was not a lord of the village of Salle, there is a memorial brass inside the village's church dedicated to him, paid for by his wife who outlived him. This brass is quite impressive and is situated in the middle aisle of the church. It represents the beginning of the rise to prominence of the Boleyn family in Norfolk.

There is a suggestion that Alice Boleyn, Geoffrey's wife, was the daughter of Sir John Bracton of Bracton, although this has not been proved as the evidence doesn't completely match up with other records.[13] Alice had her own connections to the church in the village of Salle, as she made gifts of tapestry work to the church over her lifetime.[14]

Geoffrey Boleyn's memorial brass was for his family members too. From it we get an idea of how Alice wanted to be remembered, as it was a depiction of her own choosing. Alice and Geoffrey are standing side by side, their clothing suggesting a fashionable and powerful couple. The inscription reads: 'Here lies Geoffrey Boleyn, who deed [sic] 25th March 1440 and Alice his wife and their children, on whose souls may God have mercy. Amen'. If we accept that this is the beginning of the Boleyns as a family unit, immortalised in brass, we can speculate as to whether these depictions are true likenesses. The truth of the resemblance to the sitter of portraits of later Boleyn members has been questioned in modern years.

The same Georgian visitor who visited the church in Salle and made a note of the church's window also made a note of this brass memorial. They mention being able to see all of Geoffrey and Alice's children, five sons and four daughters. This is interesting as only four sons are known to us today. Perhaps the other son had passed away at a young age and before he could make a name for himself.

In the same church as Geoffrey and his family's memorial brass there was a separate memorial brass dedicated to a Simon Boleyn. Simon's will does not mention a Geoffrey or an Alice, but he does mention a Thomas of Gunthorp. Geoffrey and Alice did have a child called Thomas, so we might think that Simon was referring to him. However, the couple's Thomas later becomes a priest and would not have been able to have children, whereas this Simon's 'Thomas' does have children.[15] This, plus the fact that no other connection between the Boleyn family and the Gunthorp family in Geoffrey and Alice's direct family line has been found, suggest that this Simon was perhaps an uncle or a great uncle to Geoffrey, or there was no direct family connection at all.

As well as a son called Thomas Boleyn, sometimes written as 'Bullen', Geoffrey and Alice also had sons called William and John. The names of the daughters of Geoffrey and Alice we are less sure about. This is mainly because Boleyn was actually quite a common surname in this area of England and at this time. The only name we can be sure of is Cecily. We know this because the couple also have another son, named after the father, Geoffrey Junior. This Geoffrey becomes important to the story when focusing on Cecily; when this Geoffrey buys a manor that becomes well-known in the tale of the later Boleyns, he takes his then unmarried sister Cecily to live with him. We know of this because there is a brass memorial in the church next door to Blickling Manor that describes Cecily as his sister. This place was important to the Boleyn family for many reasons but is most famous for being the suggested birthplace of three siblings, Mary, Anne and George Boleyn.

It is believed that Cecily Boleyn was born in 1407 or 1408; this would have made her the youngest of the known children of Geoffrey Senior and his wife. This also indicates that Thomas was the oldest and Geoffrey Junior the second child. Cecily was buried in the church near Blickling Manor and her memorial brass depicts a woman praying in a simple pleated dress with full sleeves. The inscription states:

Here lieth Cecily Boleyn, sister of Geoffrey Boleyn, Lord of the Manor of Blickling, which Cecily, deceased in her maidenhood, of age O L [(fifty years old at the time of death] the XXVI

[twenty sixth] day of June of our Lord MCCCC VIII [1458] whose
Soul God pardon. Amen.

Cecily's brother Thomas later becomes a priest. In 1463 Thomas
had to prove he was the son of Geoffrey Senior so that he could
claim on one of Geoffrey's estates, the manor of Calthorpe. As
odd as this court case was, the fact that Thomas won it does
confirm that Thomas was a son of Geoffrey and Alice.[16] Thomas
studied at Cambridge where he was later made Seventh Master
of Gonville Hall in 1454. Thomas was ordained as a deacon
in March 1421, becoming a priest later on in the same year.[17]
He never forgot his Cambridge roots as he donated a window in
the Old Dining Hall there.

Thomas was indubitably making a name for himself in certain
circles. Thomas was asked by the King of England himself to
attend the Council of Basle in Switzerland, held by the Roman
Catholic Church to discuss the Papal Supremacy and the Hussite
Heresy, the teachings of the religious reformer Jan Hus who was
condemned by the Council of Constance (1414-18) and burned
at the stake. Thomas was again chosen by Henry VI to help the
drafting in of the Queen's College at Cambridge in 1446. These
two appointments made by the king show us once again that the
Boleyn family were gaining status at this point. Thomas's career
had taken him a long way from his family background of farming
in Norfolk.

Geoffrey Boleyn: Great-Grandfather of Mary, Anne and George

Thomas's younger brother Geoffrey, Lord of Blickling Hall,
transformed the Boleyn family status by becoming a lord of the
manor, something his predecessors never managed to do. Geoffrey
married twice, first to a lady called Dionise, sometimes spelt

as Denise. There is a lack of information about her, apart from
the fact that she was mentioned in her ex-husband's will, so she
outlived her ex-husband and maintained a good relationship with
him after the break-up of their marriage.

Geoffrey married again to Anne Hoo, who was said to have
come from nobility. Geoffrey had already taken a step away from
the family background by setting himself up in the capital of
London. He was apprenticed as a hatter but concentrated his
efforts in mercery.[18] The records for 1435 show that Geoffrey
was by then fairly successful because he was able to employ two
people to work for him, a Mr Robert Hastings and a Mr William
Brampton.[19] In 1449, Geoffrey became a Member of Parliament
for the city of London[20] and amazingly, just two years later, he
was one of five men that lent Henry VI the vast sum of £1,246 to
help fund the war against the French.[21]

In 1457 Geoffrey was made Mayor of London.[22] This role
ultimately placed him in high social circles, mixing with barons
and chief justices at special occasions. Of course, this new
'famous' Boleyn caught the eye and we can imagine it was while
he was at one of these special occasions that he came into contact
with Anne Hoo, the daughter of Lord Thomas Hoo. Geoffrey was
twenty years older than his new wife, who was born in 1425[23]
and she had been married before but was widowed at the age of
fifteen.[24] Anne's father was made Lord Hoo and Hastings in 1448
by Henry VI. He had already been made a Knight of the Garter.
He served the king as Chancellor of France for thirteen years.[25]
So Geoffrey had married into an influential family and gained a
connection with the King of England himself.

Geoffrey and Anne had five children: Thomas, William, Isabel,
Anne and Alice. Around 1452 Geoffrey started discussions for the
purchase of the lands and manor of Blickling in Norfolk from Sir
John Falstoff.[26] Geoffrey passed away in 1463 and although he

had bought Blickling Hall Manor in Norfolk, he had originally hoped to be buried in St Lawrence Church in London as it was, and still is, the official church of the Lord Mayor of London, situated next to the Guildhall in the City of London. Geoffrey was organised when it came to his passing, going into a lot of detail as to how he would like to be buried, even with a backup plan. If he couldn't be buried in London, then the church in Blickling would do. He asked for his body to be buried with black candles that had been carried alongside his body by people of the poorest households in the area. He left his wife a wealthy woman and gave each of his children three hundred marks.[27]

Anne Hoo Boleyn looked after her children and the estates after the death of her husband until her own death in 1485. She was buried in Norwich Cathedral, at one stage her remains being moved to another part of the cathedral. Her eldest son Thomas died young in April 1471 after gaining his father's manor for only a few years. This passed the manor of Blickling over to his younger brother William.

William Boleyn: Grandfather to Mary, Anne and George Boleyn

William Boleyn married Margaret Butler around 1475. For William, it was an impressive match. Margaret Butler's parentage has been debated over the years. Her father has been suggested as being Thomas Butler the 7th Earl of Ormond, or his older brother John Butler the 6th Earl.[28] The will of Thomas Butler refers to his daughters as 'Dame Anne St Leger', Margaret's sister, and 'Dame Margaret Boleyn, late wife of Sir William Boleyn', which would seem to settle the debate.[29] In her father's will, Margaret receives a bed of tapestry work and a great old carpet.[30] Margaret's family has Irish roots going back to the time of King Edward I.[31] Not only was Margaret's father the Earl of Ormond but he was also the grandson of Lord Bergavenny and Margaret's grandmother was the daughter of the Earl of Shrewsbury. All this made Margaret a very good match for William Boleyn.

Margaret and William had six children who survived into adulthood. The three sons were named Thomas, John and William Junior. William Junior becomes a priest, and he is the Archdeacon of Winchester before passing away. The surviving daughters were Anne, Alice and Margaret. The oldest, Anne, married Sir John Shelton, making her the 'Lady Shelton' we see within later records of the royal family. In 1533 Lady Shelton was placed in charge of the household of Henry VIII's daughter, the Lady Mary.[32] It has been suggested that Lady Shelton was very harsh towards Mary when she would not accept the marriage of her father and Anne Boleyn.[33] Lady Shelton was one of the ladies that was sent to serve Queen Anne Boleyn when she was sent to the Tower of London.

William and Margaret's daughter Jane died in early childhood as did an older daughter also named Anne and sons called Anthony and John. All these children are believed to be buried at Blickling Church in Norfolk.[34]

William Senior became a Knight of the Bath in 1483 at the coronation of Richard III, William was then appointed the third Baron of the Exchequer, a role that meant he could move away from Blickling. He chose the county of Kent as he had owned Hever Castle since 1479.[35] Although William had moved down to Kent permanently, he still kept his ties with Norfolk, being appointed Commissioner of the Peace there in 1483 and again two years later. He was also the Sheriff of Norfolk and Sheriff of Kent.[36]

Thomas Boleyn: Father to Mary, Anne and George
Margaret had a close relationship with her eldest son Thomas, something that continued in later life as we can see by looking

into Thomas's account books. Thomas paid nine shillings and eight pence for fur to be added to his mother's gowns in 1526, a gift from son to mother.[37] Margaret would later live with her son at Hever Castle and be there when he died. She was to stay within Hever Castle until her own death in the same year. She was ninety years of age when she passed away, passing the estate she owned at Rochford Hall to her granddaughter Mary Boleyn, the then Lady Stafford.

Thomas had another powerful woman in his life, his wife. Thomas, like the early members of his family, chose well. He married Elizabeth Howard, scion of a powerful family residing in Norfolk. The Howard family's background can be traced to Sir William Howard, a lawyer. King Edward I appointed him one of the Chief Justices of Common Pleas.[38] The family carried on improving its status and increasing landholdings through the years, gaining the title of Duke of Norfolk through marriage. John Howard fought at the Battle of Towton, as did the Fogges, a family that has its own connections to the Boleyn family, which will be discussed later. John Howard appeared at the coronation of King Edward IV in 1461 when he was appointed to the role of Carver. He would be treated well by the king and his queen, Elizabeth Woodville. We know this because the queen gave John seven yards of green velvet for one of his gowns.[39] The gifts from the king kept coming, and John was made a lord. His accounts show us that John was a very wealthy man, spending money on entertainments and expensive foodstuffs.[40]

Elizabeth's father, Thomas Howard, was a leading man in the Tudor Court. He was the 2nd Duke of Norfolk and would become the Earl of Surrey. He fought bravely and was wounded at the Battle of Barnet that ultimately helped to restore King Edward IV to the throne.[41] The Howard family maintained their power by cultivating their links to the sovereign, and when Thomas married Elizabeth Howard, he shared in some of that power.

Elizabeth probably spent her childhood with her mother, while her father was fighting battles in other countries and certainly by 1490 she was residing with her mother and brothers at their Sheriff Hutton Castle in Yorkshire.[42] As her two brothers seemed to have gained a good education, it would also seem likely that Elizabeth would have had, if not the same level of education, then at least a good grounding; she was certainly able to speak French very well. This, we can imagine, made her stand out to Thomas Boleyn, who was also fluent in languages. Sadly, the date of their marriage has not been found in records to date, although it has been suggested that it happened between 1495 and 1499 because in the records for those years, Elizabeth was given a 'life interest in the Boleyn lands in Sussex and Norfolk as well as Hever'.[43]

In 1498, possibly at the time when Thomas Boleyn and Elizabeth Howard married, Henry VII visited Norfolk. The records states that a 'Mr Boleyn' greeted the king at Blickling Hall; 'Mr', not 'Sir', so it was Thomas rather than his father who was the host for King Henry.[44] The king's visit was seen as a mark of respect to the Boleyn family. It was also a sign of how far the Boleyn family had come.

It is not often mentioned that at the time of his marriage to Elizabeth, Thomas was not a rich man. He had only fifty pounds a year to live on and if you think that the prominence of him marrying a Howard would have instantly changed Thomas's fortunes, this was actually not the case. Elizabeth did not receive her settlement from her father until a few years into her marriage to Thomas.[45] Although lacking in funds, Thomas endeavoured to be noticed at court. Luckily, Thomas was a good jouster. This brought him to the attention of the future King, Henry VIII. This we know because when Thomas was knighted, it was at a very important moment for Henry, Thomas was knighted at King Henry's coronation in 1509.

Thomas would continue to be involved in ceremonials in the role of courtier. Thomas had previously been a part of the royal escort for the wedding of Princess Margaret Tudor, the king's sister, in 1503. Thomas was twenty-six years old at the time of her wedding when he travelled to Scotland as a part of her escort. One wonders what he made of his trip? What he made of the Palace of Holyrood, where the Princess married? Would it have seemed so very different from the London palaces that Thomas would have known? One also wonders what the young Thomas thought of King James IV of Scotland, the groom, when he caught a glimpse of him for the first time.

Two years later, Thomas's father died. One wonders how this affected Thomas. Maybe to get over the grief and pain he was feeling, he threw himself into the details of his father's funeral – he was the principal organiser. Thomas had strict rules to follow; his father wished to be buried with his mother and Thomas's grandmother at Norwich Cathedral. This has led some to believe that Thomas's parents did not get on, but in reality, all this can tell us is that Thomas's father felt very close to his mother, or possibly valued his connection to Norfolk highly. Thomas was given a large piece of new tapestry and the manors of Calthrop, Mulbarton, Wykemere and the manor house in which he and his family were living at the time of his father's death, Blickling Hall.

At the age of twenty-eight Thomas was the head of his own family, and now, with the death of his father, the head of the Boleyn clan. Thomas was given Hever Castle in 1505. This castle would become the childhood home of his children, who would become the most famous of the Boleyns, so we should learn a little more about it. The oldest part of the castle was built in 1270, the gatehouse and a walled bailey surrounded by a moat with a wooden drawbridge. When the Boleyns took over the place two hundred years later, they made a Tudor dwelling to fit inside its protective walls.[46] In what is now the dining room there are decorative locks upon the doors. One is a copy, but the other is considered the original that Henry VIII had installed. This might seem odd, but for the king's safety, whenever he travelled he would have his personal locksmith make him his own locks to be applied to the doors of the rooms in which he stayed.[47] There is some debate as to whether Henry actually stayed at Hever Castle. There is a room within Hever Castle called King Henry VIII's Bedroom, however, there doesn't seem to be much to support the idea that Henry actually stayed there, other than the lock. What makes the suggestion questionable is the fact that at the time when Henry had an interest in both Mary and Anne Boleyn, he owned Penshurst Palace. This was only four miles away from Hever Castle, a short ride away. The king could have stayed in his palace whenever he wanted to see the Boleyns.

At the end of what is now the Morning Room is a set of spiral stairs that lead into what was once suggested to be Anne Boleyn's childhood bedroom. The staircase unusually spirals in an anti-clockwise fashion. On this level is the Staircase Gallery, which was designed by Thomas to connect the main house to the Long Gallery that Thomas built a year after he and his family moved in, in 1506.[48] The windows along the Staircase Gallery were designed and bought by Thomas, too. In the Tudor period to have glass made for you was a very expensive undertaking and a show of wealth. Some of the nobility even travelled with their glass to show off their wealth elsewhere, leaving the members of staff that were left behind to suffer the draught.

Looking around Hever Castle today, set in the beautiful Kentish countryside, it seems obvious why Thomas chose to move his family to this place. However, the choice probably had more to do with Thomas's position in the English court than aesthetics or comfort, as his role often took him to France, and Hever Castle was situated conveniently between the court in London and the port of Dover.

When Henry VII was coming to the end of his reign, Thomas appears in the records as a 'Yeomen of the Crown', which meant he was within the royal household and rising to a station that no other Boleyn had reached before.[49] Thomas was even one of the men at Henry VII's funeral.[50] At Henry VIII's coronation, Thomas was made a Knight of the Bath. He would have been wearing his 'blue long gown with hood'[51] on 23 June 1509 when Henry and his future queen proceeded through the streets of London on the eve of their coronation.

It is difficult to be sure of how Thomas looked because there is no definite, proven portrait of him. There is a purported portrait at Hever Castle displayed in the room that was once said to be Anne Boleyn's bedroom, but there are doubts whether this is truly him or whether it was of James Butler, the 9th Earl of Ormond. We must read between the lines of records and documents to see if we can come up with some idea. We do know that at the age of thirty-four, Thomas was part of a four-day knightly combat in which the athletic Henry VIII, Charles Brandon and Edward Howard participated.[52] This indicates that Thomas was fit enough to keep up with the younger generation of courtiers.

It could be easy to think that Thomas only got close to the king because of Henry's pursuit of Thomas's two daughters. In reality, Thomas was close to the king years before either romance started. For example, Thomas was at the celebrations for the king's first-born child, Prince Henry.[53] We also know that when this child passed away on 22 February 1511, Thomas was there to share the grief and carry the tiny coffin in Westminster Abbey.[54]

At four a.m. on 18 February 1517, King Henry and Katherine of Aragon welcomed into the world their daughter, Princess Mary, at Greenwich. A week later at the child's christening Thomas Boleyn attended the celebrations. This was the second royal christening Thomas had been invited to, proving how far the family name of Boleyn had come and that Thomas was important within his own right to the king, before the king's eyes fell upon his daughters.[55]

Although both Elizabeth and Thomas were members of court in the early years of their marriage, it would seem they were separate most of the time, with Thomas being an ambassador abroad.[56] Thomas was known for his charming personality, a trait the king used to calm the waters in other countries. It was a family trait that was passed on to his daughter Anne Boleyn.[57] Thomas became a well-known ambassador for the king, developing amity with the King of France and his family, which often came in handy to allay the tensions that often appeared between England and France at the time. Thomas's efforts on behalf of the king were very much appreciated. We know this because the king gave Thomas and Elizabeth their own manor in Norfolk as a thank you.[58] In 1513, Thomas returned from his political duties abroad, only to join the king's army and fight in France.[59] Thomas was appointed Lord Privy Seal in 1530, slowly stepping away from his role as ambassador and allowing his son to try to step into that role. He did not hold on to the Privy Seal for long upon the downfall of his daughter Anne, Thomas escaped with his life but without his status.[60]

Thomas Boleyn lies as a guardian of his family home at Hever Castle at the entrance, inside the church of St Peter. He is interred in the Boleyn Chapel in a large chest that has a brass effigy placed on top. There is a copy of this brass among the Hever Castle displays. Thomas is displayed in his knightly robes and resting on his head is a coronet. To his right is a symbol of his family, a sign two of his children, George and Anne, would use, a falcon. The falcon is wrapped around oak leaves with a braided cord. Thomas stands on a Gryphon that has its claws fully outstretched. Thomas's tomb within St Peter's Church was made from Purbeck marble, which today is worn down. As you look around St Peter's Church you can see that Thomas's tomb is not the only representation of the Boleyn family. Above the rector's seat is the Boleyn family coat of arms within a stained-glass window. This is a replica and is not something the Boleyns themselves would have seen. Although Thomas's tomb may well be the main attraction to the church for many tourists who visit the Castle, Thomas was buried near his second son, who did not reach adulthood, Henry Boleyn. That father and son are together within a small space at the entrance of their family home has a peaceful, poignant feel.

Elizabeth and Thomas had five children in total that are known to us today. Two died young, Thomas and Henry. There is a memorial brass at Penshurst Church dedicated to the young Thomas Boleyn. Upon this brass the date of Thomas's death is supposed to have been recorded, 1520, suggesting that Thomas had reached adulthood by the time of his passing. However, when I visited, I could not find this date on the brass. The overall feel of the memorial brass was that it was to remember a child rather than an adult. The brass remembering Henry Boleyn has a similar feel.

This leaves three children, Mary, Anne and George. Their dates of birth are unrecorded; however, we can use other documents to suggest dates. For example, George Cavendish, a biographer of Cardinal Worsley, wrote about George Boleyn 'years thrice nine my life had passed away' when he was a part of the Privy Council. This was in 1529 so that could suggest that George was born in 1502.[61] Anne's date of birth ranges from 1501 to 1507 depending on which source you wish to accept. This means Anne could be older or younger than her brother. Historian William Camden states Anne was born in 1507.[62] This would make Anne just six years old when she went to serve Margaret of Austria in the Netherlands. This would normally have been deemed too young to leave one's family to go into service in the Tudor period. This tends to suggest that she was born closer to 1501 than 1507. This is corroborated by a letter Anne wrote to her father in the early part of the 1500s, in which she stated her handwriting had not developed yet, but she was still able to communicate in French.[63] Anne would later state that she had lost her youth waiting to be queen, suggesting she was in her later twenties or early thirties when she became one, rather than her early twenties.

Hever Castle today uses the words 'the childhood home of Anne Boleyn' to advertise itself and although I can't help but think that this was also the childhood home of George, Mary and quite possibly Mary's children too, I do realise this is a careful choice of words. This is because Mary, George and Anne might not have been born at Hever but at Blickling Hall instead. As Thomas and Elizabeth do not move their young family to Hever until 1505, it does suggest that all the children were already born before the move.

If we look at the early records of Henry VIII's reign, there is a 'Lady Boleyn' at court, tasked with observing Queen Anne when she had fallen from grace and a 'Lady Boleyn' who was involved in finding out about Lady Margaret Douglas's relationship with Thomas Howard in 1536.[64] However, there are a few candidates for those missions. There are three 'Lady Boleyns' it could have been: Elizabeth Howard Boleyn, the wife of Thomas, Elizabeth Wood Boleyn, and Anne Tempest Boleyn, all sisters-in-law.

For a long time, it was accepted that this 'Lady Boleyn' was Elizabeth Howard Boleyn. This was mainly because of Elizabeth's standing in court. However, in recent years this idea has been debated. So, let us look at the evidence to see if we can find a clue to direct us to an answer. Elizabeth Howard Boleyn becomes the Countess of Wiltshire from 1536, so this now makes it questionable that any mention of a Lady Boleyn after 1536 would mean Elizabeth. One problem is that records from Katherine of Aragon's household are limited. These records would have given us a more in-depth look at the ladies within court at the time.

Elizabeth Wood Boleyn was the wife of Thomas's younger brother, James Boleyn. She was one of four daughters of John and Margaret Wood of East Barsham in Norfolk.[65] After Elizabeth's marriage to James Boleyn, they lived together at Blickling Manor. In 1512, Elizabeth's sister Anne came to visit them. We know that she died there because Anne has a memorial brass inside Blickling Church. The brass shows Anne dressed in the normal Tudor style of clothing for a pregnant woman, she is also holding two babies, twins. It therefore may be that while Anne was visiting her sister, she was pregnant and unexpectedly went into labour and did not survive giving birth; and that the children did not survive either and were buried with their mother.

Anne's grave shows us that Elizabeth had married James Boleyn by 1512 at the latest. Knowing this and knowing which Boleyn she married means she was not the 'Lady Boleyn' mentioned at the outset. This is because James Boleyn was not knighted until 1516, so his wife, if mentioned in the early records, would be 'Mistress' Boleyn rather than 'Lady' Boleyn. She could have been the 'Lady Boleyn' mentioned in later records during the king's reign, when Anne Boleyn was arrested and taken to the Tower of London.

Although this may seem a kind act from the king, showing the love he once had for Anne Boleyn by allowing her family members to be near her in her last days, this was not the case. The king had chosen people from her own family that did not like her, making Anne feel even more alone at the end. The ladies were under strict instructions never to speak to Anne in the Tower without Lady Kingston being there to record the conversations, and they were to repeat everything Anne said while in her cell back to the king.

Elizabeth Wood Boleyn could have been one of the ladies that followed Anne out on to the scaffold in the Tower of London and she may have been one of those who helped undress Anne after she had been beheaded and wrapped her remains in cloth for her burial. She may have even helped to carry the wooden chest – apparently an elm trunk that had been used to store arrows – to the chapel within the Tower of London for Anne to be buried under the altar.

When Thomas Boleyn, the father of Anne, Mary and George died, the Boleyn estate should have passed to his younger brother and Elizabeth Wood Boleyn's husband, James Boleyn. With that should have come the title of Earl of Wiltshire from his brother. This did not happen. Instead when Jane Parker Boleyn, wife of George Boleyn, was beheaded alongside Queen Catherine Howard, James Boleyn was given all the possessions of Jane's that she had left at Blickling Manor, making both he and his wife, Elizabeth very wealthy indeed. They were to have one child together named Elizabeth Boleyn in 1547. James died in 1561.[66]

This leaves us with the two other candidates, Elizabeth Howard Boleyn and Anne Tempest Boleyn. Anne was married to Thomas Boleyn's other younger brother, Sir Edward Boleyn and when we look into her own family tree, we find that the Tempest family was as old a clan as the Boleyn family. For example, in the fourteenth century, there was a Sir Richard Tempest who was Lord of Bracewell and Waddington.[67] Their family had a turbulent past; Richard's wife was abducted in 1385 from Roxburgh Castle by the Scots and his son, Sir Piers Tempest, fought at Agincourt with Henry V. Then there is Sir Pier's son, Sir John Tempest, who was one of the knights who helped King Henry VI in the 1460s when the king became a fugitive after being dethroned. We can connect the Tempest family to the royal bloodline as well. Sir John's son, Robert Tempest, married Catherine Wells, daughter of Leo, Lord Wells. Her uncle was John Wells, the half-brother of Margaret Beaufort, the mother of Henry VII. John himself had married Cecily of York, daughter to King Edward IV and sister to Elizabeth of York Henry VII's wife. It is from Robert's and Catherine's marriage that we can follow the family line to get to Anne Tempest, as they were Anne's grandparents.

When Anne married Sir Edward Boleyn, it really was an important and powerful match for both families. The date of their marriage is not known, which does not help us when we are trying to discover if Anne would have been 'Lady Boleyn', however, we find a clue when looking at Anne's age. By Tudor standards, a twelve-year-old bride would have been considered as a minor and unlikely to have married. Anne's twelfth birthday would have happened around the years of 1517 or 1518. This means that Anne Tempest Boleyn would have been too young and unmarried when a 'Lady Boleyn' was being mentioned in the records in the early part of Henry VIII's reign. This then, tends to lean towards Elizabeth Howard Boleyn being the 'Lady Boleyn' that was first mentioned.

With this now in mind, it was likely that it was Elizabeth Howard Boleyn who attended the coronation of Henry VIII and Queen Katherine in 1509.[68] It would also be likely that when 'Lady Boleyn' was mentioned within the queen's household, this was Elizabeth Howard Boleyn. If so, we can assume that in 1513 it was Elizabeth Howard Boleyn to whom the king gave a New Year's gift of a cup with gilt covering, weighting sixteen and a half ounces.[69] We also know that being within court at this time, Elizabeth would have been able to spend some time with her niece-in-law, Anne Shelton.[70]

The Howard family, of which Elizabeth would have been classed as still being part of, even though she had married a Boleyn, set themselves firmly by the side of Henry VIII when Elizabeth's father won at the Battle of Flodden Field against the Scots, the battle in which King James IV of Scotland lost his life. Elizabeth herself was ensconced by the side of Queen Katherine of Aragon as well, as she would be one of the ladies travelling with the king and queen to Calais to the Field of the Cloth of Gold in 1520. (Though in truth, pretty much all of the nobility of England were part of the royal entourage.)

The Field of the Cloth of Gold was a tournament held from 7 to 24 June, attended by Henry VIII and Francis I of France, meant to display a bond of friendship between the two kings after the Anglo-French treaty of 1514. As friendly as this event should have been, both kings were highly competitive and tried to outshine each other, with large, colourful tents and splendid attire, enormous amounts of food and drink, and music.

Elizabeth Howard Boleyn did not survive her time at the English court without a stain upon her name. There was a rumour that she was one of Henry's early mistresses. This will not seem hard to believe for any historian who knows the king's proclivity for making mistresses of maids in his queen's service. This was certainly what Elizabeth was within the early part of King Henry VIII's reign, we know that she was in the service of Queen Katherine, being often without her husband. If she was a mistress to the king, then mother and daughters shared the king's bed.

Did it happen, or was this just a piece of court gossip? Looking through the records, we find in 1533 that Mistress Amadas stated:

My lady Anne (Boleyn) should be burned for she is a harlot, that Master Norris was bawd between the King and her; that the King kept both the mother and daughter and that my lord of Wiltshire [Thomas] was bawd both to his wife and two daughters.[71]

This would seem very damning against Elizabeth, but we may have to look deeper into the reason behind the condemnation. Mistress Elizabeth Amadas was related, albeit through marriage, to the king's most famous mistress, Elizabeth Blount. She had given the king a son and it was thought at the time of this statement that the family may have hoped the king would marry Blount to legitimise his long-awaited and much needed son. It is worth noting this when looking back at her statement.[72]

Mistress Amadas was not the only one to have mentioned the rumour. Friar Peto was recorded as making a similar claim a year before, in 1532. There is also an interesting letter written by Sir George Throckmorton. In it he remembers his attempt to persuade the king not to marry Anne Boleyn. He dared to tell the king that 'It is thought you have meddled both with the mother and sister.' The king was apparently caught off-guard and quickly replied 'Never with the mother', four little words that have gone down in history as indicating Mary Boleyn was a mistress of Henry before his relationship with her sister, Anne.[73] As easy as it is to dismiss this as being just a piece of worthless court gossip, the fact that this rumour survived into the reign of Queen Elizabeth I, Elizabeth Howard Boleyn's granddaughter, in a statement made by the Jesuit writer Nicholas Sander,[74] begs the question, how strong was this rumour to have survived for so long? Can there be smoke without fire? However, we must be wary of Nicholas as a source. Nicholas's statements are sometimes deemed fanciful, even outrageous. For example, he suggested that Anne Boleyn was actually Henry's daughter.

We will probably never know the truth of whether Elizabeth Howard Boleyn was a mistress of the king, but the fact that so many people seemed to know the word on the street at the time and after, does suggest that it was possible. Maybe the king was seen flirting with Elizabeth on more than one occasion while they were both at court? But perhaps that was all it was? Flirtation or something more, one cannot help but wonder how Elizabeth felt when the king paid the same attention not just to one of her daughters, but both.

Elizabeth passed away in April 1538. She had been staying near Baynard's Castle.[75] Her body was taken by barge along the Thames to Lambeth, where she was buried. The barge was lit with torches and had four black banners covering it. She was buried in the Howard's Chapel within St Mary's Church.[76] This is an interesting resting place for Elizabeth, as her husband would later be buried at Hever, so it could seem that Elizabeth in her final moments chose the family Howard over the family she had married into, Boleyn. Perhaps it was not her choice. The Howards who died in the capital were all buried in their chapel at St Mary's Church, Lambeth, and the tradition may have been too strong to ignore.

When I visited the church, I was told by a volunteer at the Garden Museum the church has now become that because of the Victorian redesign, it is now impossible to know the whereabouts of Elizabeth's remains or if her body was one that had been moved since that redesign. This is a little sad, for not only was Elizabeth a link between two powerful Tudor families but she was also the mother to a queen of England, and grandmother to another who was possibly named after her. She is not the only Boleyn lost in this way.

QUEEN ANNE AND SECOND VISCOUNT OF ROCHFORD, GEORGE BOLEYN

Anne Boleyn

There has always been an air of mystery surrounding Anne Boleyn. The fact that she was an archetype of the 'other woman' is part of it, but that mystery and allure does not come solely from circumstance, it is innate.

The mystery starts from birth. Firstly, we do not know the exact year of her birth, this was not recorded, so the date must be estimated from other information; for example, the usual age at which a young lady would have entered service. Secondly, Anne's paternity has been questioned. This may be because Anne looked very different from her sister, Mary. Mary was said to have looked like her mother, Elizabeth, with blonde hair and light skin. Her beauty was acknowledged in the English court, as was her mother's. It certainly seemed that in this period, gentleman preferred blondes.

So far as we can tell, Anne was not blonde, she was dark-haired and her skin was not pale, she stood out in the English court. The personalities of the two sisters were very different too, suggesting to some that Anne was not a true Boleyn. Sander, who wrote a report on Anne, stated, 'Anne Boleyn was the daughter to Sir Thomas Boleyn's wife; I say his wife because she could not have been the daughter of Sir Thomas, for she was born during his absence of two years in France on the King's affairs.'[1] He even recounts that Thomas had asked who the father was after being told of the news and was told to ask no more, because the real father was a lot further up the social ladder than he was. 'The child Anne was the daughter of none other than Henry VIII.'[2]

There was no evidence to suggest that Sir Thomas Boleyn doubted that Anne was his daughter. Even if we take the latest suggested date for Anne's birth, this would only have made the then Prince Henry sixteen years old, a time when he was in the care of his over-protective father, still grieving the death of Prince Arthur, his eldest son. It is doubtful that the young Henry would have been allowed to have a relationship with Elizabeth Howard Boleyn, a married woman. However, as discussed earlier, a liaison at some stage cannot be ruled out.

William Camden writes in his history of Queen Elizabeth I that Anne was born in 1507.[3] The early seventeenth-century *Life of Jane Dormer*, an account of the lady in waiting to the Lady Mary, suggests the same date.[4] However, this would make Anne just six years old when she left England and went into service with Margaret of Austria, an unusually young age. The earlier suggested date for her birth of 1501 would suit Anne's timeline a great deal better. This puts Anne in the middle of her two surviving siblings, Mary and George.

It is often stated that Mary Boleyn was better looking than her sister – which is of course no more than a matter of opinion – but as so often with Anne, things are not simple. Anne may have been born with 'deformities'. She had a large mole on her neck that she took pains to hide, and apparently a sixth finger on one hand, which she covered with a long sleeve. George Wyatt wrote in his *Life of Queen Anne*; 'There was found, indeed upon the side of her nail upon one of her fingers, some little show of a nail, which yet was so small.'[5]

In 1513, Anne was sent to the Brussels court of Margaret of Austria. If she had been born in 1501, Anne would have been twelve years old. She must have been filled with excitement and feeling proud to have been chosen over her sister, who was quite possibly older than her, perhaps because of the intelligence she had already shown at her young age. She must have also felt anxious and fearful of failing in her duties.

Her new mistress, Margaret of Austria, was the only child of the Emperor Maximilian I and Mary of Burgundy. She was raised to be the wife of Charles VIII from a young age; however, she was rejected by Charles, who married the heiress to Brittany, Anne. She was then quickly shipped off to Spain to marry Ferdinand II of Aragon and Isabella I of Castile's son, John, Prince of Asturias. He was the older brother of Katherine of Aragon. This marriage was short-lived as her husband died at a young age, Margaret was then married off for the final time to Philibert II, Duke of Savoy and when he also died early, she did not wish to marry again. All this made her a very powerful and rich dowager by 1513, when Anne Boleyn came into her service. What effect did this have on the young Anne Boleyn? What did she take away from her experience with Margaret of Austria?

In a letter that Margaret wrote to Anne's father Thomas, she praised his clever young daughter: 'I find her of such good address and so pleasing in her youthful age that I am more beholden to you for having sent her to me than you are to me.'[6] This shows that Anne made a good impression quickly, and her father could congratulate himself on having made a good choice over which daughter to send. It gives us some idea of Anne's personality at a young age. Anne may well not have been considered the prettiest in the room at court, but she could still hold the attention of everyone in it with her wit and intelligence.

Anne had her father's gift for learning languages and when Henry VIII's sister, Mary Tudor, married the French King Louis XII, Anne was placed in the service of this new Queen of France in 1514. This would have reunited Anne with her sister Mary, who was also in Mary Tudor's household at the time. After the death of Louis, when Mary Tudor married again, most of her ladies in waiting travelled back with her to England. Anne, however, perhaps again because of her skills and intelligence, stayed in France and was welcomed into the service of another new Queen of France, Queen Claude. Anne would stay in her service for the next seven years.

Queen Claude was just fifteen years old when her husband Francis I came to the throne after the death of Louis XII. Throughout her marriage, she was overshadowed by her husband's mother, Louise of Savoy and her sister-in-law Marguerite of Angouleme. She had to cope with yearly pregnancies and sadly died young. Francis I had married and taken his wife's titles at the behest of his father and although he seemed to show his wife respect in public, he did not do the same in private. He had a reputation for chasing other women in his court.

Seigneur de Brantôme wrote of Francis, that he would be happy to look upon a beautiful woman, a fine horse and handsome hound: 'For casting his gaze now to one, now on the other and presently on the third, he would never be a weary ... having there three things most pleasant to look upon and admire and so exercising his eyes right agreeably.'[7] With a reputation such as Francis's, it is perhaps not surprising that both Anne and Mary were rumoured to have been his mistresses. Sander would later write of Anne being known at the French court as 'the English mare, because of her shameful behaviour; and then the royal mule, when she became acquainted with the King of France'.[8] It would seem that the writer may have confused the Boleyn sisters, as later the King of France would refer to Mary Boleyn as a great prostitute and infamous above all.[9]

When Mary was sent home owing to her behaviour at the French court, it allowed Anne some space to gain experience and to make a name for herself on her own. She would have learned some needlework, a pastime for any young lady at court, although it would be suggested later that Anne's needlework was lacking compared to that of her predecessor, Katherine of Aragon. She would have also learned to play the lute, how to sing and dance. Anne would surely have met people who changed her views on life while within the French court; people such as King Francis's sister, Marguerite of Angouleme, who was known for her reformist views. This may have been where Anne first formed her own views on religion.

Anne probably attended the Field of the Cloth of Gold. Although Anne was not mentioned by name in the records, it would have been odd if she wasn't there, as she was one of Queen Claude's ladies. This would have given her a chance to see her mother, father and sister again. She may have used this opportunity to show her family how well she had developed, without their guidance. It is a wonder that powerful men such as her father, Sir Thomas Boleyn and her uncle, the Duke of Norfolk, allowed Anne to play the role she had designed for herself later on in her life, when it could and eventually did affect them greatly. Perhaps seeing Anne in this new light at the Field of the Cloth of Gold may have persuaded her family to allow Anne to take control of the situation after King Henry VIII showed an interest in her.

This would have also been the moment when Anne would have seen her future husband, perhaps for the first time. What did she think of him? Was she intrigued by him? In 1520, Henry was in his prime. He could speak French, Latin and even a little Italian. It was said that he sang well and played instruments such as the lute and the harpsichord. He was also an athlete, a formidable jousting opponent and skilled with the bow. It would be hard for Anne to miss the King of England at this point.

Anne's time in France was coming to an end. In 1522, Anne returned to England on the orders of her father. Almost straight away she was pushed into the household of Queen Katherine of Aragon. Anne would have certainly felt the stark differences between the French court, where she had spent the last nine years of her life, and the English court she now found herself in.

There was another reason why Anne was called back to England and that was to settle her marriage to James Butler. This was actually an idea of Cardinal Wolsey's. So the Cardinal was not only involved later in Anne's life, stopping a relationship she has with Henry Percy, as is commonly known. He was also involved in setting up a marriage for her to a man she had never met. Women born into nobility would often not have a choice of husband, arranged marriages were the norm. However, Anne Boleyn was not a normal Tudor lady. She had a mind of her own and knew what she wanted, and she would not have appreciated a man telling her who she should marry, still less one from outside her own family. The marriage would have meant leaving the French court, where she was popular and well respected. In England, Anne would have to start building up her reputation again, and she would have known that her sister Mary was prominent at the English court at this time. 'This is Lady Anne Boleyn, Mary Boleyn's sister' is not the introduction a woman like Anne would enjoy.

Anne is often described as holding a grudge against Cardinal Wolsey because of his actions in preventing her marriage to Henry Percy. This grudge was said to have stayed with Anne even after she had attracted Henry's attentions. Her anger towards the Cardinal has been interpreted as proof that Anne really did love Percy. However, with the proposed marriage of Anne and James

Butler now being known as having been designed by the Cardinal before Anne's relationship with Henry Percy, we can speculate that the enmity, if it existed, actually started earlier than was thought.

In 1515 the Earl of Ormond died. He was Anne Boleyn's great-grandfather on her father's side. With this family connection, Thomas Boleyn thought he was eligible for the title and ownership of the lands of his grandfather; however, his cousin, Sir Piers Butler, declared himself Earl of Ormond and took the lands in Ireland for himself. This angered Thomas, who went straight to the king to claim his right to this title. The king was reluctant to offend the powerful Butler family, so the king had asked Cardinal Wolsey to sort the problem out without upsetting either clan. When the Cardinal discovered through Anne's uncle, the Earl of Surrey, that Thomas Boleyn had a daughter called Anne and Sir Piers had a son called James, he thought the answer to this problem would be for them to marry.[10]

Wolsey had not allowed for the extent of the ambitions of the Boleyns, both father and daughter. Anne sought to delay the marriage for as long as she could, and her father helped her in this matter. He was not happy with the title he felt was his going to the offspring of his daughter. The delaying tactics worked and by May 1523, the marriage had simply faded away. By then, Anne had already set her sights on somebody else.[11]

As much as the English court must have seemed different to Anne, so Anne seemed very different from the other ladies at the English court. The sixteenth-century biographer George Wyatt wrote of her:

> She was taken at a time to have a beauty not so whitely as clear and fresh above all we may esteem, which appeared much more excellent by her favour passing sweet and cheerful and these

both also increased by her noble presence of shape and fashion, representing both mildness and majesty more than can be expressed.[12]

Although Anne was meant to have married James Butler, after a few months of her arrival in England she had set her sights on a bigger catch, Henry Percy, heir to the title of Earl of Northumberland.[13] Anne and Percy's relationship has been portrayed as being one of unconditional love on his part, as Anne was of lower status to him, while Anne's feelings for him were less sure. Anne thought herself worthy of more than her peers, certainly more than what her sister had made for herself. Although the fact she was angry with Cardinal Wolsey when he broke this relationship up might suggest some feelings for Henry Percy, it may be that the anger was due more to her not getting her own way and losing the status she would have gained, rather than any romantic feelings for Percy.

It seems that Anne wasn't satisfied with seeing Wolsey banished from court later on in her life. When Wolsey was sent to the Tower of London, it was none other than Henry Percy the king sent to take him there in 1530. There were people the king could have asked who were more suited to the task and we can speculate that it was Anne's doing, she wanting to remind the Cardinal of his meddling, and that she now had the king's ear, not him. (To squeeze the metaphor to within an inch of its life, the Cardinal was a red rag to a bull.) Henry Percy would be a part of Anne's life until her death. He was actually at her trial in 1536 and had to leave early as he was unable to cope with what was happening to her.

Anne and Percy's relationship reached the ears of the king at a time when the king had no real interest in Anne, but he was angry that this match was developing without his permission. So it was actually the king who had asked Wolsey to stop it. The Boleyns were a powerful family, but not powerful enough to have one of their daughters marry the son of the Earl of Northumberland. Percy was instead forced into marrying Mary Talbot and Anne was sent to Hever in disgrace. Did Anne ever find out that Wolsey was actually following the orders of her future husband, the king?

We can only guess what Anne thought of returning to her childhood home of Hever Castle. Did she start to hate the place because of the reason she was there? Was it like a prison to her, when all she wanted was to be back in the court, where she could feel special, where she felt she had some control? If this was so, it was the opposite to how her sister Mary felt about the castle. She often returned to it when wanting to disappear from court, and she brought up her children there.

Anne was allowed to return to court and the queen's household in 1521. Within moments of her arrival, another admirer was paying her attention. This time it was Sir Thomas Wyatt, a poet and courtier, he would have known Anne through their fathers, both owning lands in Kent and both being made Knights of the Bath at the same time at King Henry's coronation in 1509. Being neighbours of a sort, perhaps the affection between the pair actually started when Anne was banished from court and returned to Hever.

Thomas Wyatt was born to Anne Skinner and Sir Henry Wyatt in 1503, in Allington Castle, Kent. He was known to be tall, being over six feet, handsome and physically strong. He was also a poet and ambassador within the king's service, Thomas Wyatt was an important man at court owing to his friendship with the king.[14] Thomas went to Rome with John Russell, Earl of Bedford, to help annul the king's marriage to Katherine of Aragon. It is suggested that while travelling, Thomas was captured by the armies of Emperor Charles V. He managed to escape and make his way back to England. Thomas was knighted and appointed High Sheriff of Kent in 1536.[15]

Thomas had a closer relationship with the Boleyn family than being a neighbour, a friend or an admirer of one of their daughters – he actually married into the family. Thomas married Elizabeth Brooke, the daughter of Thomas Brooke, Baron of Cobham and Dorothy Heydon. Dorothy was daughter of Sir Henry Heydon who married a daughter of Sir Geoffrey Boleyn. As well as Thomas's wife Elizabeth being a relation, albeit loosely, of Anne Boleyn, she would also later be mentioned as a candidate for Henry VIII's sixth wife, as her name appeared in Spanish dispatches as a lady the king took an interest in.[16]

By 1521, Thomas and Elizabeth have their one child, Sir Thomas Wyatt the younger, who would become famous after the death of his father. He led what became known as Wyatt's Rebellion against Queen Mary I, in response to the queen's choice of a Spanish husband, Philip. Thomas Wyatt the younger gained public support in Maidstone, Kent, close to the castle where he was born and lived when not at court. By the time Thomas and his supporters had reached London, the tide of emotion had turned against them, making it impossible for Thomas and his rebels to cross the Thames at London Bridge. Thomas did, however, manage to cross the river at Kingston and once across, fought against the inhabitants of Ludgate and lost. Thomas surrendered and was executed on 11 April 1554. It has been suggested that through torture, Thomas proclaimed that Princess Elizabeth, Anne Boleyn's daughter and half-sister to Queen Mary I, knew about the rebellion. This caused Elizabeth to be sent to the Tower of London on charges of treason, a prisoner of her own half-sister facing death, and aware that her mother never left the place when she had entered it under similar circumstances. Eventually, Thomas claimed on the scaffold that the princess was not involved and because there was no other evidence against her, Princess Elizabeth was released from the Tower and placed under house arrest at Woodstock.

This rebellion also caused the death of Lady Jane Grey. Before the rebellion, Jane was a prisoner within the Tower that Queen Mary did not know what to do with, as a previous queen of England. The rebellion almost certainly had nothing to do with her, but it highlighted the threat Jane was to the Tudor throne and so she was executed.

Thomas Wyatt the elder admired the work of Geoffrey Chaucer, author of *The Canterbury Tales*, something reflected in his own works. His poems hint at his flirtation with Anne Boleyn. He wrote about a mistress called Anna: 'And now I follow the coals that quent / from Dover to Calais with willing mind.'[17] This could refer to Anne's trip to France with King Henry before her marriage to him. Wyatt accompanied Anne and the king to Calais in 1532.

In May 1536, Thomas was in fact imprisoned in the Tower of London for allegedly committing adultery with Anne Boleyn.[18] He would have witnessed the execution of the other accused – Henry Norris, Sir Francis Weston, Mark Smeaton, William Brereton and George Boleyn, Anne Boleyn's own brother – from his prison cell window in the Tower. The trauma stayed with him forever and he wrote the poem *Innocentia Veritas Viat Fides* about the experience. Each verse ends with the Latin phrase circa Regna tonat, which translates as 'Thunder rolls around the throne'. Thomas managed to survive either through his own friendship with Thomas Cromwell, or his father's friendship with him.

In a poem of 1530, Wyatt declares his love for an 'unknown' woman. The first letter of each line spells out SHELTUN (sic). Mary Shelton was Anne Boleyn's first cousin, who rejected Thomas's advances. Thomas Wyatt died on 11 October 1542, at the young age of thirty-seven and was buried at Sherborne Abbey in Devon.

Thomas's suggested flirtation with Anne came at a time when Thomas was unhappily married. The fact that he was married would have allowed Anne to flirt with him knowing nothing would ever happen, and perhaps this took her mind off the loss of Henry Percy. Anne was clearly attractive to men at court and so perhaps she was more of a beauty than we first have been led to believe. Anne was arguably the whole package, combining wit, intelligence, learning, fashion and beauty. The fact that the king's friend, Thomas Wyatt was attracted to Anne would have helped to focus the king's attention on her. Henry VIII loved the chase, and he loved to win.

In a playful manner Thomas appears to have stolen a jewel from Anne. She had tried to get it back without success. Later, the king took a ring from Anne and wore it on his little finger, we can assume she didn't try to stop him. Now she had the problem of two men with items belonging to her that could be seen as love tokens. A few days later the king was losing a game of bowls with Thomas, but although he was losing he said to Thomas, 'Wyatt I tell thee it is mine,' pointing to the bowls with his finger that had Anne's ring on it. Thomas replied with a certain bravura, 'If it may like your majesty to give me leave to measure it, the distance between the bowls, I hope it will be mine,' showing the jewel he had taken from Anne. The king was not pleased and declared, 'It may be so but then am I deceived,' and left the game.[19] This seemed to have ended the flirtation between Thomas and Anne. Who actually ended it we cannot be sure, as Anne may have ended it to keep the king happy with her and Thomas may have ended it knowing he was no match for the king. It does seem that as soon as Henry showed more interest in Anne than a meaningless flirtation, her other suitors fell by the wayside.

Anne may have liked the attention she got from the king and not just because of his status. In 1536, King Henry was still fit and healthy; it was only after an accident he had while jousting that year that his health deteriorated and he became overweight and the man most think of today when his name gets mentioned. All the suitors Anne had in her life before the king proved she liked attractive men, so the flirtation between Henry and Anne was surely real to both of them at the start.

However, the way Mary Boleyn had been used and cast aside by Henry must have played on Anne's mind. She was able to see at close range the distress caused to the whole family when the king became bored with Mary, and this must have coloured Anne's actions from the start of the relationship. Anne may well have thought of herself too worthy to be cast to one side like her sister, who was now without any honour, gifts or good reputation. It is often suggested that Anne played hard to get with the king, when she ran back to Hever Castle during the early flirtation. This may well be true, but if she didn't want to end up in the same situation as her sister, she had no choice but to retreat when the king's pressure became too great.

In the love letters from the king, not only did he sound like a teenage boy who was in love for the first time, but he also seemed confused by Anne's actions. Other ladies had always said yes to him, for he was the King of England, but here was a lady of the court, of his wife's household, who seemed to like to be in his company, but was saying no to him in the firmest way by her absence. This confusion seemed to intrigue the king further. The fact that Anne said no to being the king's official mistress, which would have given her high status in court, showed she was aiming very high indeed. It then became clear to the king that if he wanted to bed Anne, only marriage would do.

The stress was huge. The political issues raised would reverberate for many more years than they both expected at the time. The wait may have also caused a few cracks to appear in Anne's armour. She was reported to have said in court that 'she wished all the Spaniards to be at sea,' meaning Katherine of Aragon and perhaps even her daughter Princess Mary, and that she 'did not care anything for the Queen and would rather see her hanged than acknowledge her as her mistress'.[20]

It is easy to feel sympathy for Anne Boleyn at this moment. She was unable to marry the man she claimed to have loved and who would move heaven and earth to be with her, and now she was being denied marriage yet again. She was wasting time that could have produced children. She may have even thought that she wasn't getting any younger and if this marriage wasn't going to happen, she would be too old to find someone else.

Cardinal Wolsey had dragged his feet on this matter, so she had to get rid of him. She may have thought this would have solved the matter, but Katherine and her daughter Mary always stood in her way. Perhaps Anne genuinely – and arrogantly – could not understand Katherine's actions; if she loved the king as much as she claimed, surely she would have wanted the king to be happy? And in Anne's eyes, the king was happy with her.

In 1527, the king was meant to have met up with Cardinal Wolsey to hear his advice, but to please Anne the king decided instead to travel to Richmond Palace so that they could be together. Anne more than likely travelled to the palace by boat, along the Thames. It must have seemed to be a very grand and elegant palace to Anne, not only in its structure but in its history. The palace meant a lot to the king as the place where both of his parents had spent their final days together. Later Richmond Palace would be a favourite of Anne Boleyn's daughter, Queen Elizabeth I, even after being held prisoner there before being taken to Woodstock in her early years, it was the place in which after her very long reign Queen Elizabeth died. The only part of this palace that still exists today is the main gate and a part of the outer range by the green; the wall was once a part of the Royal Wardrobe inside the palace.

By 1528, Anne was once again back at Hever in Kent. This time, however, the reason was because of illness. A Sweating Sickness outbreak had hit the capital, and when Anne showed symptoms, the king immediately sent her back to Hever Castle, writing to her daily. Anne was not the only one of her family to have caught this illness, her brother-in-law William Carey caught it and did not survive. Thomas Boleyn, Anne's father, also caught the Sweating Sickness at this point and although the chances of survival were low, both Anne and her father recovered, possibly being nursed by Elizabeth Howard Boleyn.

When Anne returned to court, she came to Windsor Castle. This castle would play an important part in Anne's life. On 25 February 1528, the king held a sumptuous banquet in honour of Anne's return. It would also be the place where King Henry left Katherine of Aragon, riding out through Windsor Park with Anne Boleyn, never to see his first wife again. Windsor Castle would be Henry's final resting place; he chose to be buried next to his third wife, Jane Seymour.

When Anne returned to court she probably stayed with the king at Bridewell Palace.[21] Built in 1515, this Tudor palace with its two brick-built courtyards and three storeys was up-to-the-minute. It was positioned well within the City of London, on the west bank of the river Fleet and south of Fleet Street. Bridewell Palace was near Blackfriars, where the annulment trials between King Henry and Katherine of Aragon took place. The inner courtyard contained the Royal Apartments on the second floor, the king's rooms were on the southern end of the building with the queen's rooms on the opposite side. When the king took possession of Hampton Court in 1529, he seemed to lose interest in Bridewell Palace, and by 1530 it was mainly used by French ambassadors.

More than twenty years later, King Edward VI gave the palace over to the City of London governors for the housing of homeless children. This was soon fully taken over by the City, who turned it into a prison, hospital and workrooms, becoming a part of the Bridewell and Bethlehem Hospital.[22]

When Anne returned to court, she had to cope with the gossip of the Tudor court, knowing that everyone thought of her as 'the other woman', being called 'the lady' or 'the concubine' rather than 'queen'. It could be said that Anne believed she was entitled to have what she wanted, that she did not expect to be told no and did not truly see what she was making happen as being wrong. In this Anne Boleyn was very much like the king himself, the key difference being their different social levels. Could this also be another reason for their mutual attraction? Could their similarities also show us in some way what ultimately broke them apart?

It could also suggest that there was something childlike about Anne, that she was a spoilt juvenile, used to being pampered. There was perhaps even something infantile in her actions. Does this make us feel even more wretched for her seeing her as an innocent child or do we think that she caused her own problems because she had not grown up and this caused her own terrible downfall? As fiery as Anne was, she played with fire, possibly without even knowing it. On one occasion Anne was furious that Katherine of Aragon was still mending the king's shirts, behaving as if she was still his wife. Anne threw herself at the king in a rage that had never been seen in court before.[23]

During the years waiting for the king's divorce, the relationship between Henry and Anne can be seen as a game played to decide who would get the upper hand. This could also be said of the struggle between Anne and Katherine of Aragon. For example, Anne asked for the queen's jewels so that she could wear them, and the Queen's response was that it was 'against her conscience to give her jewels to adorn a person who is the Scandal of Christendom'. However, Anne always had one card up her sleeve to use for precisely such occasions and it was quite a powerful card: the King of Hearts. When Henry personally asked for the jewels himself, Katherine was forced to hand them over.[24]

It would seem that as the divorce dragged on, Anne's social armour began to tarnish. Even with her own family, Anne's mood began to change and as a consequence some of the high-ranking members of her clan began to fall out with her. However, the spats were always short. We may think that this was because of the closeness of the Boleyn family, but it was probably more to do with the power Anne wielded through the king, rather than actual affection. Her family benefited from Anne's position. In 1529, her father Thomas was made the Earl of Wiltshire and Ormond. George, her brother, was appointed Keeper of the Palace of Beaulieu in Essex. His wife Jane received a New Year's gift in 1532 from the king of a gold plate.

On 25 January 1533, the king apparently married Anne Boleyn. He married her, it is suggested, at Whitehall Palace. This place would have meant a great deal to the couple, it was here that Anne first entered into the English court after completing her service at the French court. At the time the building was called York Place and was owned by Cardinal Wolsey, but after the Cardinal's failure to get the king an annulment, the Cardinal had tried to stay on the king's good side by giving him properties, and this was one. Once the king owned the place, both he and Anne would spend a lot of time there redesigning it at Christmas 1529. York Place became grander than it ever was before and was renamed Whitehall Palace. Sadly, the only parts of the palace that both King Henry and Anne designed together that still exist today are a few corridors, fireplaces and an underground room, possibly used as the king's wine cellar, that only a handful of people have ever been allowed to visit.

In the eyes of the world King Henry was still married to Katherine of Aragon, but the reason for this secret marriage became clear when on 7 September in the same year, Anne Boleyn gave birth to a daughter. She was named Elizabeth after the child's grandmothers on both sides of the family. However, a problem arises with this 'secret' wedding date, if Anne and Henry had secretly married in the January of 1533, it would have meant that the child Anne was going to have would have been conceived out of wedlock. Would the king who moved heaven and earth to be with Anne Boleyn, the lady who could provide him with an heir to the throne, have really allowed the heir to be conceived out of wedlock? Would he have risked further issues this might have brought later on?

There is another suggestion that actually Anne and Henry secretly married on 14 November 1532. The Tudor chronicler, Edward Hall writes: 'The King after his return (from Calais) married privily the Lady Anne Bulleyn on Saint Erkenwald's Day, which marriage was kept so secret that very few knew it, till she was great with child at Easter after.'[25] Saint Erkenwald's Day was 14 November 1532, the day after the couple had returned to Dover from their time spent at the French court. If their wedding actually happened at this time instead of 25 January 1533, it would mean Anne's child, the future Queen Elizabeth I, was conceived within wedlock. This also meant that at the time of Anne's coronation procession on 31 May 1533, Anne was six months pregnant, something to remember as we describe her procession through the streets of London on a summer's evening.

Much of London has changed since Anne's procession almost five hundred years ago, but amazingly we can still walk most of it today. As she left the entrance to the Tower of London, she headed towards Trinity Gardens, passing what is now the memorial plaque for the people who were beheaded on Tower Hill. We can keep walking with Queen Anne to Cooper's Row, then along Crutched Friars and Lloyd's Avenue to reach Fenchurch Street. We carry on towards Leadenhall Market, turn left on to Cornhill, cross over Bank Junction and turn right into Cheapside. From New Charge we enter Carter Lane, then move onto Fleet Street and from there make our way towards Westminster Hall. Admittedly, Anne Boleyn took breaks and was carried in a litter, but even still that is a long way for a woman who was perhaps six months pregnant wearing layer upon layer of Tudor clothing on a warm summer's evening in the City of London. It is not often mentioned that it was also a rarity. From the days of William the Conqueror until this very day, no monarch has normally been allowed to enter London's 'square mile' without permission from the city's lord mayor.

On 1 June 1533, Anne was crowned Queen Consort of England at Westminster Abbey, the place where her sister's descendants would be buried. Anne would be the last Queen Consort to be crowned on a different day to her husband and she was crowned with St Edward's Crown, normally used for crowning male heirs to the throne.[26] This was probably done because Anne was visibly pregnant and assumed to be carrying a boy. The original crown was melted down during the English Civil War and a replica was made for the coronation of King Charles II. Although a girl was not the answer to Henry's dynastic needs,[27] the parents were soon in love with their daughter. Anne was a good mother, caring fondly for her child.

In early 1534, Anne was pregnant again, but it is likely that Anne suffered from a still birth. At least with the birth of Elizabeth, Anne proved that she could hold a child full term and if she could do this with a female, there was nothing stopping her doing it for a male. However, this still birth may have begun to change the king's thinking and he may have been questioning why he had been waiting so long for this woman, only to have received the same outcome as with his previous wife. In the last months of 1535, Anne was pregnant again, so the king had not entirely given up hope on Anne Boleyn producing him a son. This pregnancy was not to last either. Anne was to suffer a miscarriage on the day of Katherine of Aragon's funeral – and the child Anne miscarried was a boy.[28]

At this news, the king's patience was wearing thin. He stormed into Anne's room, where she was still crying over the death of the child and shouted that he 'would have no more boys by her'.[29] Anne would later claim it was the strain that she was under after hearing that Henry had suffered an accident while jousting where he nearly died that caused her miscarriage. At the same time, Anne also claimed it was seeing the king with a lady a few days before that had caused the loss. Anne was certainly laying the blame at the king's feet as best she could.[30] This lady was Jane Seymour, who would become King Henry's third wife, Anne's second cousin.

It has often been suggested that this miscarriage was the beginning of the end for Anne Boleyn, but perhaps it had started some time before this, and the miscarriage was the final straw. Anne was soon taken to the Tower of London, being accused of adultery, incest and treason, the last because she was accused of referring to the king's death. Anne was taken to the Tower on 2 May 1536 by barge. It is likely that Anne entered through the Court Gate in the Byward Tower rather than the Traitor's Gate. In *A Chronicle of England during the Reigns of the Tudors from AD 1488 to 1559*, Volume One, the contemporary author Charles Wriothesley states: '...and when she came to the Courtgate, entering in, she fell downe.' The term 'Courtgate' means the

Towergate and a plan of the Tower from 1597[31] shows that the part of the Tower labelled 'The Tower at the Gate' is today known as the Byward Tower. This entrance was used for royalty and although Anne was a prisoner, she was still a queen, so it would have made sense for her to have used this entrance rather than Traitor's Gate. We also know that years later, when Anne Boleyn's daughter Princess Elizabeth was brought to the Tower as a prisoner, she was taken through the entrance of the Byward Tower.

Once in the Tower, Anne collapsed, demanding to know where her father was, the question of a frightened child.[32] She had travelled a similar route almost three years before, when she used the Tower to get ready to be crowned Queen Consort at Westminster Abbey.

One myth surrounding Anne Boleyn's final days survives today, that she spent her final days in a stone cell. As much as this might help to magnify the downfall of Anne Boleyn, the lady that had gained so much and lost all, this is not true. Hauntingly, Anne was given the same rooms she once had as she prepared for her coronation. She was given the rooms within the Royal Apartments that sadly no longer exist. The Royal Apartments, with a Great Hall and kitchen, were built by King Henry as a wedding gift for Anne Boleyn and stood where there is now a green beside the White Tower.

A few days after being taken to the Tower, on 6 May 1536, Anne wrote her last ever letter to her husband. She did not sign the letter as Queen of England, instead she writes, 'Your most loyal and ever faithful wife, Anne Boleyn'. Eight days later, on 14 May 1536, Anne was stripped of her title and her marriage was voided, making her daughter, Elizabeth, illegitimate.

Anne would have known all too well what this meant for her baby girl, after seeing – and possibly being involved in –

the making of Katherine of Aragon's daughter, Mary, a bastard. There was nothing Anne could have done for her daughter. On 17 May 1536, five men said to have been involved with Anne were beheaded, one of them her brother George. It is commonly suggested that while watching this, Anne knew she would be next to the block, however this would be another myth. As Anne was not placed in a tower cell but in the Royal Apartments further inside the Tower, it would have been impossible for her to see her brother and the other men being beheaded on Tower Hill. So, unless she was taken out of her apartments on that day to see her brother's death as a cruel additional punishment, this could not be true.

William Kingston, the Constable of the Tower, stated that Anne seemed happy and ready to be done with life when he came to collect her. Perhaps after everything she had seen, there was a part of her that wanted her suffering to end. It is a wonder that in a last sign of any feeling the king had for her that Henry commuted Anne's sentence from burning to beheading. And rather than having a queen of England beheaded with the common axe, he had brought an expert swordsman from France to perform the execution. The fact that the French swordsman arrived only a day late for the official execution date and knowing the amount of time it would have taken to fetch him, this suggests that this was something the king ordered before Anne was found guilty. Her execution was delayed as they waited for the swordsman to arrive.

It is believed the modern-day memorial of the site of Anne's beheading is not positioned correctly, a Victorian mistake. Tower Green was actually much larger during the Tudor period than it is today, stretching further around the White Tower. Anne's scaffold was actually placed on the north side of the White Tower, by the entrance to the Waterloo Barracks on the parade ground. It was not placed on the western side of the White Tower where the memorial is placed. This 2006 memorial of a glass pillow states:

> Gentle visitor pause awhile: where you stand death cut away the light of many days: here jewelled names were broken from the vivid thread of life: may they rest in peace while we walk the generations around their strife and courage under these restless skies.

On the morning of Friday, 19 May 1536, Anne Boleyn was brought out from the Queen's House to the scaffold. She wore a red petticoat under a loose, dark grey gown trimmed in fur, and a mantle of ermine. She was accompanied by two female attendants and after Anne had climbed the scaffold, she made a speech to the crowd:

> Good Christian people, I am come hither to die, for according to the law, and by the law I am judged to die, and therefore I will speak nothing against it. I am come hither to accuse no man, nor to speak anything of that, whereof I am accused and condemned to die, but I pray God save the king and send him long to reign over you, for a gentler nor a more merciful prince was there never: and to me he was ever a good, a gentle and sovereign lord. And if any person will meddle of my cause, I require them to judge the best. And thus, I take my leave of the world and of you all, and I heartily desire you all to pray for me. O Lord have mercy on me, to God I commend my soul.[33]

The execution, which consisted of a single stroke of the sword, was witnessed by Thomas Cromwell, Charles Brandon, the king's illegitimate son Henry Fitzroy, the Lord Mayor of London, as well as aldermen, sheriffs, and representatives of the various craft guilds. She was executed at nine o'clock in the morning and buried that afternoon. It has been suggested that the reasons for the delay was firstly, to allow the ladies enough time to removed Anne's clothing and jewellery for those items to be given to the Tower officials, as was customary. Secondly, this burial of a queen of England was not as one might expect – pre planned meticulously – and someone had to lift the stones up from the floor of the church and dig a shallow grave for her after her death.[34]

She was buried in an unmarked grave in the chapel of St Peter Vincula. Some believe she was buried next to her brother George, others that the Boleyn siblings were buried quite a distance apart. It wasn't until her skeleton was said to be identified during renovations of the chapel in 1876 that 'Anne's grave' was given a marble floor.[35] The renovation of the church of St Peter Vincula began after Sir Charles Yorke, the then Constable of the Tower, submitted plans to Queen Victoria that included repairing the drains, Her response was that 'The chapel should be, as far as possible, architecturally restored to its original condition and also suitably arranged as a place of worship.'[36]

Describing the bones that were found, Dr Frederic Mouat, a surgeon, chemist and prison reformer, stated:

> The bones found in the place where Queen Anne Boleyn is said to have been buried are certainly those of a female in the prime of life, all perfectly consolidated and symmetrical, and belong to the same person. The bones of the head indicate a well-formed round skull, with an intellectual forehead, straight orbital ridge, large eyes, oval face and rather square full chin. The remains of the vertebrae, and the bones of the lower limbs, indicate a well-formed woman of middle height, with a short and slender neck. The ribs show depth and roundness of chest. The hands and feet bones indicate delicate and well-shaped hands and feet, with tapering fingers and a narrow foot.[37]

He noted that 'Anne' was five foot three inches in height and there was no evidence of any sixth finger. If Dr Mouat is correct, it is satisfying to have at least one hard fact about Anne's appearance, her height. The fact that Dr Mouat *looked* for the sixth finger in the Victorian period tells us that the detail had become firmly embedded in the Boleyn story.

However, when Dr Mouat was brought into the investigation, it was assumed these bones were Anne Boleyn's before he looked at them. And when the slab flooring was lifted the bones of the female were 'not lying in the original order, but ... had evidently for some reason or other been heaped together into a smaller space'.[38] The bones of George Boleyn and Catherine Howard were not found, leading to speculation that in the eighteenth century their remains were removed, or that Catherine's bones had dissolved in quick lime as traces of it were found where her grave should have been.[39] This all casts doubt on the identification of Anne's skeleton.

Dr Mouat 's description of 'Anne's skeleton' as being of a woman aged around twenty-five to thirty years of age with a square, full chin contradicts some things already known about Anne. If we believe Anne was born around 1501, this would have made Anne roughly thirty-five when she died. If this was the case, then the bones of a female 'about thirty to forty years of age' found at the time that Dr Mouat claimed to be Lady Rochford, George's wife, would actually suit Anne better, especially as George's wife was thought to have been born around 1512, making her age more in the range of the skeleton thought to be Anne.

A square chin? Which portrait do you believe depicts Anne most accurately? As to Dr Mouat's description of 'delicate and well-shaped hands and feet, with tapering fingers and a narrow foot',[40] Queen Elizabeth I was proud of her long, elegant fingers, which she could have inherited from her mother. The debate hinges on Anne Boleyn's date of birth. If you believe Anne was born around 1507 then Dr Mouat was right in his notes, however if you believe Anne Boleyn was born around 1501, then the marble slab that states Anne Boleyn is buried here is actually over the remains of Jane, Lady Rochford, Anne's sister-in-law.

For someone as ambitious as Anne, this was not the way she would have liked to be remembered, a mystery surrounding her place of death as well as birth; but one thing we do know. She gave birth to one of the greatest English sovereigns, Queen Elizabeth I.

George Boleyn

George Boleyn, even from a young age, was under pressure. He needed to succeed more than his sisters because he was male, a *surviving* male after several losses. Thomas and Elizabeth Howard Boleyn had more children than the three we know about. The other children did not survive into adulthood, and they all happened to be males. As the only male child of Thomas and Elizabeth Howard Boleyn to have survived into adulthood, a lot was riding on George's young shoulders.

George's date of birth has been debated, much like his sisters'. Some say it was in 1503,[41] some April 1504.[42] It is generally accepted that it was in 1504 because George Cavendish, best known for his biography of Cardinal Wolsey, states that George Boleyn is twenty-five years old when he gains his position on the Privy Council in 1529.[43] We know that by 1514, George Boleyn was a Page in the King of England's service, and from that time on he is a member of the English court.[44] At the Christmas celebrations of 1514 a 'Master Bollen' was mentioned in Edward Hall's records of Henry VIII's court. Edward also mentions the attendance of Thomas Boleyn, George's father. The fact that Thomas Boleyn is mentioned does suggest that the 'Master Bollen' was George, however, it is possible this was a reference to Edward Boleyn, George's uncle, who was also at court at the time and was only eighteen years old.[45]

In 1524 George's family were in talks with Henry Parker, the English ambassador to Germany, for George to marry Henry's daughter, Jane. This was an unusual match for the Boleyn family. The Boleyns had always used marriage to improve their status, however with this marriage they seemed to have married within their own social circle. Two years later, as Cardinal Wolsey tried to save money within the royal household, George's role changed to Cup Bearer with a wage of twenty pounds a year.[46]

As we have seen, in the early stages of Henry's and Anne Boleyn's flirtation, Anne was sent to Hever Castle on the orders of her father Thomas. George then became a messenger between the king and his sister. Seventeen of the king's love letters to Anne survive. What did George think about the situation he had been placed in as he travelled from court to Hever and back again? Did he feel like he was being used, or that he wasn't being used to his full potential? Did he worry his sister could ruin his career but that he was powerless to stop it? Did he fear that his sister and her ambitious ways would lead to his downfall?

After the sweating sickness of 1528, which affected many including George's father, sister Anne and brother-in-law, William Carey, George had the opportunity of advancement within the court. By the end of September that year, he was made Esquire of the Body, being round the same age that his father was when he assumed the same role. Later, George was made Master of the King's Buckhounds, a very high honour indeed, and he also became Keeper of the Palace gardens and Wardrobe of Beaulieu. These appointments show how well-respected George was at court, or at least how important George may have become through his connection with his sister, Anne. Being the Keeper of Beaulieu would have had some special meaning for George Boleyn. It was once owned by George's great grandfather and other family members had also performed the role.[47]

The Palace of Beaulieu was once called New Hall, which coincidentally is how it is named today, being a part of New Hall School. New Hall in the early years was once owned by Thomas Butler, Earl of Ormond. When Thomas Butler died, it was given to Lady Margaret Butler, Thomas Boleyn's mother and George Boleyn's grandmother. Situated twenty-seven miles from London, the New Hall sat in the beautiful countryside of Essex, so very different to the busy city milieu of the court. The Butler's entertained the king there in 1510.

Six years later the king remembered this place and, liking what he remembered, he bought it in February 1516. King Henry began improving the New Hall by purchasing Flemish tapestries, beds and items such as blankets and sheets. In early 1517, the king changed his mind about the residence and instead of improving it, he decided to knock the whole building down and rebuild it. From March 1517 to June of 1521 New Hall went from being a courtier's home to a grand royal palace. The king felt it needed a grander name and so it became the Palace of Beaulieu, 'beautiful place'.

The king stayed in his palace a number of times, but it was his sojourn there in the summer of 1527 that is most significant. As well as taking a large group of his friends to stay with him there, the king also took Thomas Boleyn and his brother-in-law, Thomas Howard. Cardinal Wolsey's authority was on the wane and the king, because of Anne, was turning more and more towards her family for guidance. So, it is small wonder that George Boleyn was given the role of Keeper of the Palace of Beaulieu just a year after this meeting, a position that was once held by Mary Boleyn's first husband William Carey. It was a way for the king to keep the palace indirectly within the family to whom it once belonged.

Later, the palace fell out of favour with the king and upon his death it was given to his daughter Mary, who used it on a number of occasions in her reign. It was then passed on to Anne Boleyn's daughter, Queen Elizabeth I, who gave it to one of her favourites, the Earl of Sussex, Thomas Radclyffe. Elizabeth could not bring attention to her mother Anne Boleyn the traitor, and her own consequent illegitimacy. But by giving the palace to the Earl of Sussex, Elizabeth was actually handing the place back to her mother's family, as Thomas Radclyffe was the nephew of Elizabeth Howard Boleyn, the mother of Anne Boleyn and the grandmother of the queen herself.[48] Later, the Palace of Beaulieu was bought by Oliver Cromwell for five shillings.[49]

In a relatively short space of time compared to other courtiers, George's status grew. He was appointed Governor of Bethlehem Hospital in 1529. Founded during the reign of Henry III in 1247, the hospital was not originally the notorious bedlam it was in the seventeenth to nineteenth centuries, when it was governed by authorities rather than the crown.[50] When it was run by the crown, Bethlehem was a basic hospital with no specialism. In 1546 the Lord Mayor of London, Sir John Gresham, started a petition to grant the hospital to the people of the City of London and Henry VIII reluctantly gave the 'custody, order and governance' of the hospital over to the 'occupants and revenues' of the City of London, making the role that George Boleyn once had obsolete.[51]

George was also appointed to be the new ambassador for France in October the same year. These were very important roles for a young man of twenty-five; his father was ten years older when he was first sent abroad.[52] George was maligned, perhaps unfairly, before he had even left England to start his new role. Other members of the court considered his unmerited ascendancy as owed solely to the influence of Anne Boleyn, the woman who had the king's ear and heart. They called him the 'petit prince'.[53]

When George was sent abroad in his new role as ambassador, he was accompanied by John Stokesley, a well-respected ambassador in his own right and a church figure, the Dean of the Chapel Royal. As George and John's orders were to talk to the King of France about the possibility of organising a General Council of the Church to further the king's annulment, having a churchman on the case was good planning on King Henry's part. They were told to gain votes from the country's universities, so that they could persuade Francis I to be in favour of the annulment. This plan failed and George arrived back in England on 20 February 1530 a disappointed man. However, what George did manage to do successfully was befriend Chapuys, the Spanish ambassador who would spend most of his time at the English court. Chapuys would later describe George as 'charming, exceeding courteous ... his frank mind was refreshing'.[54]

While George was establishing himself at court, he and his wife Jane lived at Rochford Hall, a place George's sister Mary would later own just before her death. George was invited to be part of parliament for the first time on 5 February 1533, sitting beside his father and uncles. After a few months George was given another chance to work with the French embassy, travelling to France in March 1533. He was a part of the special envoy rather than a resident ambassador this time.[55]

He was now twenty-nine years old and seemed to be growing into his role. He led the envoy.[56] George had letters written by King Henry which he was to hand over to Francis. In these letters, Henry was, perhaps surprisingly, too frank: 'From his anxiety to have made issue for the establishment of his kingdom, he has proceeded effectually to the accomplishment of his marriage.'[57] Henry was basically telling the French king that he wanted to marry again to have a son. Making George the go-between in this Great Matter shows the king trusted him, at this point anyway.

George returned to England in April of the same year, a short enough time abroad to complete all of his tasks. He returned with two thousand crowns from Francis as an early wedding gift, which looks like a success; but as nothing much else was done, his second trip to France could also be seen as not being hugely effective. After George's trip aboard, he went straight back into his duties as a Privy Councillor[58]. This was not to last, as within weeks of George returning home, he was then sent to France yet again. This time he would be travelling with his uncle, the Duke of Norfolk.

The duke had always been deemed to be a little rough in his manner, more suited to parleying with the Scots than the French. It was probably thought wise to send George Boleyn with him, to calm any issues that may arise. This meant that George was not there to see his sister be crowned Queen Consort of England.

One wonders how George felt about this. It has always been said that George and Anne were close and the fact that George was sent away at this moment must have affected him in some way. Anne, too, may well have been saddened not to have her brother there, as just days before her coronation relationships with other family members, such as her own father, were tense.[59]

On this trip to France, George was to meet with the King of France's sister, Marguerite, but their conversations were unrecorded. The duke fell ill during the trip and travelled with the embassy to Lyon to recover, George meanwhile carried on with the mission he had been set. Perhaps this was a sign of his father's strong and prominent nature starting to shine through in George.

Did George want to prove that he did not need his uncle or any family member to help him? George was showing the independent nature that all the Boleyn siblings shared.

Before George could get on with the mission, he and his uncle learned that the pope had nullified the Archbishop of Canterbury's statement that king Henry was divorced. The king had six weeks to leave Anne and go back to his legal wife, Katherine of Aragon. George was sent home quickly in the belief that if the news was broken to a very pregnant Anne by her brother, she may be able to cope with the shock better. George arrived at Windsor Castle where Anne and the king were holding court on 28 July 1533 with the bad news.[60] After he had informed Anne of the situation, George was ordered back to France. The king was treating George like the messenger he had once been during the early part of Anne and the king's relationship. Perhaps George in the back of his mind knew he would never be more than a messenger to the king and no more.

George's new orders were to prevent a meeting that the King of France, ambassador Francis Bryan and John Wallop had planned with the pope. Hopefully, this would send a signal to the pope that Francis I was on Henry's side. At this point the King of France was becoming uneasy with Henry's constant demands for his support. Francis said the planning for the meeting was already too far ahead to stop it from happening. For Henry, this was infuriating. For George, it meant that another mission to France was a failure.

The Boleyn family must have been dismayed by George's constant attempts to better himself seemingly coming up short, almost every time. Maybe there was a family meeting. Was George beginning to seem like a failure, like his sister? Did this also mean that all hopes now lay at Anne Boleyn's door?

On the positive side for George, he was also tasked to inform the King of France's sister, Marguerite that although the two kings had planned to meet for the third time in their reign, Anne would not be there as she was pregnant.[61] So when George came back to England on 27 July 1533 with the bad news that Francis was not going to change his plans with the pope, he could at least say that Francis was happy to wait another year before he saw King Henry again. One can imagine with all the constant failed coercion Henry had recently tried on the King of France that this was true for reasons other than Anne's pregnancy.[62]

On 7 September 1533, Princess Elizabeth was born to George's sister. George would be at the new princess's christening, carrying the canopy of 'crimson satin, fringed with gold' over his niece's head.[63] This should have been a day of family celebration, perhaps a day for the Boleyn family to hold their heads up high, to show how far they had come from such humble beginnings. Maybe on the outside, this is exactly how they portrayed themselves. However, what were they feeling privately? If all hopes were pinned on Anne to save the family name and position, the fact that Anne had given birth to a girl when the king needed a son must have hung heavy on all the family members. Tensions were surely running high within the family at this point.

George may have felt like a failure, he may have been told he was, he may have believed he was. So, could George have looked for an outlet for his feelings? Could he have wanted to prove himself in other ways? This may be why George was also known to be a musician and poet? Perhaps his outlet, like his friend Thomas Wyatt before him, was a creative one.

George Cavendish wrote 'God gave me grace, dame nature did her part, Endowed me with gifts of natural qualities, Dame eloquence also taught me the art, In meter and verse to make pleasant ditties' when describing George's good looks and skill in poetry.[64] The court chronicler Raphael Hollinshed said 'he wrote divers songs and sonnets'.[65] Unfortunately, none of his poems actually survive with his name on. However, one poem has been suggested as being his, originally in the manuscripts of John Harington dated 1564. Horace Walpole, the fourth Earl of Orford, in his *Catalogue of Royal and Noble Authors of England, Scotland and Ireland*[66] identifies George as the author: 'I have long lamented our having no certain piece by Anne Boleyn's brother, Lord Rochford. I have found a very pretty copy of verse by him in the new published volume of the Nugae Antiquae, though by mistake he is called Earl of instead of Viscount Rochford.'[67] The poem is called 'The Lover Complaineth the Unkindness of his Love'.[68] The poem ends with the line 'My lute be still, for I have done.'[69] At this moment perhaps George would have liked events to be a little less dramatic, a little more still.

In 1534, George received a temporary promotion. He was made Captain of Guisnes Castle in the Pas de Calais when Lord Sandys became ill. This would have given George a salary of 1000 pounds a year. Lord Sandys recovered sooner than expected and George was given a new role as the Constable of Dover Castle on 16 June 1534.[70] This was the same position held by King Henry when he was but three years old and he held it until he was nineteen, when he became king.[71]

Talks now began concerning the King of France's son marrying the Princess Elizabeth. George was once again sent over to France to sell the idea to, Francis.[72] George's task was a delicate one. He had his own personal reasons for making this trip a success, as his other forays into France were not as wonderful as they could have been. He also had an interest in making a marriage connection between England and France through his niece, one that would have been invaluable in protecting his own family.

Yet again, things did not go right for George. He discovered via a courtier travelling with the French ambassador, Fitzwilliam, that the King of France now seemed to be showing signs that he believed the marriage between Henry and Anne to be invalid. This made Princess Elizabeth unimportant to Francis and he would prefer to have his son marry the Princess Mary instead.[73] George would have known what this could have meant. The King of England would be angered, as would Anne, and George himself would seem to have failed again. There was nothing George could do; he was still fully accepted at the French court, unlike his father before him. The Bishop of Faenza would later write, 'He came here for eight days, but, as far as could be seen, did nothing. It is only from his relation with the Queen that he is employed for the King has very few to trust in.'[74] No doubt George tried his hardest to force the issue, but as the queen's brother and nothing else, he held no sway.

The view of the French king had not changed during those eight days, so when George arrived back in England he went straight to his sister to tell her the bad news and then he went on to the king. Luckily, the king took his anger out on the French representative, Jean Dinteville, rather than George. He returned to his duties as the Constable of Dover Castle and gained a reputation for harshness in the role. Perhaps he wanted to impose himself because of his failure at the French court. His actions meant George clashed with Thomas Cromwell, one of the king's most trusted advisors and the person who would later bring about George's downfall.[75]

As the Constable, George faced problems. The king wanted to update the defences of the castle and the port, now that he finally knew that the King of France was against his marriage to Anne, in case France invaded. The work was George's to complete. The labourers were not happy with a wage of just six pence a day, below the going rate, and a riot ensued. Instead of negotiating, George decided to instead round up the four ring leaders of the riots and throw them into the prison inside Dover Castle's walls.[76]

To celebrate George's role as Constable of Dover Castle he sent Anne eighteen dotterels that had been killed on the beach of Dover and it was said that the queen liked them very much. Dotterels are small wading birds, now more native to the northern side of Scotland than the Kent coast. The next person to take over the role of Constable of Dover Castle was the king's son with Elizabeth Blount, Henry Fitzroy, who died in the same year he was given the role in 1536. The post was then given to Sir Thomas Cheyne, Treasurer of the Royal Household. He would welcome Anne of Cleves to Dover Castle before she was made the king's fourth wife.[77]

When Katherine of Aragon died on 7 January 1536 at Kimbolton, it seemed as if luck was with the Boleyns. Chapuys, inimical to the Boleyns at this point and a loyal friend to Katherine of Aragon, wrote: 'No words can describe the joy and delight which this King and the promoters of his concubine have felt at the demise of the good Queen, especially the Earl of Vulcher (Wiltshire) and his son, who much have said to themselves, what a pity it was that the Princess (Mary) had not kept her mother company.' This was translated by Garrett Mattingly from the Spanish Calendar.[78] We cannot know if there was in reality any celebration of Katherine's death by the Boleyns. In the version given in the *Letters and Papers*, Chapuys was meant to have written: 'You could not conceive the joy that the King and those who favour this concubine have shown at the death of the good Queen, especially the Earl of Wiltshire and his son, who said it was pity the Princess did not keep company with her'.[79] Still bitter, but a little less vicious.

To celebrate Anne's new pregnancy (and perhaps obliquely the death of Katherine of Aragon), tournaments were held on 24 January 1536. George was a part of these jousts and performed well. This was the the joust during which Henry was thrown from his horse, with the steed landing on top of him, rendering him unconscious for two hours. Thereafter the king suffered from a leg sore, possibly due to an earlier injury. It would plague him for the rest of his life, causing him to have constant infections, to gain weight – and possibly it exacerbated his irascible, dangerous nature. As mentioned earlier, when Anne was told of the news of the king's accident in a blunt manner by her uncle, it was suggested she miscarried a baby boy. Or Anne was desperately searching for a reason for the loss and came up with the story.[80]

George went back to his duties at Dover Castle, perhaps wanting to keep away from court when he sensed tension in the air. George was said to have returned to court briefly to help his family trick the Spanish ambassador, Chapuys, into acknowledging Anne as Queen of England by trapping him in the chapel and making him bow before her. This is the story as usually told.[81] However, if we look at the Spanish Calendar documents and what was actually stated by Chapuys, we find something different: 'I must say that she (Anne) was affable enough on the occasion for my being placed behind the door by which she entered the chapel, she turned round to return the reverence which I made her when she passed.'[82] Chapuys bowed to her and she returned the acknowledgement. There doesn't seem to be any forcing or trapping here. That same evening George dined with his father and Chapuys, which also indicates that there was no bad feeling between the Boleyns and Chapuys after the encounter.[83]

Unbeknown to the Boleyn family, Thomas Cromwell had already set their downfall in motion and George was arrested in the early afternoon on 2 May 1536 and taken to the Tower of London, accused of treason. He would end his life there.[84] The treason law passed in 1532 did not class adultery as treason, so adultery – even incestuous – would not normally have resulted in execution. The fact that George was executed for adultery would have appeared anomalous to the public at the time. But they would have understood how George could be seen as an accessory to anything his sister Anne may have done, and that was why he was treated so harshly.[85] George and his sister were tried at different times on 15 May 1536, with their uncle presiding over both. The trials were a family affair; as well as their uncle, their cousin and George's father-in-law, Henry Parker, sat on the jury.[86]

Chapuys wrote of George's trial that 'No proof of his guilt was produced except that of his having once passed many hours in her (Anne's) company and other little follies.'[87] This was actually a very common opinion and many thought George would eventually be spared. Although George was vociferous in his own defence, showing his naturally confident nature perhaps, he also seemed to know what the outcome would be, knowing the king wanted rid of the Boleyns altogether in order to remarry. Although George was firm in his responses, he was oddly quiet when asked if he thought Princess Elizabeth was the king's child. It was an interesting reaction. George was executed on 17 May 1536.[88]

There is a suggestion that George left behind a son named after himself, George Boleyn. For his own safety, this son was taken to one of the domiciles still owned by the family, Clonony Castle in Ireland. This would be where George's son would grow up and have children of his own. George junior was said to have had a son called Thomas Boleyn named after his grandfather. This Thomas had two daughters, Mary and Elizabeth Boleyn.

All this information comes from the headstone of the grave of these two ladies, found about three hundred feet from the castle itself.[89]

Here under leys Elizabeth and Mary Bullyn daughters of Thomas Bullyn son of George Bullyn the son of George Bullyn Viscount Rochford son of Sir Thomas Boleyn Earle of Ormonde and Wiltshire [sic].[90]

This grave was found by local labourers who were gathering stonework in the nearby area in 1803. Within a cave nearby, a coffin of limestone was said to have been found containing two bodies, known as the monument of Queen Elizabeth's cousins.[91] As there is no other evidence that George Boleyn had a child, we cannot be sure that the epitaph is accurate. Nevertheless, it has been suggested that George's son was the Dean of Lichfield, son of George's wife Jane, Lady Rochford, or born illegitimately[92] and there are some good reasons why. George Boleyn, the Dean of Lichfield, was known to the Carey family and the Knollys family; both families were descendants of George's sister Mary. He even named Henry Carey, Mary's son, as executor of his will.[93] However, the theory begins to be undermined because of the Dean's age. Like many of the Boleyns before him, his date of birth is not known with certainty but may have been 1537, one year after the execution of George Boleyn. There is no mention of the Dean gaining any inheritance from the Boleyn family at any point and when later George Carey, the second Baron of Hunsdon and grandson to Mary Boleyn, claimed the Earl of Ormond title as a relation of Mary Boleyn, there was no counterclaim that the title should go to the Dean of Lichfield.[94]

In purported portraits of Mary and Elizabeth Boleyn, the clothing of the ladies seems to be more Stuart in period rather than Tudor. Some think the portraits are of Margaret and Elizabeth Clere, who have a connection to the Boleyn family through Alice Boleyn. A comparison of these portraits with the suggested portrait of Katherine Carey, Mary Boleyn's daughter, and even with the portrait of Lettice Knollys, the granddaughter of Mary Boleyn, does seem to show some family resemblance. Therefore the grave of these ladies does at least leave the suggestion open that the Boleyn name may have carried on through George and that Elizabeth and Mary Boleyn could have been the great-granddaughters of George Boleyn.

To end on a different, less sombre note, George was very good at all the Tudor sports and games that would have made him noticed in court, such as archery, bowls and even the shovelboard, often winning large amounts of money from his challengers, one of them being the king.[95] It is tempting to think that everyone in his court was terrified of 'England's Nero', and would allow the king to win at every sport, but here we have a courtier competing and – more often than not – winning. For example, on 5 April 1530 George received money '...for 4 games which he won of the King's grace at tennis at 4 Agells a game'.[96]

The number of times George played some kind of sport with the king shows that they were often in each other's company. Surveying the records of events day-by day in isolation, George could be seen as just the king's messenger boy, promoted only because the king fell in love with his sister and sometimes failing in his duties; but if this picture is correct, would the king have wanted to spend that much time with George when he didn't have to? Was George actually the king's friend on his own merits?

Much of the focus has been on the king's execution of the woman he had done so much to win, and rightly so. But George's death was as shocking. The king was murdering a friend, a person he may have felt close to, someone he had spent a lot of time with, someone he trusted. This was surely an early expression of the tyrant Henry would become.

MARY BOLEYN, LADY CAREY
AND STAFFORD

Blickling Hall had been owned by the Boleyn family for some time prior to the birth of Mary Boleyn. Mary's grandfather, William Boleyn, had spent most of his time there and it would probably be where William's son Thomas's three surviving children, Mary, Anne and George, were born. Two miles from Aylsham in Norfolk, Blickling Hall is surrounded by woodlands, parks and gardens, but much of what Mary Boleyn would have remembered about the place has long since gone.

Deciding where the children of Thomas and Elizabeth Howard Boleyn were born depends on when you think they were born. Much like her sister, Anne, Mary's date of birth has been debated because there are no records as yet discovered. It is suggested that Mary was actually older than Anne because George Carey, Mary's grandson, fought for the rights to claim a title at the expense of Queen Elizabeth I, and could do so only if Anne was younger than Mary. Mary was probably born around 1498, three years or so before Anne.[1] When Anne arrived, we know the Boleyn fortunes were improving. For example, Thomas, Mary's father, attended Prince Arthur's marriage to Katherine of Aragon at St Paul's Cathedral on 14 November 1501.[2] When Thomas's father William passed away on 10 October 1505, Thomas inherited many manors including Hever Castle in Kent. The Boleyns lived off the profits of the estates, only visiting them occasionally, but Hever Castle was home when they were not at court or on the king's missions.[3] Mary Boleyn was probably around seven years old when Hever Castle became her new home, closer to the court than Blickling Hall.

The proposed birthplace of the Boleyn siblings was once home to King Harold I. After 1066 the manor at Blickling passed to the Bishops of Norwich. By the fifteenth century Blickling was owned by Sir John Fastolfe and, as we noted earlier, Sir John sold Blickling to Geoffrey Boleyn in 1437. The connection with the Boleyns did not stop after Sir Thomas Boleyn died, as the estate passed to the Cleres family, relations of the Boleyns. When Sir Edward Cleres died in 1605, he left his widow penniless. She tried to hold on to Blickling for as long as she could but eventually had to sell it to Sir Henry Hobart.[4]

The Hobarts were proud of the history of the place and what better story was there than that Anne Boleyn, a queen of England, was born there?[5] To bolster the narrative, the Hobarts added certain items to the estate: for example, a piece of black cloth, said to come from the bed that Anne Boleyn was born in. Later tests suggest that the cloth dated to the 1560s, roughly thirty years after Anne Boleyn's death.[6] In the Great Hall are two eighteenth-century carved wooden figures standing on plinths. One is a female in questionable Tudor period clothing. Inscribed on the plinth are the words *Anna Boleyn Hic Nata*, 'Anne Boleyn was born here.'[7] The other is of her daughter, Queen Elizabeth I. In 1925 and 1938 Anne was remembered through the production of celebration masques. The 1938 masque was attended by the then patroness of Blickling Hall, Queen Mary. In the grounds of Blickling Hall is St Andrew's Church, situated to the south-east of the Hall. The church has brass plaques dedicated to Cecily Boleyn, the sister of Geoffrey, and to Anne Wood, who died unexpectedly while visiting her sister Elizabeth Boleyn, wife of Sir James Boleyn.

There is a ghostly tale attached to Blickling Hall involving Anne Boleyn. As the clock strikes midnight on the anniversary of Anne's death, headless coachmen and headless horses bring a carriage to the entrance. They are of course, delivering Anne Boleyn, also headless, home to meet her father, who also haunts the place. His ghost, distraught because he did not try to stop the king from killing his two children when he was alive, attempts to cross the twelve bridges from Blickling to Wroxham before sunrise.[8]

On 11 May 1509, Henry VII died. Thomas Boleyn served as the Esquire of the Body at his funeral at Westminster Abbey[9] and on the coronation of the next king, Thomas was given the title of Knight of the Bath and the Knight of the Body to King Henry VIII.[10] This meant that Thomas was Henry's bodyguard, sleeping outside the king's chamber.

This enabled Thomas to give his children a good education. We have already seen what this level of education did for Mary's siblings; however, with Mary, the most we know was that she could read and write. It may be that Mary was not as intellectually precocious as Anne, which is why Thomas favoured Anne over his older daughter.[11] Although it would be unusual for the oldest not to receive the same level of education as her younger siblings, or at least her younger sister.

Sadly, only two of Mary's letters survive, which does not give us much of an idea of the level of education she received. However, we can tell from these two letters when comparing them to the vast array of letters from her sister, that Mary seems less elegant in her writing skills, her words do not flow easily, her vocabulary is limited and her handwriting itself is less fluid.[12] Mary did seem to like reading, however. In one of her letters Mary explains that she had been reading 'old books' on kings and queens. As quite often Mary and her family are mentioned in 'kings and queens' books today, it almost as if –as she plays out her own drama – Mary is breaking the fourth wall!

Mary did speak French fluently, maybe better than her sister. Mary may have been jealous of her when her father chose Anne to be sent first into the world; but in reality, there is no real evidence the sisters were even close to each other[13] in the first place.

Was Mary in fact pleased to have her sister sent away? Maybe Mary felt that with the 'star' of the family, idolised by her father, absent, she could be more like herself and breathe a little more easily. Maybe she felt she didn't have to work so hard to prove herself, or to keep up with her sister. Alternatively, it has been suggested that Mary found life at Hever Castle tiresome. If she did exhibit some disgruntlement, this might have been an expression of sororal jealousy.[14]

Descriptions of Mary Boleyn vary. She is 'dark haired'[15] or 'stately and golden-haired',[16] even 'dimpled and red-cheeked with lightish-brown hair'.[17] Tresses notwithstanding, she was attractive enough to win one or maybe two kings' hearts at a young age, if only for a while.

In the summer of 1514, Mary's chance to enter service came when Mary Tudor, the king's sister, was to marry the King of France, Louis XII. Henry needed high-born ladies who spoke French to travel with his sister when she voyaged across the Channel. Anne, Mary Boleyn's sister was also chosen.[18] This underlines the importance of Thomas Boleyn, his position acknowledged by two of his children serving the King of England's sister. Mary Boleyn would also spend some time in Henry's household in 1514, as she attended 'the lady of honour' Lady Jane Guildford, the former wife of Sir Richard Guildford and a woman of high status, formerly the lady in waiting to Elizabeth of York, Henry's mother.

At the death of King Louis XII only eighty-two days after the wedding, his brother, Francis I, took the throne. Mary is supposed to have been his mistress. Where did this suggestion come from? A letter dated 10 March 1536 written by Rodolfo Pio, Bishop of Faenza – more than twenty years after the purported liaison – is the main source: 'The French King knew her in France for the great whore and infamous above all.'[19] There is some doubt as to whether this refers to Mary Boleyn or her sister. The Bishop would have been hostile to the Boleyns, after everything that the 'king's great matter' had done to the church. If there was an affair, it was probably of brief duration, judging by the lack of commentary on it.

Mary Tudor, the king's sister, married for the second time to the Duke of Suffolk. Henry reluctantly had a second wedding for them at Greenwich Palace on 13 May 1515, for they had married first in secret. Mary Boleyn was still in Mary Tudor's service and she probably travelled back to England with the king's sister. There is no record of Mary Boleyn anywhere from 1515 to 1520, the year in which she married, so we can only assume that she had returned to England.

Mary's marriage to William Carey had the king's blessing, as he was one of the guests at the wedding.[20] They were perfectly suited in the eyes of their peers. William was a rising star at court. He was marrying a woman of similar age, the daughter of a powerful man. They married on 4 February 1520.[21] Thomas Boleyn was not there to give her away as he was working for the king abroad.

They married in the Chapel Royal, Greenwich Palace, a significant location for the entire Tudor dynasty.[22] The palace was originally called Bella Court when Humphrey of Lancaster, the Duke of Gloucester, had the place built in 1443. Four years later, when the duke was arrested for high treason, Henry VI gave the place over to his wife and queen, Margaret of Anjou, and she renamed it the Palace of Placentia. Henry VII rebuilt the palace between 1498 and 1504, adding running water and three large courtyards, making his renamed Palace of Greenwich very large indeed. It covered the area of the whole of the Royal Naval College, from the Thames to where the Queen's House is today. Henry VII would use this palace on a regular basis, and it would be the birthplace of his son, Prince Henry.[23] Henry VIII married his first wife there in the same chapel, and his daughters Mary and Elizabeth were born there. He would quit the palace leaving Anne Boleyn alone there at a joust, to be arrested for treason. From Greenwich Palace Anne would travel to the Tower of London and eventually meet her death.[24] Henry's son, King Edward, died there of tuberculosis. Queen Mary I spent her childhood and some time as queen there. It would also be important to Mary Boleyn's niece, Queen Elizabeth I. She bade farewell to Sir Francis Drake at the palace as he went on his voyages. Queen Elizabeth signed the death warrant of her cousin, Mary, Queen of Scots there, and gave orders for the English to attack the Spanish Armada.[25]

The chapel itself was one of the most important places within the palace. The choristers and officers of the Chapel Royal would have led the noble congregation to the place of worship, with the king observing everyone in the chapel from his Privy Closet on feast days, such as Christmas, Easter and Maundy Thursday, when the king gave Maundy Money to the poor who gathered outside.[26]

Although plans were known of what the Tudor palace would have looked like, the precise location was not one hundred per cent certain. This changed in the winter of 2005, with a project to landscape the car park on the eastern side. Tudor bricks began appearing in a trench dug for a new water drain. This find instantly stopped work and the Museum of London Archaeology Service was brought in. After two weeks of digging, the side of the chapel and the Tudor flooring within it began to emerge, a copy of which can be seen at the Visitor Information Centre at Greenwich.[27] Sadly, there are not many places left where we can envisage Mary Boleyn, but here in the car park of the Royal Naval College in Greenwich was the black-and-white tiled floor that Mary Boleyn would have walked down as a bride.

Why were Mary Boleyn and William Carey permitted to marry in such a place? There was no doubt that Thomas Boleyn was a significant figure at court, so this is part of the answer. It is possible, however, that there could be other reasons. William Carey was the second son of Thomas Carey and his wife Margaret Spencer. William's maternal grandmother was Eleanor Beaufort, the first cousin to Margaret Beaufort, who was the grandmother of Henry VIII. This means that William was related to the king, they were third cousins. In addition, there is a suggestion that one or both of William Carey's children with Mary Boleyn were in fact not William's but actually Henry's, from the time when Mary was the king's mistress. As we are following Mary's family tree down to modern-day descendants, this will be discussed in more detail later. Whoever the father of Mary's children actually was, the fact that William Carey was related to the king means the children were. This ultimately means that the modern-day descendants that we will be discussing were not just related to the Boleyn family but also to the royal Tudor family. As William was related to Margaret Beaufort, it means that William was also related to Margaret's father, John Beaufort, Duke of Somerset. the great-grandson of King Edward III.

The notion that William Carey was 'paid off' for his silence in allowing his wife to lie with the king is often put forward. The way he was compensated was apparently through promotions and endowments. Though there is a sound counter-argument to this in that William was an established member of court at the time and may have earned these gifts by doing his duty to the king. In view of the family connection, it could be argued William gained these rewards because he was related to the king. So, there are several possible reasons why Mary married in the Chapel Royal.

At the time of the marriage, William Carey was twenty-four years old, a young man with a promising career in court to look forward to. But he would have known the pitfalls of court life. William's grandfather, Sir William Carey of Cockington, had chosen unwisely in the War of the Roses and fought for the House of Lancaster at the Battle of Tewkesbury. The outcome of being on the losing side was that Sir William was beheaded on 6 May 1471, when William's father, Thomas Carey, was eleven.[28]

Going by the date and age given on William's known portrait, William was born around 1496, which would mean his career at court started in 1519.[29] Within a short time, William was given a post that Mary Boleyn's father once held, Esquire of the Body to his royal master, Henry VIII.[30] It has been suggested that this was around the time that Mary Boleyn became the king's mistress, but we have no solid evidence of this. We cannot be sure when Mary's relationship with the king started, if it ever did, nor can we be sure how long it lasted.[31] It could have been any time between 1510 and 1525, a period of fifteen years. However, there's one clue that points to 1522.[32]

On 2 March 1522, there was a tournament to celebrate the marriage of the Emperor King Charles V's son and Henry's daughter Mary. Henry took part in the jousts, his horse was dressed in caparisons on which the words 'Elle mon Coeur a Navera', 'she has wounded my heart', were embroidered.[33] It is impossible to know who had 'wounded' the king's heart but it is suggested this wasn't meant for his wife and the date seems to suit the time that Mary Boleyn had caught his eye. The words used imply that whoever the lady was, she may have, at this point at least, rejected the king's advances, which would seem to suit the circumstances, as Mary was already married.

We have another clue from 4 March 1522, at a feast attended by the two Boleyn sisters. Anne had just returned from her time in France. When the food was cleared away, a pageant called 'The Assault on the Castle of Virtue' was performed.[34] Within the scene, hanging from the castle were three banners, one having broken hearts on it, another had a lady's hand holding a man's heart and the third had a lady's hand turning a man's heart.[35] The king liked to flaunt his fancies using codes and symbols, in part so as to not upset the queen. Were these banners for Mary Boleyn, who would have seen them, as she was a part of the pageant?

Whether Mary went willingly to the king's chamber or whether she was forced into going is debatable. Her own family may well have forced her to the king's bed to enhance their own positions at court, but this might not be the case. Cardinal Pole, who had the ear of the pope and who also might have had access to papers about the king's affair from the Vatican library, wrote in the *treatise of 1536*, that the king had 'violated' Mary Boleyn.[36] The word 'violated' meant in the Tudor period what it means today. We cannot be sure whether the cardinal mentions this as another reason to reject the king's marriage to Anne Boleyn, there may be an alternative motive here. However, it does make the suggestion that Mary slept with the king to gain rewards for herself or her family, as portrayed in some films and TV programmes, a little more doubtful. While being interrogated for treason in September 1537, William Webbe told the Privy Seal, that he was out riding one day near Eltham Palace when he came across the king in the woods. He said the king had taken a girl into the woods and had forced himself on her.[37]

As for the suggestion that the king and indeed her family forced Mary Boleyn to go to the king's chamber to enhance the family status, people such as her father and her husband seemed to have gained rewards through their own merits rather than because of anything Mary did. It is also interesting to note that Sir John Blount, the father of Elizabeth Blount, who was a mistress to the king and whose relationship with the monarch probably lasted far longer than Mary's did, received no gifts or rewards. This was even after his daughter bore the king a son.

There is no proof of the patrimony of Mary Boleyn's children.[38] Although there is no factual evidence that Mary ever bore the King of England a child,[39] that did not stop the rumours, both then and now. The rumours that Mary Boleyn's son Henry Carey was indeed the king's child were ostensibly first recorded six years after his birth, in 1531, when Lodovico Falier, the Venetian ambassador at Henry's court, stated: 'The King has also a natural son, bore to him of the widow of one of his peers; a youth of great promise, so much does he resemble his father.'[40] The Venetian ambassador could have been describing Mary Boleyn's child, or he could be referring to Elizabeth Blount's child. Elizabeth bore the king a son and was a widow at this time.

However, we do not just have Lodovico Falier's word, we also have John Hale's. He was the Vicar of Isleworth Church and he ended up begging the king for forgiveness after being arrested and taken to the Tower for treason. While in the Tower, John Hale wrote to the king, 'I have maliciously slandered the King and Queen and their Council; for which I ask forgiveness of God, King Henry VIII and Queen Anne, and shall continue sorrowful during my life, which stands only in the King's will.'[41] One of the many statements John had made, claiming that a 'Mr Skidmore' had told him this and he was only repeating it, was that Master Carey 'was our Sovereign Lord the King's son by our sovereign lady, the Queen's sister'.[42] John Hale said that Henry Carey looked very much like the king. Perhaps Master Carey, at the age of nine, was sporting the famous Tudor red hair.

After Thomas Cromwell's spies reported the conversation, John Hale and Robert Feron, the Vicar of Teddington, were taken to the Tower of London. John was hung, drawn and quartered at Tyburn on 4 May 1535, in front of a huge crowd, with five other men, all clerics, he had named as party to the slander. John Hale was later regarded as a martyr and is still remembered on 5 May, his feast day. Robert Feron survived by turning king's evidence.

Henry never admitted to Mary Boleyn being his mistress, whereas he did with Elizabeth Blount, she was made his official mistress and her son was claimed by the king as his own, so the fact that the king never claimed Henry Carey might suggest the king knew that Henry wasn't his. There were similarities between Elizabeth Blount's position and Mary Boleyn's, but the crucial difference was that Elizabeth Blount was widowed at the time the king recorded her as his mistress, whereas Mary was married when the rumours started. If his affair with Mary had been common knowledge, Katherine of Aragon would have certainly used it against the king through their annulment process.

The king admitting to an affair with Mary Boleyn would have harmed his side of the annulment with Katherine of Aragon. The king's future marriage to Anne Boleyn would be seen as almost incestuous, if the king admitted to his affair with Mary. The king had nothing to gain from admitting to this affair. With Elizabeth Blount, he needed a son to be his heir at a time when he had no other option. When Mary Boleyn was purported to be his mistress, the king already had the son from Elizabeth Blount to fall back on.

It has also been suggested that Mary's daughter Katherine Carey was the king's child. The portrait said to be of Katherine Carey was in the Knollys' family collection until 1944, when they sold it. It is claimed that the sitter is in her thirty-eighth year, which would place her date of birth around the year 1524, suggesting she was conceived in the summer of 1523. All this will be discussed further.

If the sitter was Katherine Carey, it would make Katherine the older of Mary's two children, with Henry born around 1525. It is possible that it was the birth of Katherine that ended the affair with the king, as did the pregnancy of Elizabeth Blount. If so, this counts against Henry Carey being the king's child. Katherine was born at the time Mary was, potentially, having an affair with the king. It is no more than a possibility, but what supports the suggestion is the portrait. The sitter looks very much like Henry VIII. The shape of the sitter's eyes, the winged eyebrows, the pronounced chin and the round jaw seem to be very similar to the Tudor king. There are traces of his brother Prince Arthur, and of Henry VII and their mother Elizabeth of York, too. There is a little red tuft of hair showing from under the sitter's coif and wired hood. Red hair was prominent in the Tudor family and important to its history too, as it was said that King Henry only accepted Elizabeth as his daughter because of her bright red hair.

Does all this suggest to us that Mary Boleyn was the king's mistress and that her two children were actually the King of England's rather than her husband's? We will probably never know. What we do know was that there was a rumour of the affair extant into the reign of Queen Elizabeth I, which suggests that something happened. Whether this was a full-blown affair or a passing flirtation, Mary Boleyn had caught the King of England's eye in any case.

William Carey died of the Sweating Sickness at Greenwich Palace. He caught the disease at the same time as Anne Boleyn and her father, who both survived. He died on Monday, 22 June 1528[43]. He was only thirty-two years old, and it is not known where he was buried, perhaps because of a hasty interment to stop the disease from spreading. If William had survived, in all probability he would have continued on his way to a peerage and wealth, which would have made Mary Boleyn a well-known and rich lady. But with the early death of her husband, Mary fell out of favour; Mary was in debt with two children to bring up, a hard position to be in in any period.

The lands already given to William within his lifetime were not passed on to his widow but to their son Henry Carey, who was only three years old at the time. They were worth roughly £107,000, making Henry a very rich toddler. This net worth would then be passed on to Henry's heir, Mary would never receive any of it, leaving her with only the rents from her Essex manor. This was not enough for her to live on as she asked her father several times to help her financially. He initially refused.

This issue was not left to the family to sort out, it was under the control of the king, and he decided to give the wardship of Henry Carey over to Mary's sister, Anne, so that he would enjoy a better education than his own mother could give him. So Mary's husband had died at a young age leaving her poor, her father had abandoned her when she needed him, her son was given into the care of her sister, whom she may or may not have liked – and she still had another child to try to bring up on her own. Eventually, by the order of the king – who at the time was probably listening to Anne Boleyn more than anyone else in 1528 – Mary's father had no choice but to allow Mary to live with him and his wife at Hever Castle.[44]

In December that year, the king also gave Mary an annuity of one hundred pounds, which was the same amount he had given

Mary's husband when he was alive. It is notoriously difficult to equate historic and contemporary monetary values, but this would be about £32,000 per year. This was an odd order for the king to make, a widow would not normally have the same wage that her deceased husband had, so this does look like a 'pay off'. However, it could simply have been the result of Anne's hold over the king at this time.[45] In 1532, the Boleyn family received New Year's gifts from the king. Mary received a piece of gilt plate, either in a form of a cup, salt cellar bottle or goblet.[46]

In October that year, King Henry rode from his palace at Greenwich to start his journey to Calais to meet with Francis I. With Katherine of Aragon sent away from court at the time, King Henry took Anne with him, as well as a few thousand lords and ladies, one of them being Mary.[47]

From London, they stopped at Stone in Kent and then on to Canterbury, where the 'Nun of Kent' shouted prophecies of how Anne Boleyn would be the ruin of the king. The nun was Sister Elizabeth Barton, born in 1506 in the village of Aldington, close to the City of Canterbury. By the age of nineteen she began to have visions while working as a domestic servant for Thomas Cobb, a farmer. She was believed to have predicted the death of a child in the household. She urged people to remain with the Roman Catholic Church, to pray to the Virgin Mary, and to reject the demands of the king, who by then wanted to be the Supreme Head of the Church of England. Many people believed in her and her prophecies, including Archbishop William Warham and Bishop, later Cardinal, John Fisher.[48] Elizabeth was becoming so well known that she had a private meeting with Cardinal Thomas Wolsey, who was regarded as the second most important man in England at the time, and even met with King Henry twice, before they met in Canterbury.

The king seemed quite happy with Elizabeth in the first two meetings because she wasn't saying anything that displeased him at this point.[49] This was soon to change once the king began proceedings for an annulment, and it became clear he wanted to gain control over the church. She openly opposed his wishes, stating that if the king was to marry Anne Boleyn he would die within a few months and go to Hell. Considering Elizabeth was prophesying the death of a king, it is amazing that she went unpunished for almost a year. This led some at the time to think that the king believed her. However, there were also rumours that many people, like Thomas More, thought she was harmless, putting her visions down to mental illness.[50]

As the visions continued and because of the support Elizabeth was gaining, she was eventually arrested for treason in 1533 and forced to admit her visions were untrue. She was hanged at Tyburn on 20 April 1534. She was only twenty-eight years old. Although her body was buried at Greyfriars Church in Newgate, London, her head was placed on a spike on London Bridge. She was to be the only woman treated thus,[51] an indication of the king's wrath after the public scene she made at Canterbury before Anne and Mary.

After the royal party's visit to Canterbury, they stayed at the house of Sir Christopher Hales. He had prosecuted Thomas Wolsey two years before and would later appear for the king in the trial of Thomas More, John Fisher and Anne Boleyn, watching them all being found guilty and sent to their deaths. From there, they travelled on to Dover Castle, a place the king knew well. At the age of three, the then Prince Henry had been appointed the Lord Warden of the Cinque Ports and the ninetieth Constable of Dover Castle, a position he held for sixteen years, visiting the place and even personally taking up an office. After he became king in 1509, the position went to Sir Edward Poynings.[52] George Boleyn assumed the role in 1533, the year the king apparently secretly married Anne. George would have been the ninety-fourth

Constable of Dover, a role that caused some trouble for him, as we have already discussed.[53] The king would update the castle's defences along the south coast between 1537 and 1540, and a series of artillery forts were added with at least three batteries.[54]

From the Port of Dover, the party travelled on a ship called the *Swallow* to France, landing in the French town of Calais, where they were greeted by a royal salute.[55] After a large celebration meal, the ladies, including Mary, were led by Anne in a masque, during which the ladies danced before the two kings. It is quite possible that it is here that Mary first meets William Stafford, who would become Mary's second husband. His name appears on the list of 200 people within the king's retinue who were at the event.[56]

On the way back, they stayed at Dover Castle and Stone Castle, arriving at Eltham Palace on 24 November 1532.[57] Eltham Palace was again a place King Henry would have known well. As a young prince, he grew up there and in 1499 Henry met with Desiderius Erasmus Roterodamus at the behest of Thomas More. Erasmus would later write of the meeting:

I had been carried off by Thomas More, who had come to pay me a visit on an estate of Mountjoy's [the house of Lord Mountjoy near Greenwich] where I was staying, to take a walk by way of diversion as far as the nearest town [Eltham]. For there all the royal children were being educated, Arthur alone excepted, the eldest son. When we came to the hall, all the retinue was assembled; not only that of the palace, but Mountjoy's as well. In the midst stood Henry, aged nine, already with a certain royal demeanour; I mean a dignity of mind combined with a remarkable courtesy... More with his companion Arnold saluted Henry (the present King of England) and presented to him something in writing. I, who was expecting nothing of the sort, had nothing to offer; but I promised that somehow, at some other time, I would show my duty towards him.[58]

When Anne Boleyn first appeared in public as queen at Easter 1533, she was given ladies in waiting. One of these was her sister Mary, as well as Lady Rochford, their sister-in-law, Margaret Douglas, Mary Howard, Frances de Vere, Mary Shelton, Elizabeth Wood, Anne Savage, Lady Berkeley and Elizabeth Browne.[59] Mary's role as her sister's lady in waiting did not last long before she was banished from court. This was because Mary had become pregnant by William Stafford in September of 1534, and it is suggested that she had married William just a few weeks before she was showing with child.[60]

Not only was Anne not best pleased with her sister, but the timing was not good for Anne herself. Anne, who had just lost a child full term, was quickly losing favour with the king. The Boleyn family were angry with Mary for allowing herself to get in this position, still more so when Mary told them that she had in fact married the plain William Stafford, without their permission; permission the family would have never given as they believed he was below her station.[61] The family tree of William Stafford in fact indicates that although William was a farmer, he was attached to a family with some status. Maybe the Boleyn family were a little too quick to judge him.

William Stafford was born around the year of 1500 to Sir Humphrey Stafford and his wife, Margaret Fogge, daughter to Sir John Fogge of Ashford in Kent.[62] William's grandfather Sir John Fogge was born in 1417 and was named after his father, John Fogge Sr, who was the second son to Sir Thomas Fogge, a soldier of fortune, willing to fight for anyone who would pay. He was successful enough to be able to buy lands around Canterbury, Harbledown, Boughton under Blean and Chartham. In 1360, he was knighted and became a Member of Parliament for Kent, serving in this role eight times. Sir Thomas Fogge passed away on 13 July 1407 and was buried inside Canterbury Cathedral. He left enough money for his family to be provided for, meaning when Sir John Fogge was born, ten years after his grandfather's death, he entered into a family with wealth.[63]

In the early 1440s John married Alice de Criol, daughter of Sir Thomas de Criol of Westenhanger, near Folkstone, Kent. (When Sir Thomas de Criol was beheaded after the Second Battle of St Albans, Westenhanger Castle was given to his daughter and her husband, John Fogge.) They had one son together, John Fogge the younger.[64] In February 1447, when other members of his family had passed away, John gained the same lands that his grandfather had bought before him and three years later, being a nobleman with lands, John was able to become an Esquire to King Henry VI, being involved in the Rebellion of Jack Cade.

This rebellion was fomented by the abuse of power of the King's Men and anger over the country's debts incurred from the constant battles with France.[65] Jack Cade had gathered an army from Kent to march on the capital. However, once his men had entered the capital, their urge to loot the place took over. Many people turned on the rebels because of the looting, helping the king and indeed the King's Men, including John, to fight back. This ultimately caused a bloody battle upon London Bridge. Jack Cade fled the scene, only to be captured later. He was so badly wounded from the battle on the bridge that he died before reaching London for his trial.[66]

Three years after this failed rebellion, in 1453 John Fogge was made Sheriff of Kent, one of the oldest crown appointments that is still in use today.[67] In 1458, John Fogge married again, this time to Alice Haute. This marriage linked John and the children he had with Alice to royalty. Alice Haute was the daughter of William Haute and Joan Woodville.

Joan's brother, Richard Woodville, was the grandfather of Elizabeth Woodville, wife of King Edward IV and mother of Elizabeth of York, wife of Henry VII. With this family connection in mind, we can perhaps understand the future actions of John Fogge more clearly.

Despite his earlier service under King Henry VI, when the future king, Edward IV, landed in Britain in 1460, John Fogge turned coat and joined his side at the Battle of Towton. The fact that Edward IV was successful in this battle, becoming king afterwards, meant that John profited from being on the winning side. John was given the manors of Tonford in Thanington and Dane Court in Boughton under Blean, as well as being knighted. In 1461, John was given the office of Keeper of the Writs and was the Treasurer of the Household to King Edward IV until 1468.[68]

When King Edward IV gained the throne for the second time from King Henry VI, who was then imprisoned in the Tower where he passed away in suspicious circumstances,[69] John was given a number of gold and silver mines in Devon and Cornwall in acknowledgement of his loyalty.

However, events soon took another turn for Sir John Fogge, when in 1483 the future King Richard III became Protector of King Edward's son and heir to the throne, Edward V. Perhaps John was sensing dark times ahead as he decided to take sanctuary, even though the new King Richard III was prepared to treat him favourably. He was also conceivably staying true to the previous king by being a supporter of Richard Guildford, who was garnering backing for King Edward's son, Edward V, to take the throne away from Richard.

Following the failure of what would become known as Buckingham's Rebellion, John lost much of his lands and property but somehow managed to keep his head. The loss of some of his property was only for a short time however, as just two years later, in 1485, John was pardoned and four of his manors were returned to him because of his good behaviour.[70]

Yet, sensing the tides were turning once more, Sir John Fogge changed sides to support Henry Tudor and was purported to have played an active role in the Battle of Bosworth Field. This is of course where Richard III lost his crown, Henry Tudor became King Henry VII, and the Tudor dynasty began. It was because of this last 'betrayal' that Sir John Fogge regained all the lands that he had previously lost during the short reign of Richard III.

John Fogge's children with Alice Haute also had their own connection to the Tudor dynasty, as their first-born, Thomas Fogge, became Sergeant Porter of Calais under King Henry VII and later under his son, Henry VIII. Their daughter, Margaret Fogge, would marry Sir Humphrey Stafford, thus making the connection that William Stafford had to the Tudor family.

Sir John Fogge passed away on 9 November 1490 and because he had built the main church in Ashford town in Kent, St Mary's, as well as the college nearby, he was buried beneath a grand altar-tomb in the church. He is celebrated in a memorial window there, and upon the wall of the church by his tomb is a jousting helmet that belonged to him.

Sir John Fogge was a man who rubbed shoulders with royalty, even becoming a part of the royal family himself through his second marriage, albeit distantly. He changed sides in wars and battles and managed to survive with his life intact, only losing lands and manors temporarily. He built St Mary's Church and helped build Ashford College, a building that still stands today, now a part of Ashford's Museum. There is a Sir John Fogge Avenue in Ashford. This man was the grandfather to William Stafford, Mary Boleyn's second husband So the Boleyns were perhaps wrong to dismiss him so easily. Would all this history tied to William Stafford have actually meant something to them? Had Mary chosen wisely, possibly without truly knowing it – while also choosing for love – without needing her family's help? We do know that Anne did not want to see her sister after the news was broken that Mary had married and was pregnant, as Mary noted: 'As far as I can perceive, her Grace is highly displeased with us both.' [71] As much as her sister's displeasure may have hurt Mary's feelings, the fact that her allowance was cut as she was no longer a widow may have hurt her more.[72] Mary was banished from court, something that would become a family tradition, as Mary's grandchild, Lettice Knollys, would also suffer the same expulsion.[73]

It may be that Mary and her new husband were also banished from Mary's childhood home of Hever Castle at this point, as now with a new husband Mary was not the responsibility of her father anymore, so it is very possible that Mary went to live with her father-in-law while she put a case together to fight to get some money back in her purse.

We know she fought for her rights as she writes to Thomas Cromwell, and although the letter is not dated it was probably written in the latter part of 1534:

Master Secretary, after my poor recommendations, which is smally to be regarded of me that am a poor banished creature, this shall be to desire you to be good to my poor husband and me. I am sure that it is not unknown to you the high displeasure that both he and I have, both of the King's Highness and the Queen's Grace, by reason of our marriage without the knowledge, wherein we both do yield ourselves faulty and acknowledge that we did not well to be so hasty nor so bold without their knowledge. But one thing, Master Secretary, consider; that he was young and love overcame reason: and for my part I saw so much honesty in him that I loved him as well as he did me; was in bondage and glad I was to be at liberty.[74]

The letter continues in the same vein, begging and pleading with Cromwell to reinstate her new husband at court. The lament seemed to go unheard, as no one, not Thomas Cromwell, the king, or indeed her own sister did anything to help Mary and her new husband. Unbeknown to them, their absence from court distanced them from the cataclysm that was about to engulf her sister, brother and, to some extent, her father.

What does this tell us about the nature of Mary Boleyn? Mary has been portrayed as someone quiet, meek even, which is understandable when she is compared to her sister, who rightly or wrongly has been portrayed as more clever, ambitious, maybe more devious. However, Mary was a Boleyn after all, and here we might catch a glimpse of the Boleyn steel at work. Mary had lost almost everything at this point because she had chosen to go after what she wanted, rather than what her family wanted for her – like her sister. Mary had displeased her father and her sister, which in truth Mary might not have cared about if it wasn't for the fact that her sister was now the queen of England. Mary had lost her standing in court, her money and her home. She does not give up. She tries to gain favour for her husband at every turn. She may not have had the intelligence her sister was claimed to have had, but she did know what to say and how to say it, to make her case. This, as we have seen earlier, is very much like her father, Sir Thomas Boleyn. Look out for the quiet ones, even at court.

Rodolfo Pio, Bishop of Faenza, stated that Anne had not in fact given birth to a still-born child in January 1536 but had lied about her pregnancy and had faked the miscarriage to keep up the deceit. In consequence, 'She would allow no one to attend her but her sister,' so Mary was granted permission to return to court. However, there are other accounts and descriptions of a child then being born by Anne, and a strong possibility that Mary was living in Calais at the time of this birth, which does put his statement – and for that matter, any of his other statements – into question.[75]

William and Mary spent the rest of their lives more or less in obscurity compared to the rest of her family and in relative poverty.[76] A child was born to them in 1535, and they named her Anne. That could suggest Mary and her husband were trying once again to return to the king's and queen's good graces, however, it was common in the Tudor period to name one's child after whoever was king or queen at the time, and the queen just happened to be Mary's sister. There was also a claim that Mary and William had a son, unnamed in any records found to date, who died in 1543.[77] It was always thought Mary Boleyn only ever had one son, Henry Carey.[78]

At this point in 1535, Henry Carey had been taken away from her and was living at Syon Abbey at Isleworth in Middlesex, now aged ten. His guardian was his aunt, the queen, and she gave him a fine education. Perhaps wanting the same level of education for him that Anne herself received, she hired the well-known French humanist and poet Nicholas Bourbon to tutor him. Nicholas was already known to Anne after he had fled persecution in France some years before. He would later write a series of poems lauding Anne as one of God's beloved servants.

Regarding the trials of George and Anne, it would be interesting to know how Mary felt about the suggestion of incest between her sister and brother, and how she felt about the downfall of both being helped along by her sister-in-law and, in a small way, her own father. What an extraordinary turn of Fortune's Wheel, almost incomprehensible.

George was beheaded on 17 May 1536 and buried beneath the altar in the Royal Chapel of St Peter of Vincula within the Tower of London. Before Anne was to suffer the same fate, her marriage was declared invalid and her daughter, Elizabeth was declared a bastard. These final actions by the king imply that he wanted Anne to know that she had failed in all she had wanted for her family, that everything she had done to gain power was in vain.

The king finally used his relationship with Mary against Anne, to gain an easier annulment of his second marriage compared to his first.[79] After all, Anne and the Boleyns had no family relations to fall back on to hinder him, unlike Katherine of Aragon, who was a princess royal and the aunt of the King of Spain, someone who could have started a war with England over the issue.

Anne Boleyn may have thought she was gaining power, the Boleyns may have thought they had some importance because of Anne's rise to fame, but in reality, they could be easily pushed to one side if the king chose so to do. The king had sometimes been portrayed as under the influence of Anne Boleyn, almost as if he were in a trance – the king himself had suggested witchcraft. In reality, he had all the power all along. Power, as we learn from the deaths of Anne and George Boleyn, that he was not afraid to use.

Were the Boleyns guilty of vaulting ambition? If they had settled for the high status they had already achieved before Anne pushed for being more than a mistress to the king, perhaps they would have gained even greater standing and power anyway. Would they have all survived? Perhaps a more important question is, would Queen Elizabeth I have reigned without Anne demanding to be the king's wife rather than a mistress?

Augustus Hare, writing in 1878, says that Mary's daughter Katherine was one of the ladies who served Anne Boleyn while she was in the tower, but there are no corroborative documents. Katherine would only have been twelve years old. Katherine would in fact become a maid of honour to a queen in 1540, when she served Henry's fourth wife, Anne of Cleves. There also seems to be no evidence that Mary ever visited her sister at the Tower or was at her execution, scenes irresistible to dramatists.

So where was Mary Boleyn at this time? Although it has been suggested that Mary and William stayed at Rochford Hall for years after their banishment from court, there is actually no evidence in reports or letters that Mary's father allowed this to happen. Mary could have stayed in the French town of Calais at this point, as her husband was working with Lord Lisle in the February of 1537.[80] This, plus the fact that William was one of those who welcomed the King of England's fourth wife, Anne of Cleves, to Calais in 1539, does suggest Mary and William were living in France after their banishment from court.[81]

In a letter dated April 1537 written by Robert Blakeney, the then new Prior of Tynemouth, he expresses the wish to stop paying Mary an annuity of one hundred marks as, with her diminished status, she was no longer of any use to Robert's house.[82] However, the annuity was still paid to Mary even after the priory was dissolved in 1539. So indirectly, the king was still providing for Mary and possibly his own daughter, Katherine. After all, the king looked after Mary's other child Henry Carey after the death of Anne Boleyn, accepting the wardship and continuing his education to a high level, employing different tutors.

After the death of Mary's father, Thomas Boleyn, in 1539, Mary was able to claim half of the Boleyn estate, the other half (including Hever Castle) went to the crown. The castle was then given to Anne of Cleves after her divorce, surely a painful moment for Mary. William Stafford was slowly allowed to re-enter court after his banishment, By 1540, he was recorded as a Gentleman Pensioner in the king's household. To be a Gentleman Pensioner meant that he was to guard the king and keep watch on his chamber.[83]

Mary would have to wait a long time for her grandmother's, home, Rochford Hall, and both Mary and her husband became frustrated with how long it took for Mary to claim on her inheritance. However, on the death of Mary's father, the king did give Mary the livery lands of Southborough in Kent, including the Manor of Great Bounds,[84] all the lands of Hever excluding the castle itself, and the lands of Brasted. These lands provided roughly the equivalent of £150,000 today per annum.[85]

In the same year as gaining those lands, Mary's sixteen-year-old daughter married Sir Francis Knollys, a twenty-six-year-old Gentleman Pensioner of the king's household working with William Stafford.[86] The king seems not to have given the newly married couple a gift, which would have been strange if you believe that the bride was his own daughter. However, the king did have an involvement in an Act of Parliament that meant the couple were given Rotherfield Greys estate and title. Greys Court would be where Mary's daughter would make her home with her new husband.[87]

In 1541, Katherine gave birth to a daughter. She named her child Henry, possibly after Henry VIII as he was on the throne at the time. As we have mentioned before this was a common occurrence. So Mary's first grandson was probably named after the man who had caused so much heartache for Mary personally and for her close family members. Of course we cannot know Mary's reaction to this, as she could not admit to any ill feeling without risking arrest for treason.

Also in 1541, Mary's husband was promoted to Esquire of the Body and the couple would exchange the manor in Henden, Kent, for the manor of Ugthorpe near Whitby.[88] The couple probably spent most of their time in Southborough nevertheless, because William sold the manor of Ugthorpe almost as soon as he had it, to Roland Shakerly.[89] This would also make sense because the place in Southborough that Mary was given, called Great Bounds, was once the home of her brother George Boleyn and was only a two-hour walk from her childhood home of Hever Castle. [90]

We also know that the family – Mary, William, Katherine and her husband – sold houses, outbuildings and gardens, 700 acres of land, fifty acres of meadow, sixty acres of furze and heath, common pasture for 1000 sheep, and the rent in Fulborn. We know this because the Stafford family were not actually allowed to sell the land without asking the King of England first. A case was brought in the Justices of Common Pleas at Westminster on 23 October 1542, and the family was fined.[91] At this time Mary also gave the manor of Filby in Norfolk to her uncle Sir James Boleyn. The family was trying to raise funds as the claim to Mary's grandmother's estate of Rochford Hall was still not settled. In May 1543, Mary finally received the estate.[92]

On 5 April 1543, William was caught eating flesh on Good Friday. He was sent to Fleet Prison and dismissed from Council meetings.[93] This, as well as the fall of Queen Catherine Howard, who was related to Mary and whose demise must have reminded Mary of her own sister's fall from grace, would have made 1543 a cruel year for Mary, were it not for her belated move to Rochford Hall.[94] Finally, Mary had a place to call her own. This was not to last.

After waiting for the deeds to be finalised and allowing for the time it took to move in, Mary was mistress of Rochford Hall for perhaps only a few days. She passed away on 19 July 1543.[95] This meant that Mary only officially owned Rochford Hall for two months and four days. Her death was deemed sudden at the time. The reason was unknown – a fatal accident, or even a seizure of some sort? Perhaps simply the stress of being a Boleyn and all that had meant for Mary was the cause of her death. Her demise meant that Rochford Hall went to her son Henry Carey. In her will Mary gave the manor of Arbinger in Surrey and dwellings in London and elsewhere to her husband William.[96]

Mary's last resting place – which will come as no surprise – is a mystery. Some have stated that she was buried in the grounds of Hever Castle, however, for her to be buried in unconsecrated ground would have been bizarre. Westminster Abbey, where her children lie, is an interesting suggestion. However, there is no mention of her being there. St Andrew's Church in the grounds of Rochford Hall is another possibility, but the church has no record. However, this could be explained by the fact that the church changed a lot in the Victorian period and the burial records do not go back that far. If she is there, there is sadly no sign of her today.

Personally, I feel the idea that Mary was buried in the grounds of Rochford Hall does not ring true. Mary either liked this building for its own sake or because of family connections to it, but in the latter case, was there somewhere else that would have fitted the bill better for Mary's last resting place? It is interesting that of all the estates and lands Mary had sold off to get money for Rochford Hall, she kept Great Bounds in Southborough near Tonbridge in Kent. We know this because upon her death, her son, Henry Carey, received Great Bounds and he spent money on the land to improve it. Mary gained Great Bounds around 1539 and Rochford Hall in 1543, so there were four years where she could have enjoyed her time at Great Bounds, close to her childhood home and where she could have possibly brought up her daughter. Would she have been happy to be within the rolling hills of the Kent countryside once again, at the end of her life?

The original building was demolished for the first time in the 1600s,[97] but the extant gated entrance and lodge is very much Tudor in style[98] with its tall, thin chimney stacks reminiscent of Hampton Court Palace. I toured the local churches within the area to search for some answers, when I came in contact with Roger Evernden, the churchwarden of St Thomas Church, a church near to Great Bounds once was. A member of the committee of the Southborough Society, Roger explained that although Tudor records are sadly few and far between, there was a possibility that Mary or a representative of hers chose this area of Kent rather than the area of Rochford Hall in Essex for her interment.

The Boleyns were well known and well established not just in Kent but this particular area of Kent. Roger Evernden pointed out that that all of the churches in the immediate area of Great Bounds, in Tonbridge and Tunbridge Wells, were Victorian.[99] Was there a church that was built within the required timeframe? The answer came, as it quite often does, by accident.

I was looking over some old maps of the area of Hever Castle for a piece I was writing for *Historic Houses,* wanting to visualize the distance from Penshurst Place to Hever Castle for the story. On one map,[100] slightly to the east of Hever Castle and west of Great Bounds, was a very crude drawing of a church. Isolated on a hill in what looked like a field, the church was labelled – Bidborough.

A little more research revealed that this particular church was Norman and would indeed have been in the right parish, the church of St Lawrence in Bidborough. Sadly, any Tudor records have disappeared, so the suggestion of Mary Boleyn being buried at St Lawrence Church will probably remain just that, a suggestion. However, it is hopefully an idea that can stand beside all the other proposals for her last resting place. I went to St Lawrence Church to lay some Myosotis flowers, forget-me-nots, in memory of this formidable lady, just in case. It is comforting to think that Mary could be buried somewhere near her childhood home of Hever, with its memories of a time away from the royal court, a time when she might have been able to be herself and to enjoy being a daughter, sister and quite possibly a mother.

It is possible that Mary was looked down upon somewhat by her own family, they may have forced her to become the king's mistress to better their own fortunes, at the same time remaining disappointed in her lack of ambition and her lowly position at court. Although she may have lived in the shadow of her younger sister for most of her life, Mary's fall from grace was less catastrophic than that of other family members, and she managed to live the rest of her life with the love of a husband and to die in her own bed. Which Boleyn sister actually had the better life in the long run?

From the month of Mary's passing, William led one hundred foot soldiers for the next four months as the king fought and took Boulogne in France.[101] Within two years, William was fighting in Scotland under the banner of Edward Seymour and it might be for this that William was knighted on 23 September 1545.[102] It may have also have been through William's connections with Edward Seymour that he held his position in court when Henry VIII's son took the throne, as Edward Seymour became the child king's Lord Protector. William sat at the new king's parliament in 1547 and became the king's standard bearer, granted an annuity of one hundred pounds.[103] His career was not all plain sailing, as he managed to get into a fight with another soldier called Adrian Poynings in November 1554 and once again found himself in Fleet Prison.[104]

It seems that William was in mourning for the woman he had risked so much for, as he does not remarry until 1552, to Dorothy Stafford, a distant relation. She was fifteen years old at the time of the marriage. Dorothy was closely connected to a Plantagenet part of the family with a notorious background. Her grandfather,

Edward Stafford, 3rd Duke of Buckingham, was thrown into the Tower and executed for treason in May 1521. Dorothy did not have much money to her name because of her family background. Did William marry for love again? After all, William had married Mary Boleyn for love rather than status or riches, surely the reason why Mary Boleyn had chosen to be his wife against her family's wishes.

William and Dorothy would go on to have three sons and two daughters, all garnering high positions in Queen Elizabeth's court. One of the daughters, Elizabeth, possibly named after the queen, became a part of Queen Elizabeth I's household as her Lady of the Bedchamber.[105] However, not all of the children remained in the good graces of the monarch. The younger William Stafford, born in 1554, became a French spy working for the French ambassador, Châteauneuf, who had plans to kill Elizabeth with a poisoned gown or saddle. William Stafford was arrested and taken to the Tower of London where he was questioned by the queen's spymaster Sir Francis Walsingham. William Stafford confessed to conspiring to poison the queen, but extraordinarily enough was released in August 1588 with no charges being brought against him. This strongly implies that William became Walsingham's double agent, unless it was simply the family connections to the Walsinghams, or to the queen herself, that saved his life.[106]

When Mary I came to the throne, the Protestant William Stafford Senior decided to leave the country in March 1554 and lived the rest of his life in Geneva, Switzerland, with his wife and children. William died on 5 May 1556; his second wife went on to serve Queen Elizabeth I for another forty years. She would pass away in 1604, having a tomb in St Margaret's Church in Westminster, something that sadly William's first wife, Mary, does not have.

Dorothy's inscription on her effigy reads:

Here Lyeth the Lady Dorothy Stafford, Wife and Widow to Sir William Stafford, Knight, Daughter to Henry, Lord Stafford, the only son of Edward, the last Duke of Buckingham: Her mother was Ursula, Daughter to the Countesse of Salisbury, the only Daughter to George, Duke of Clarence, Brother to King Edward the Fourth. Shee continued a true Widow from the Age of 27 till her Death. She served Queen Elizabeth 40 Yeeres, lying in the Bedchamber, esteemed of her, loved of all, doing good, all she could, to every Body, never hurt any; a continual Remembrancer of the Suits of the Poor. As she Lived a religious Life, in great Reputation of Honour and Vertue in the World, so she ended in continual fervent Meditation, and hearty Prayer to God. At which Instant, as all her Life, so after her Death, she gave liberally to the Poore, and died aged 78, the 22. of September 1604. In whose Remembrance, Sir Edward Stafford, her sonne, hath caused this Memorial of her to be in the same Forme and Place as she herselfe long since required him.[107]

Mary's son Henry Carey had a prince's education given to him first by his aunt Queen Anne Boleyn and then by Henry VIII. In 1545, two years after the death of his mother, Henry joins the king's household.[108] In the same year Henry marries Anne Morgan, a wife chosen for him by the king. Anne was sixteen years old at the time of her marriage, daughter of a Welsh gentleman called Sir Thomas Morgan of Arkstone, Herefordshire. Henry married Anne on 21 May 1545.[109] This match chosen by the king was not a high-status union compared with the one he had chosen for his bastard son, Henry Fitzroy. Fitzroy was married off to a daughter of a duke, Henry Carey was married to a daughter of a gentleman. This indicates Henry Carey was not the king's son, or at the very least, that the king did not think of him as his own. We also have the fact that the king did not give Henry Carey any gifts for his wedding.[110] Henry and Anne would have twelve children and he was able to claim on his inherited lands in Buckingham, Essex, Hampshire and Wiltshire, which included Rochford Hall. By 1546, Henry had become an MP for Buckingham, a role he would hold for four terms.[111] In 1552 he would sell Rochford Hall, the place his mother had waited so long to have, to Richard Lord Rich, who then changed the Hall design greatly, leaving little that Mary Boleyn would have recognised.[112] The records of Elizabeth's time spent at Hatfield Estate show that Henry was within her personal circle of friends. The records also show us that Elizabeth sent a gift of money at the christening of Henry Carey's child.[113] The relations of Mary Boleyn were no threat to Queen Elizabeth, unlike her relations on her father's side, so Elizabeth was content to have the Boleyn side of her family close to her. Both Henry and Katherine Carey entered the service of Queen Elizabeth almost as soon as the queen took the throne in November 1558. Their loyalty was surely the main reason why they were later to receive grand funerals at Westminster Abbey.[114]

Henry Carey was knighted in 1558 and just two months later, in January 1559, the queen gave him the title of Baron Hunsdon, which not only brought him money but also the royal palace of Hunsdon House in Hertfordshire.[115] In 1560, he was given the role of Master of the Queen's Hawks and a year later he was made a Knight of the Garter. Events in 1562 probably cemented the closeness between the queen and her cousin Henry. It was thought that Elizabeth was going to die from smallpox, and it was Henry who summoned a German doctor, an expert, to treat her. When the doctor had given up hope, stating the queen was unlikely to survive, Henry is supposed to have forced the doctor to continue the treatment – at knife point.[116] If this event is true, it indicates an inner strength and unshakable loyalty to his cousin. Maybe he inherited these characteristics from his mother.

Henry was sent to watch over the Insignia of the Garter to Charles IX of France in 1564 and for many years was deemed an important presence at court. He became a Privy Councillor in 1577 and was made Captain of the Gentlemen Pensioners, being the queen's personal bodyguard, in 1583. He even became the Lord Chamberlain in 1585, gaining many more titles along the way. As Lord Chamberlain, in charge of the Queen Elizabeth's household,[117] one perk was that he could have suits made to order for himself![118]

However, Henry never seemed to be a rich man; he never asked for more than he needed, and his large family meant that he was always short of money. The queen seemed to like him because he kept his own counsel, something that his mother had done before him, though when he was asked his opinions he was blunt, even when directly speaking to the queen. This characteristic Henry may have taken from his grandfather, Thomas Boleyn, who dared to follow the same approach with Henry VIII.[119]

In 1568, Henry was one of the commissioners at the trial of Mary, Queen of Scots, in York. A few years before, Henry's eldest son, George, had been mooted by Queen Elizabeth as a new husband for Mary. As a Lieutenant General, Henry was instrumental in the defeat of the Northern Rebellion of 1569.[120]

If Henry Carey was devoted to the queen of England, he was not so to his wife. He was known to have at least two mistresses and fathered many children with them, one of which, Valentine Carey, would grow up to become a soldier under Henry's own command. Valentine would later become the Dean of St Paul's Cathedral and the Bishop of Exeter. When he died in his London townhouse in Drury Lane, he was buried at St Paul's.[121] Any monument he may have had was destroyed in the Great Fire of London in 1666, but there is still a likeness of him in Exeter Cathedral.[122]

Henry was in Tilbury when the queen made her famous speech – 'I know I have the body but of a weak and feeble woman, but I have the heart and stomach of a king, and of a King of England too, and think foul scorn that Parma or Spain, or any Prince of Europe should dare to invade the borders of my realm' – before the troops went to confront the Spanish Armada. [123]

Henry Carey was the first patron of the Lord Chamberlain's Men, with whom William Shakespeare acted.[124] Shakespeare would write of Henry Carey twice in his plays, once as the Philostrate Master of the Revels to King Theseus in *A Midsummer Night's Dream* and also as victor over the Northern Rebellion in 1569 in *Henry IV Part One*.[125]

Henry Carey died on 23 July 1596 at his lodgings at Somerset House in London, being the Keeper of the place at the time, in the same week of his brother-in-law's death.[126] Henry was buried in a large tomb in St John the Baptist's Chapel, Westminster Abbey.[127]

In conclusion. we return to Mary. There are many portraits said to be of her. One of them hangs at Hever Castle, for many years labelled as another painting of her sister, Anne Boleyn. However, it now hangs as a one of a pair, Mary and Anne, although the Anne portrait is still under debate. There is a suggested portrait of Mary Boleyn hanging at Warwick Castle, one in Southside House in Wimbledon, another at Henden Manor in Kent and one, possibly two, in the Royal Collection. Although all of these do look like the same person, they were all painted after Mary's death. Mary Boleyn always seems to be retreating from our view behind suggested portraits, suggested events, suggested dates.

In 2020, Mary Boleyn reappeared and caused quite a stir. Historian and author Alison Weir was enthused: 'I am delighted that the sitter in the portrait has been identified at last.'[128] So where was she hiding for all these years? In plain sight.

On 31 May, The Jorden Van Dyck Panel Paintings Project announced their findings concerning a portrait in the Royal Collection at Windsor Castle. Originally titled 'Portrait of a Woman', it was thought to be possibly a copy of a lost picture by Hans Holbein. It had been in the Royal Collection for hundreds of years, part of a group of fourteen portraits categorised as 'Beauties' that had been hanging in Queen Anne's Bathing Room at Windsor Castle over 300 years ago. It had been taken down in the nineteenth century because the sitter and the way she was painted looked so different from the other thirteen. Although all fourteen had been painted in the seventeenth century, this one stood out because the sitter was wearing clothes of an earlier era. The other thirteen were moved to Queen Victoria's Drawing Room before travelling to Highgrove, the private residence of the Prince of Wales and the Duchess of Cornwall. The fourteenth portrait went to Hampton Court Palace in the nineteenth century, before travelling to Holyroodhouse in Edinburgh in 1995 – where it still hangs in Mary, Queen of Scots' bedroom.

Now, through dendrochronology, the testing of the wood it was painted on, provenance and comparative analysis, the sitter of the portrait has a name, Mary Boleyn. 'It's been a voyage of discovery,' said Justin Davies, a British art historian and Jorden Van Dyck Paintings Project co-founder. 'The results were remarkable and unexpected. Six of the 14 panels had been made from the same oak tree. The tree had started growing in southwest Germany before 1393 and was cut down between 1651 and 1671. In itself, this constitutes a world record – six panel paintings from the same tree had not been recorded before.'[129]

In the nineteenth century the portrait had been catalogued as a Holbein portrait of Anne Boleyn and by 1861 that description had changed to 'a portrait of a lady of the Court of Henry VIII', a mysterious Tudor lady.

Justin Davies did some research at the Heinz Library and Archive at the National Portrait Gallery, where he found two photographs of paintings in a private collection. One was identified as Lady Herbert and the other, Mary Boleyn. This Lady Herbert was married to Thomas Carey, the great-grandson of Mary Boleyn, before remarrying after Thomas's death to Sir Edward Herbert. It was through these paintings that a comparison could be made, leading to the finding that the Holyroodhouse portrait is of Mary Boleyn. As it looks very much like all the other suggested portraits of her, including the one hanging in her childhood home of Hever Castle, this reinforces the identification.

It is from Mary that we trace a lineage to modern-day royals, through her daughter, Katherine Carey.

3

KATHERINE CAREY, LADY KNOLLYS

Henry Carey had a sister and as we learn about her, we step down one more level on the family tree. Katherine's brother's birth date looks quite easy to work out because he is mentioned in William Carey's inquisition post-mortem notes as being his heir, 'aged two years, fifteen weeks and 5 days on 22nd June 1528'.[1] This makes his date of birth 4 March 1526; but even this evidence isn't watertight for some, who suspect that the date was written down incorrectly and that actually Henry was one year older, making his birth date 4 March 1525. This is because upon his tomb in Westminster Abbey it states that he died in his seventy-second year in 1591.

Katherine's birth is a little harder to pinpoint as of course she wasn't William Carey's heir, being female, and she wasn't a royal birth.[2] In *Letters and Papers of Henry VIII Volume XIV Part II*, 572, Katherine Carey spelt with a 'K'[3] was listed as a maid of honour to the king's new wife, Anne of Cleves.[4] Normally, maids of honour to a queen would have been aged sixteen and above because they were expected to know how to entertain the queen with music or dance. To do this, they must have already had an education. This narrows the range a little for her birth date.

She was mentioned in the *Letters and Papers XVI 498* documents for April 1540, when she gained the Knollys Manor at Rotherfield Grey in Oxfordshire on the death of her mother-in-law. This proves that by the early part of 1540, Katherine was certainly married. A Latin dictionary found among items belonging to the Knollys family has an inscription written by Katherine's future husband. It states, 'Francys Knollys and Katern, his wyffe that were married ye xxvi daye of Apryle anno. 1540',[5] 26 April 1540. Just knowing Katherine's marriage date doesn't of course tell us her date of birth, but it would have been anomalous for a Tudor marriage to have been consummated before the age of sixteen. Katherine has her first child on 'the Tuesday before Easter day in 1541'.[6] The same Latin dictionary informs us that Katherine has her last child, Dudley, in 1562. This information may well be important as it is the same year that a painting of a pregnant courtier, suggested as being Katherine, was painted by Steven Vander Meulen. He provided an inscription stating the sitter was in her thirty-eighth year. If this portrait was indeed of Katherine, this points to her birth being in the early part of 1524, which would accord with all the other indicators.

This date can help in resolving the question of her patrimony. Mary Boleyn being the mistress of King Henry is common knowledge now because of historical fiction and films, but in fact, at the time the affair was not widely known or written about. However, Pope Clement (1478–1534) wrote a dispensation on 1 January 1528 to the effect that, if Henry's marriage to Katherine of Aragon was made void, he could marry someone who was related to a person he had already slept with. This dispensation surely refers to Mary.

This also means that Mary must have been the king's mistress before he showed signs of his attraction to her sister. This could roughly make 1526 the year of their affair, two years before the king was asking for dispensation from the pope. We could also suggest that she became his mistress after the birth of Henry Fitzroy, King Henry's illegitimate child with his mistress Elizabeth Blount in 1519.

In the purported portrait of Katherine paid for by her brother, Katherine looks very much like certain portraits of Henry VIII and even of portraits of his daughter Queen Elizabeth. Her face seems softer than William Carey's, and as previously mentioned, just peeking out of her coif is hair of a distinct red colour. Mary Boleyn has been described as fair or dark, but never a redhead, the Tudor trait. As much as this might sound like proof of Katherine being the king's daughter, it must be remembered that through her mother, Katherine shared the same DNA as Queen Elizabeth, no matter who her father actually was. Another possibility is that the artist van der Meulen was deliberately making a sly reference to her potential royal blood. The jury is still out, perhaps forever.

Where Katherine was born is unknown. Mary may have been sent away from court to give birth, perhaps in one of the manor houses in Essex. However, Mary may have been allowed the luxury of giving birth at the court, as Mary and William held important roles at the time, even if we dismiss the idea that she was giving birth to the king's child. All things considered, it would seem likely that Katherine was born at her mother's childhood home of Hever Castle in Kent, where Katherine's grandparents were still living. If this is correct, it is likely Katherine spent the first four years of her life there.

When Katherine was four years old, William Carey, the man she would have known as her father, died on 22 June 1528 of the Sweating Sickness.[7] The king reacted to the news by writing to Anne, telling her that he hoped their father would do his duty and look after Mary. He placed Mary's son in the wardship of Anne, while Mary and probably Katherine were sent away from court to live at Hever. Of course, we cannot know if mother and child formed a close bond, but when they were both away from court and coping with William's death it would seem likely.

So, Katherine and her brother, Henry, are separated. Henry's education would have been quite different to Katherine's. He studied at a Cistercian Monastery and knew the French poet, Nicholas Bourbon, whom his aunt, Anne, admired.[8] Katherine and Henry may have visited each other but this would have been a rarity and it is very likely that they did not form a close relationship after the death of Anne. Although during the reign of Elizabeth I they both held important roles at court at the same time.

Mary did return to court and was there when Katherine's aunt became queen in 1533. We can assume that Katherine then visited her mother from time to time at court. However, it is interesting to note that Mary left court again for a considerable time after Anne became queen. When she returned in September 1534, it seemed to cause such a scandal that Mary was once again sent away.

Katherine was not recorded at court during this time and some historians have suggested that Katherine might have been sent to Hatfield to be part of her cousin Princess Elizabeth's household. Although this seems reasonable, there is no record of her being there either. Mary may have returned to Hever Castle, or she may have lived with her new husband, William Stafford's family, travelling with him to Calais where he was working as a Spearman to Viscount Lisle. Was Katherine with her mother at Hever Castle, or did she travel to France with her?

Katherine's first mention at court was after the execution of Anne Boleyn in the *Chronicle of Calais Note 572 Volume 14*.[9] Katherine was one of six women sent to meet King Henry's new wife, Anne of Cleves, upon her arrival in England. With hindsight, there is an irony in the greeting, for Katherine was sent to meet Anne with Catherine Howard.[10] Perhaps Katherine and Catherine Howard formed a friendship while they were maids of honour to

Anne of Cleves, something that would have secured Katherine's continued role at court when Catherine Howard became queen herself.

On 3 January 1540, Anne was greeted at Greenwich by her ladies in waiting at the pavilion in Greenwich Park, which was decorated with cloth of gold and filled with food and drink. After the new queen had dined, the ladies helped to change her clothes for her official meeting with King Henry. The king travelled on horseback to the park with trumpeters and privy councillors by his side to meet his new bride. Two days later, Katherine most likely would have been one of the ladies who dressed the queen in a cloth of gold gown for her wedding. After the wedding had taken place, Katherine would have then attended the wedding feast before she probably was sent to undress the new queen, while the priest blessed the bed. Katherine would have spent much of her service in entertaining the queen, perhaps playing cards, or reading.[11]

Katherine and her future husband possibly met when Francis Knollys was sent by the king to meet Anne of Cleves when she arrived from France.[12] Katherine and Francis married soon after the event, on 26 April 1540, with Katherine giving birth to her first child, Henry, in the same year. Katherine seems to then retreat from court. We know this because her name does not appear in any court record at that time and we know Katherine later gave birth to her daughter, Lettice, at Greys Manor, a place given to the married couple in 1540.[13]

When Katherine was pregnant with her second child, her friend and relation, Queen Catherine Howard, was stripped of her title as queen on 23 November 1541 and imprisoned in the new Syon Abbey, Middlesex, formerly a convent, where she remained throughout the winter of 1541. She was taken to the Tower and executed on 13 February 1542. The king was once again without a queen, meaning that Katherine could well have spent more time with her own family. Katherine's husband's role continued within court and in March 1544, Francis leaves his wife and his five children to be with the king at the first Siege of Boulogne.[14] This siege would carry on until 13 September 1544. This may well have been the first time that the family were separated.

Katherine retired from court after the king's death. The next monarch, King Edward VI, did not marry so there would have been no need for Katherine to come back to court. However, her husband's role continued as he was at the Battle of Pinkie, fighting against the Scots. He was also at the Battle of Roxburgh, where he was knighted by the Duke of Somerset on 28 September 1547.[15]

After King Edward died, his sister Mary I took the throne. With a Catholic monarch in England, the Protestant Knollys family went into exile. They chose to live in Frankfurt in Germany, staying at the home of John Weller, a merchant originally from London.[16] Katherine was pregnant with her sixth child. The exile would end with the death of Queen Mary I and the beginning of the reign of Katherine's first cousin, Elizabeth I. Elizabeth appointed Katherine Chief Lady of the Privy Chamber and her husband was made Vice Chamberlain of the queen's household. As Chief Lady of the Privy Chamber, Katherine was in charge of the queen's jewels and a keeper of any gifts the queen received. In 1565, Kat Ashley, the queen's governess, passed away and the queen gave her role over to Katherine Knollys; Katherine was now the Chief Lady of the Bedchamber. This meant that Katherine had to spend some nights sleeping on a pallet beside the royal bedroom and she would have privately dined with the queen. She was one of the ladies who dressed the queen. She was therefore one of the very few who knew what the queen actually looked like in her declining years, when others only saw the regal image her ladies created for her.

In May 1568, Francis was given a very important role, one he would grow to dislike, perhaps, because of the time he would be away from his wife to play it. Francis had the task of keeping Mary, Queen of Scots imprisoned at Carlisle Castle. Queen Elizabeth assigned Francis this essential task because members of her family, especially on her mother's side, stood in good stead in Elizabeth's court.

Francis was not inimical to his prisoner, being apparently 'considerably seduced by the charming personality of his captive'.[17] Francis discovered in her 'a woman of innate intelligence, blessed with an eloquent tongue and full of practical good sense'.[18] Within the *Calendar of State Papers* relating to Scotland, it is noted that Francis found Mary's character admirable.[19]

Mary would be later moved to Bolton Castle in Yorkshire, as it was thought that Carlisle Castle was too near to the Scottish border and thus conducive to an escape. Francis went with her, and it was he who had to cope with the Scottish queen's temper after hearing that she was to be moved. However, Francis was patient with her and she slowly relented. The journey took two days, with halts at Lowther Castle and at Wharton. When Mary finally reached her new 'home', she told Francis that there would be no more outbursts from her and she would be quiet in his company.[20]

While in his care, Mary was taught how to write and understand English[21] and it is here that is it suggested the teacher fell in love with his student: 'It was obvious from his letters that propinquity led Knollys to fall a little in love with his glamorous prisoner.'[22] If he did feel this way, it was clear he still did not want to fail in his task, as he drew up a map of the castle and sent it to London in the hope that a new and better security arrangement could be made.

The threat to Elizabeth from Mary's claim to the throne – apart from its potential to destroy the body politic! – meant that Francis could not return to his wife and family. One idea he had to solve this problem was to marry Mary off to his wife's nephew, George Carey. George paid a visit to the Scottish queen with his father, the governor of Berwick, and although George was received by the queen very well, she seemed to treat him as a messenger from and to his father, rather than as a suitor.

All the while Francis was away, he was indeed thinking of his wife, as letters to William Cecil, Queen Elizabeth's secretary, show. In one letter he writes 'the enclosed to my wife', presumably some kind of gift.[23] The reply from Cecil contained alarming news. He tells Francis his wife has fallen ill. Francis then writes directly to his wife: 'I am very sorry to hear that you are fallen into a fever. I wish to God I were so dispatched hence that I might only attend and care for your good recovery.'[24] Katherine recovered from the fever but seemed to fall into depression, possibly because of being away from her husband for so long, as Francis writes 'I pray you comfort my poor wife's disease of the mind.'[25] Francis's worries may have made him open up to the Queen of Scots as in September, Mary gave Katherine a gift of pomander beads.[26] Francis communicated his frustration to Queen Elizabeth about his role; in doing so he was sailing very dangerously close to the wind. He even threatened that if the queen did not allow him to join his wife, after all the love Katherine had shown her and the loyalty he had exhibited, he could see no alternative but to leave the queen's service and the court.[27]

This shows us Francis's true feeling for his wife. Had Francis really fallen under the spell of his prisoner, the powerful – and some would say beautiful – Mary, Queen of Scots? Or was it a Tudor myth, one that emphasised Mary's beauty; or quite simply, was Francis just playing the game? The courtly game of love was played out in the Elizabethan court, so perhaps it was played in Mary's court, too. Perhaps Francis extolled her beauty, or at least the beauty Mary thought she had, to control her, and was intelligent enough to allow Mary to think she had the upper hand over her gaoler. The show of defiance of Elizabeth's wishes indicates strength in Francis's personality, but it also shows us the intense feeling he had for his wife. Francis was a member of the queen's family through the queen's own mother, but he was still risking everything.

Katherine died within a few weeks of Francis's last letter to Elizabeth.[28] Francis's loyalty to the queen did not waver, however, and he guarded Mary until she was moved to Tutbury Castle in February 1569. Francis's grief ran deep. His brother, Henry Knollys, took over matters of business and even communication with Elizabeth.[29] Francis spent the next twenty-seven years watching his sixteen children grow to adulthood and never remarried.

Katherine's first child was born a year after their marriage, the next ten children are born at yearly, or two-year intervals. From the Latin dictionary mentioned earlier we now know that Lettice was their third child, as Francis kept a note of the births within it. The Latin dictionary and a memorial plaque of Katherine both state that Katherine had sixteen children. The first child was a son named Henry, probably named after Henry VIII, born in 1541. Henry was schooled at Magdalen College near his family's home near Oxford. Like his father he served his monarch, Elizabeth I, in battle against northern rebels. In 1565 he married Margaret Cave, in Durham House on the Strand, the wedding attended by and paid for by the queen. Related to the queen, serving the queen and with his wedding paid for by the queen, small wonder that one of his daughters was called Elizabeth. The other was named after his sister, Lettice.[30]

Katherine and Francis's next child was a girl named Mary, born around 26 October 1542, probably named after her grandmother, Mary Boleyn. Not much is known about this Mary Knollys, however it is suggested that she may have appeared in the accounts of the Duchess of Suffolk in the early 1560s, however that has not been verified as yet. The next child that comes along is Lettice, the best known of all Katherine's children, or at least the most documented; more on Lettice later.

The next child, William, was born on 20 March 1545, perhaps named after Katherine's 'father', William Carey or even her stepfather William Stafford; though William was simply a popular name at the time. As this William Knollys grew to manhood at the English court, he grew a tricoloured beard, earning him the nickname 'Party Beard'.[31] A song was written about him and his whiskers[32] and it was even thought that he was the inspiration behind William Shakespeare's character Malvolio in *Twelfth Night*. a vain and pompous man. Perhaps this is unfair as Sir Thomas Posthumous had also been put in the frame for it.[33] William became first Baron Knollys in 1603 and this was not the only title bestowed upon him. While in service for a new monarch and a new royal family in the reign of James I, William became first Viscount of Walkingford and the first Earl of Banbury.[34]

William married twice, first to Dorothy Bay. They had no children. With his second marriage to Elizabeth Howard, he had two children, but there was a rumour that these were in fact not William's but the offspring of Elizabeth's affair with Edward Vaux. Edward was an English peer investigated in the aftermath of the Gunpowder Plot of 1605, which was the reason why he decided to travel aboard. He returned to England only to be thrown into Fleet Prison for not taking the Oath of Allegiance to King James. After losing his lands and being put in the custody of the Dean of Westminster, he was later released on the payment of a thousand pounds. Edward was actually promised to Elizabeth Howard at the young age of seventeen, but after the association with the Gunpowder Plot of Edward and his mother, the Howard family decided against marrying their daughter into the Vaux family and chose to marry her to William Knollys instead, who was then forty years older than their daughter. Five weeks after the death of William,[35] Elizabeth finally married Edward Vaux in June 1632.

Edward was born on 18 October 1546 according to the Latin dictionary. Edward was to become a Member of Parliament but would die at twenty-six in Ireland in 1572, while working with his brother-in-law, Walter Devereux.[36] Maud Knollys was born on 31 March 1548. Nothing is known of her. She may have been accidently confused with her sister Mary, as Maud was another name for Mary. Next was Elizabeth, born on 15 June 1549. Her name and the fact that she had pale skin and bright red hair were probably why Queen Elizabeth took a shine to this child. Elizabeth Knollys entered unusually early into the queen's service, at just ten years old.

Robert Knollys was born next on 9 November 1550. Possibly named after his grandfather, Robert filled many positions during his career, including being the MP for Reading and Breconshire, Porter to the Tower Mint, and Keeper of Syon House, Isleworth, Brentford, Twickenham, Heston, Whitton, Sutton and Aylestone's Woods. He was also a gentleman of the Privy Chamber and Esquire of the Body to Elizabeth I.[37] These important roles continued into the next monarch's reign.

Richard was born on 21 May 1552. Sadly again, not much is known about Richard Knollys, apart from him becoming the MP for Wallingford and Northampton.[38] Francis fils was born on 14 August 1553. He became the MP for Oxford when his brother Edward passed away and also became the MP for Berkshire and Reading. He fought against the Spanish Armada, becoming the Commissioner for Musters.[39]

Anne was the next daughter to be born, on 19 July 1555. Anne became a maid of the chamber in the same year that her mother,

Katherine, died, possibly remaining in this role until her own death. Thomas was next, born on 26 January 1558, when both of his parents were in exile. Katherine was born on 21 October 1559. She, too, went into the queen's service in 1575. Finally, the last child Katherine and Francis were to have was named Dudley, born 9 May 1562. He was named after his father's close friend, Robert Dudley. Dudley died in June 1562, just a few months old.[40]

Living apart from her husband and at times her children and in the service of a demanding queen who liked to have her ladies around her at all times, surely put a great stress upon Katherine. And of course, her multiple pregnancies must have taken their toll. She died on 15 January 1569 at Hampton Court, still attending her queen. Elizabeth paid for her funeral at a cost of £640, which was held at Westminster Abbey.[41]

Katherine's coloured alabaster monument in St Edmund's Chapel in the Abbey has a Latin inscription which translates as:

O, Francis, she who was thy wife behold, Catherine Knolle [sic] lies dead under the chilly marble. I know well that she will never depart from thy soul, though dead. Whilst alive she was always loved by thee: living she bore thee her husband, sixteen children and was equally female and male (that is, both gentle and valiant). Would that she had lived many years with thee and thy wife was now an old lady. But God desired it not. But he willed that thou. O, Catherine should await thy husband in Heaven.[42]

The monument has four shields which include the coats of arms of Knowles, Carey, Spencer, Beaufort, Boleyn, and others. So ends the life of Katherine Knollys, the daughter of Mary Boleyn. Katherine's daughter Lettice Knollys is the next Boleyn scion to consider.

LETTICE KNOLLYS, COUNTESS OF ESSEX AND LEICESTER

Before we go into the many tragedies and dramas that surround Lettice Knollys's life within and beyond the royal court, one remarkable fact has to be mentioned at the outset: Lettice lived until the age of ninety-one. This is remarkable even today, but the average age for a woman in the Tudor or even the Stuart period to reach was roughly forty-five. This means that Lettice effectively lived through two lifespans, and we shall see what full and varied lives they were. Born in the reign of Henry VIII, she died in the reign of Charles I, so she lived through the reigns of seven different British monarchs, if you count Lady Jane Grey.

Again, according to the Latin dictionary, she was born at her parents' home at Greys Court in Oxfordshire's quaint village of Rotherfield Grey. Her father Francis Knollys writes that Lettice was born on 'the Tuesday present after All Hallows Day', making her birth date 6 November 1543. 'Lettice' was an interesting choice; a popular Victorian name, it could well be a nod to her paternal grandmother, Lettice Knollys neé Peniston.

Lettice was three years old when Henry VIII died, a watershed moment for the Knollys family for several reasons. Firstly, if we believe that Lettice's mother was the illegitimate child of the said monarch, Lettice had just lost her real grandfather. However, even without this family connection, the death of the king also meant changes for the family. They may have hoped to gain greater influence at court under King Edward VI, as Lettice's father had already served as the Prince's Master of the Horse and the Knollys family openly followed the same faith as the new monarch. This at first seemed to be the case as Lettice's father became a Justice of the Peace in 1547, while also gaining the Constableship of Wallingford Castle, which was not far away from his home at Greys Court, and he was awarded the stewardship in Ewelme in 1551.[1] With these responsibilities and attending court at the same time, Francis Knollys was a very busy man. This probably meant that Lettice and her siblings hardly saw their father while they were being raised and educated at home. Little is known about Lettice's early years, but it was presumably down to her mother to sort out the education of all of her children while her husband was so often away.

Katherine, as already mentioned, would have had no reason to return to court as King Edward had no queen, so she would have taken this opportunity to attend to her children's needs. Katherine may have given the role of tutor to Lettice to Magdalen College scholar Julius Palmer, as John Foxe, historian and author of *Acts and Monuments*, wrote that Palmer was 'a teacher of children in the house of Sir Frances Knollys'.[2] However, Foxe does not say which children Julius Palmer actually taught. We do know that four of Lettice's brothers were educated at Eton and Magdalen College, but records for females are not as detailed. Luckily, we do have her letters, held originally at Longleat House. Her handwriting is elegant, clear, and she writes with confidence.[3]

She would have also been tutored in all the skills a lady at court should have, like dancing and playing music. One of Lettice's daughters would be fluent in Spanish, so perhaps Lettice, too, would know how to speak a second language. Religion was central to her father's life, and he would have wanted his children to follow suit. Francis was of the opinion that 'experience teaches what foul crimes youthful women fall into for lack of orderly maintenance. My will is good, they cannot lack as long as I have it, but there is no more to be had of a cat but the skin.'[4]

In 1552, Lettice was still at home and had eight siblings to play and interact with. Greys Court at this time was a hive of activity and this was the first experience Lettice had of looking after younger children, something that she would be known for later on in her life. A year later, events changed her family's lives forever. On 6 July 1553 King Edward died suddenly. The Knollys family had experienced the death of a monarch before and all had turned out well for them, but this would be different. There was unrest over who would take the throne. Although Francis at the time was not a part of the king's council, so did not have to pick a side, he may well have favoured Lady Jane Grey. Francis was a strongly Protestant man, the same religion as Lady Jane Grey; the alternative was the Catholic Mary Tudor, who had stronger claims to the throne and who threatened to return the country to the Roman faith.

Eventually, Mary became queen. Francis Knollys went to Geneva to see how Europe would be for himself and his family, and after assuring himself that his family would be safe, he must have wanted his family to move there immediately. However, by the summer of 1555, Katherine had given birth to her eleventh child. Moving a family of that size was not going to be easy with the many dangers travel could bring, a journey that could take weeks. So, the difficult decision was made to leave some of the children that were old enough behind. On 10 June 1557, Katherine, Francis and five children left England for Frankfurt.[5] The children were not named in the records, so we don't know if Lettice was one of them, but considering her age at the time, she may have been left behind, perhaps with other members of the Knollys family that the parents trusted. Gaps continue to appear in Lettice's timeline at this point. In November of 1556, Lettice would have been thirteen, old enough to be in Tudor service. If this was the case, which household did she join?

Some historians have suggested that Lettice joined the household of Lady Elizabeth, the future Queen Elizabeth I, at Hatfield. This is mainly based upon the wording on Lettice's tomb in St Mary's Church, Warwick, part of which states: 'In her youth she had been Darling to the maiden Queen.' We cannot know when that was. However, we do know that when there was a chance of Lettice leaving England, Elizabeth was most upset. She wrote a letter to Lettice:

> Relieve your sorrow for your far journey with joy of your short return, and think this pilgrimage rather as proof of your friends, than leaving of your country. The length of time, and distance of place, separates not the love of friends, nor deprives not the show of goodwill ... when your need shall be most you shall find my friendship greatest. Let others promise, and I will do, in words not more, in deeds as much... I am driven by need to write, farewell, it is which in the sense one way I wish, the other way I grieve. Your loving cousin and ready friend, Cor Rotto [broken heart].[6]

This is arguably the most affectionate letter Elizabeth would ever write. Considering what was to come between the pair, it is important to remember this moment.

On 17 November 1558 at six o'clock, Elizabeth's sister Queen Mary I died at St James's Palace. Lettice's friend and cousin had gained the throne and because of the new queen's religion and the family connection, Lettice's family could return from exile, which they did by the December of 1558.[7] It was not only Lettice's close family members travelling back to England at this point; Dorothy Stafford, Lettice's step-grandmother, also returned to become part of the queen's household.

By 14 January 1559, Francis Knollys, Lettice's father, had been sworn in to Queen Elizabeth's Privy Council and a year later, on 3 January 1560, Lettice became Gentlewoman of the Privy Chamber.[8] The job paid 33 pounds per year, which is about £12,000 today. Her role would have included washing and dressing the queen and arranging her hair. Lettice would have served the queen her food. She was in constant contact with the queen from a very young age. Lettice would have also been expected to play cards, to dance, to talk and read to her as the queen wished.[9] Being a queen's lady, Lettice would have been expected to dress a certain way, in finery but not better than the queen herself. Elizabeth forbade her ladies to wear black or white because in some way this helped to 'emphasise her peerless beauty'.[10]

Lettice was not alone at court, her mother Katherine was by her side, as was her sister Elizabeth and her cousins Katherine and Philadelphia Carey. As time when on, Elizabeth and Lettice became closer. Lettice looked very like the queen, almost a twin with the same flaming 'Tudor' hair. This, and similar traits of stubbornness, perhaps even arrogant ways, could have been reasons for later events; but the similar looks and characteristics did not seem to matter to either of them at this early stage.

Lettice was of marriageable age and it was probably at court that Walter Devereux saw her and 'soon became captive to the charms of Lettice Knollys, a fore maiden of the court, celebrated for her beauty and spirit'.[11] Walter Devereux was the eldest son of Sir Richard Devereux and his wife Dorothy Hastings. The Devereux family had roots that went far back into royal history. They were with William the Conqueror at the Battle of Hastings in 1066 and Walter's grandfather was not only in the good offices of Henry VIII but also favoured by Edward VI. On 2 February 1550, Walter's grandfather was given the title of Viscount Hereford by Edward VI and the title eventually passed to Walter himself. His grandfather would continue to do well in court until he chose the Lady Jane Grey party and Queen Mary imprisoned him in the Tower. In 1554 he was released and retired to his manor house at Chartley in Staffordshire.[12]

His grandson Walter was born on 16 September 1539 at Carmarthen Castle.[13] It is rare to know when a person, peasant or peer, was born, and where, in the Tudor period, but with Walter we even know when he was christened, on 18 September 1539 in the church of St Peter in the town.[14] The family moved to Lamphey Manor in Pembrokeshire, where Walter's parents both passed away, first his father Richard in 1548 and then his mother in 1566. Walter's grandfather the 1st Viscount Hereford died on 17 September 1558. With Richard Devereux already dead, the Viscount's titles went straight to Walter at the age of nineteen.

Walter became Viscount Hereford and Lord Ferrers of Chartley, Bourchier and Louvaine. As he was only nineteen, Walter was not allowed to look after his estates or finances by himself, he had to wait two more years for that. But Walter was a young man with a bright future ahead of him and amidst the grandeur of the Elizabethan court, he looked the part. Between October 1559 – when he was twenty years old – to May 1561, he spent 150 pounds, about £50,000 today, on clothes. It can be easily imagined that when Walter walked into the room, people noticed.[15] One of them was probably Lettice Knollys. Despite all that was about to ensue, this love match, or some part of it, may have survived Walter's death. Although Lettice remarried, some years later Walter's portrait was still recorded in Lettice's household possessions.[16]

When Walter turned twenty-one, he gained his full inheritance of 200 pounds per year, enough money to be able to support a wife and family. Walter knew who he wanted for a wife and that

1. Norwich Cathedral, where Anne Hoo Boleyn, the great-grandmother of Mary, Anne and George Boleyn, and William Boleyn, their grandfather, were buried. (Courtesy of Jorge Pena Ramos)

2. Blickling Hall. Owned by the Boleyns since 1452, it is the suggested birthplace of Mary, Anne and George Boleyn. (Courtesy of DeFacto)

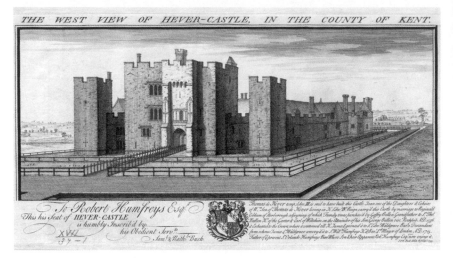

3. Hever Castle, the childhood home of Mary, Anne and George Boleyn. This could also be where Mary brought up her daughter, Katherine, in her early years. (Courtesy of the British Library)

4. Penshurst Church. This was where Thomas Boleyn, Mary Boleyn's brother, was buried. (Courtesy of Ethan Doyle White)

Ormond

5. A portrait by Hans Holbein, said by some to depict Thomas Boleyn, father of Mary, Anne and George. (Courtesy of the Rijksmuseum)

6. Henry VIII. (Courtesy of the Rijksmuseum)

Anna Bollein Queen.

7. Anne Boleyn depicted by Hans Holbein. (Courtesy of the Rijksmuseum)

Tho: Moor L'Chancelour

Left: 8. Thomas More, who refused to recognise Henry's marriage to Anne. (Courtesy of the Rijksmuseum)

Below: 9. The Tower of London. This map shows the Royal Apartments, where Anne Boleyn stayed, preparing for her coronation and when she was a prisoner. It also shows the Great Hall where Anne and George Boleyn had their trial. These two buildings no longer exist. It also shows the placement of George Boleyn's execution in the far left-hand corner. (Courtesy of the British Library)

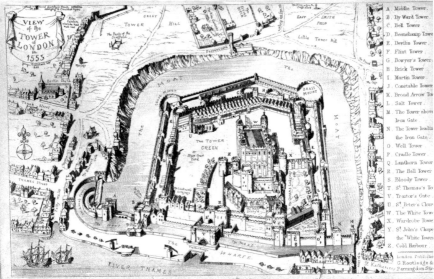

Above: 10. St Peter ad Vincula, where Anne, George Boleyn and Robert Devereux were buried. (Courtesy of the British Library)

Below: 11. This map of Kent shows how close Mary Boleyn was, living at Great Bounds near Tonbridge, to her childhood home of Hever Castle and the close proximity of these two important places to Bidborough, where at St Lawrence church she could be buried. (Courtesy of the British Library)

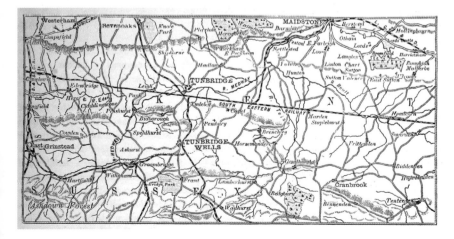

12. Carlisle Castle, where Mary Boleyn's son-in-law, Francis Knollys, was entrusted to keep Mary, Queen of Scots by Mary Boleyn's niece, Queen Elizabeth I. (Courtesy of CompleteAnonymity)

13. The tomb of Lettice Knollys and Robert Dudley at St Mary's church in Warwickshire. (With kind permission from Mary Adams; picture courtesy of J. Guffog & J. Hannan)

14. Elizabeth as queen. (Courtesy of the Rijksmuseum)

15. Katherine Knollys (nee Carey), chief lady of the bedchamber to Elizabeth I and mother to Lettice Knollys. (Courtesy of Yale Center for British Art)

Above: 16. Robert Devereux, Earl of Essex and one-time favourite of Elizabeth. (Courtesy of the Metropolitan Museum of Art)

Right: 17. Frances Walsingham, daughter of Elizabeth I's Secretary of State Francis Walsingham and wife of Robert Devereux.

18. Hampton Court Palace, where William Seymour attended to King Charles I when the king was imprisoned there in 1647. (Courtesy of the British Library)

Above left: 19. Frances Seymour's bust in Bedwyn's church as it is today. (By kind permission of Graham Bathe, author of 'The Seymour Legacy')

Above right: 20. A sketch of Frances Seymour's monument in Bedwyn's church as it was originally designed. The cherubs at the base were stolen at a later date. (By kind permission of Graham Bathe)

Below: 21. Chiswick House, the summer home of the Boyle family, where Richard and his wife, Dorothy passed away. (Courtesy of Michael Coppins)

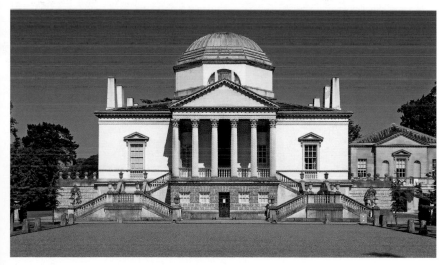

Above: 22. The cover of a paper chronicling Lord Charles Bentick and Lady Anne Abdy's criminal damages case. (Courtesy of Yale Law Library)

Below: 23. Glamis Castle, home of the Bowes-Lyon family and one of the suggested birth places of Queen Elizabeth The Queen Mother. (Courtesy of Rev Stan)

24. Statue of King George VI and Queen Elizabeth The Queen Mother in St James's Park, London. (Author's collection)

Above: 25. From left to right, King George VI, First Lady Eleanor Roosevelt and Queen Elizabeth (prior to becoming Queen Mother) in London in 1942. During the war, Nazi leader Adolf Hitler is said to have called Elizabeth 'the most dangerous woman in Europe' because of her popularity. (Courtesy of the US National Archives and Records Administration)

Below: 26. Buckingham Palace, the London residence of the royal family until this very day. (Courtesy of David Iliff)

was Lettice Knollys, who had just turned seventeen. This would have been considered as a good match within the Elizabethan court as both of them came from important families. Both families followed the same Protestant faith – and the bride and groom both seemed to have the same fiery temperament.

Although the queen liked her ladies to remain single, there is no evidence that the queen objected to Lettice and Walter getting married. The date of the wedding is unknown, but it is thought to have taken place between the time Walter gained his full inheritance and the early months of 1562.[17] The household records of Queen Elizabeth show that in 1561 Lettice's salary stopped, indicating that she had left the queen's service then, owing to her marriage.

Lettice and Walter moved into Walter's family seat at Chartley Manor in Staffordshire.[18] It would be at Chartley that Lettice would spend her first years as a married woman, only coming back to court on special occasions such as the New Year celebrations. For example, in 1564 Lettice was at court to give the queen a New Year's gift of 'a smock with a square collar and a rail wrought with black silk and gold'.[19]

Lettice gave birth to her first child in January 1563 at Chartley. The child was a girl and although Lettice and Walter decided to go against the Tudor norm and not name their child after the queen, naming her Penelope instead, when they asked the queen to be their child's godmother she still accepted. Penelope was christened on 3 February 1563. We know this from the queen's accounts, which show she sent a gift 'for the christening of Viscount Hereford, his child'.[20] The queen gave Penelope Devereux a 'gilt cup with a cover'.[21]

Lettice was very protective of her children and they would grow up knowing they always had their mother's support, no matter what they did. At the time of Penelope's birth, Walter was hardly at court as he did not have an official post, so Penelope was lucky enough to have both of her parents around her early in life.

On 17 September 1564, Lettice gave birth to another daughter, again at the family home of Chartley. They named her Dorothy, after Walter's mother.[22] Just under a year later, Lettice was pregnant again, but she managed to travel to London for the wedding of Henry Devereux to Margaret Cave on 16 July 1565. This was a fashionably grand affair held at Durham Place on the Strand. It was there in May 1553 that Lady Jane Grey had married Guildford Dudley, a relation of Robert Dudley's. Lettice was once again in the presence of the queen.[23] Walter and Lettice did not return home straight away, instead, the couple decided to spend the rest of the summer at court, even though Lettice was pregnant. It is suggested that it was at this time and while Lettice was six months pregnant that she caught the eye of Robert Dudley. Some think his flirtation with Lettice only began because he was using her to make the queen jealous. Sir Nicholas Throckmorton had previously advised Robert to pretend 'to fall in love himself with one of the ladies of the palace and watch how the Queen took it'.[24] Robert chose well in the person to flirt with; a lady of the court and daughter to the queen's first cousin. Queen Elizabeth could not have failed to notice her favourite turning away from her toward Lettice. Although it is suggested that Lettice and Robert's relationship started secretly from this point on because of a report written by the Spanish ambassador, Guzman de Silva, there is really no other evidence. With Lettice six months pregnant, an affair seems unlikely.

It is unclear how Lettice reacted to this flirtation but we do know how the queen felt at first: 'The Queen was in a great temper and upbraided him (Robert) for his behaviour ... for his flirting with the Viscountess in very bitter words.'[25] Although

Robert had to 'give up' Lettice to remain in the queen's favour, at this point it was probably something that both Robert and Lettice thought was nothing but harmless flirting, so they were not giving up much. The fact that the queen makes no move against Lettice implies the flirtation was casual. Just because it may have seemed a trifling matter to the queen does not mean it was seen as such by Lettice's husband, Walter Devereux. But it is interesting that when Lettice gives birth to her third child, Walter and Lettice still name him Robert and make Robert Dudley the child's godparent. This could suggest that there was no problem between Walter, Robert and Lettice at this time; but the date of birth of Lettice's third child has opened doors to a possible Tudor scandal. There are some indications that Robert Devereux was born on 19 November 1566 or 10 November 1567, and if so, Robert could actually be the son of Robert Dudley rather than Walter.[26] However, most believe Robert Devereux was born on 10 November 1565 at Netherwood Manor in Herefordshire, owned by the Devereux family at the time.

There was genuine sibling affection. Penelope and Robert would stay close when they worked together later. Dorothy signs off a letter to her brother with 'your sister that faithfully loves you'.[27] All of Lettice and Walter's children started their education at home under the tutelage of Lettice herself and possibly Walter, but as they grew up the children were assigned tutors. Robert's education was very formal as expected, but his sisters Penelope and Dorothy didn't lose out. Lettice arranged for a Cambridge tutor, Mathias Holmes, to teach her daughters.[28] Because they were female students, their lessons would also focus on social skills. Penelope could speak French, Spanish and some Italian. In 1598, translator Bartholomew Young dedicated his translation from the Spanish of Jorge de Montemayor's pastoral romance, *Diana*, to Penelope, describing her as having a 'magnificent mind' and saying her 'perfect knowledge' of many languages was 'well known'.[29] Penelope would gain admirers wherever she went as she could sing and dance beautifully. One such admirer was King James VI of Scotland, later James I of England. He would mention how impressed he was by Penelope Devereux and 'commended much the fineness of her wit'.[30]

In 1569 there is no record of Lettice or her husband sending New Year's gifts to the queen, as the couple had done in previous years. This was at a time when Lettice was losing the support of her parents. Francis was the guardian of Mary, Queen of Scots and her mother Katherine was showing signs of depression due to her separation from her husband. The close-knit family that Lettice was used to, that she may have relied upon, was being pulled apart because of the queen. Could this have affected Lettice's feelings for the sovereign?

On 15 January 1569, Lettice's mother passed away suddenly at Hampton Court. Katherine was without her husband and without her daughter Lettice, who was at Chartley. Perhaps for Lettice, at that moment loyalty to the queen ultimately didn't amount to much. Lettice was pregnant with her fourth child when her mother died, a time when any daughter would want to be near her own mother.

At this moment, when Lettice surely felt some resentment towards the queen, Walter was ordered to leave his family home and his wife by the sovereign. It was thought that Mary, Queen of Scots was plotting an escape. Walter and his cousin, Henry Hastings the Earl of Huntingdon, were tasked with dealing with the matter. The Scottish queen was not the least bit happy to see them; there is no record of Walter's reaction on first seeing the queen. Walter searched Mary's coffers for evidence of a planned escape but there was nothing to be found. This may have been because Mary had already burned some papers.[31] All the while that Mary's rooms were being searched, Mary complained of her foul treatment and no doubt Walter came in for the brunt of it.[32] Walter returned home just in time to be there for the arrival of his fourth child on 31 October 1569. The boy was named Walter after his father. This would be the last surviving child that Walter and Lettice were to have; another child, named Francis, died in infancy.[33]

Lettice would not have her husband around for long. With the Northern Rebellion becoming an increasing threat, it was thought best to move Mary, Queen of Scots, and Walter was tasked to do this. He and Henry Hastings travelled with the Scottish queen to Coventry, where extra guards were waiting to take over. Walter returned home, but once again his stay was short lived. The rebellion was still ongoing, and he must have felt that his family was at risk at Chartley. But Walter was unable to move his family because Lettice was too weak after giving birth, so all he could do was to assign 150 horsemen to the queen's army and join the fight. Walter was given orders to take his horsemen to the Earl of Leicester and on 27 November 1569 he wrote to the queen stating he would do as ordered, he would 'repair with all the forces that I have levied, as speedily as it is possible unto Leicester, and so forward to what place it shall please them whom your majesty hath appointed to have government of your army'.[34] On the way to the earl, he first stopped at Lichfield, where he gained 3,000 men. He then arrived in the City of Leicester, where he met up with the Earl of Warwick around 1 December 1569. We know this because the earl wrote to William Cecil, Queen Elizabeth's secretary, to let him know that Walter had arrived.[35] The earl offered Walter the post of Marshal of the Army in the North, or 'High Marshal in the Field', but Walter was reluctant to take him up the prestigious post. He was worried about his lack of experience. something the earl communicated to Cecil.[36] Under pressure from the earl, Walter finally agreed.

In the same year Walter became Lord Lieutenant of the County of Stafford, a reward for his recent services to the queen.[37] Would this have been enough for Lettice? At this point quite a few of her members of her family were in service to the queen, risking their lives in the suppression of the rebellion. Her father was leading the queen's army, her elder brother Henry and her young brother William were soldiers, and her husband was heavily involved. This must have exacerbated Lettice's already strained feelings towards the queen. In addition, as the queen had begun to think of Walter with high regard, she knew this meant he would be called upon more and more, and there would be nothing Lettice could do or say about the matter. She was in the same position as her mother before her. This would happen soon. The queen ordered Walter to take part in the trial for treason of the 4th Duke of Norfolk.

In January 1572 Walter travelled from Chartley to London, but this time he took his wife with him. They had no London home to call their own, so they stayed at Durham Place. On 16 January 1572, the Duke of Norfolk stood trial and Walter was one of the peers who oversaw it. The duke was found guilty of being part of a plot to put Mary, Queen of Scots on the throne following a Spanish invasion, and the queen signed his death warrant on 2 June 1572. The reason why the queen had taken so long to decide whether or not to execute the duke, even though Walter and others had found him guilty, was because he was her second cousin. The duke was executed on 2 June 1572, claiming that he 'never willingly offended the Queen'. [38]

On 23 April 1572, Walter was made a Knight of the Garter. This was and still is the highest order of chivalry in the realm. On the death of his cousin Anne Bourchier and Anne's father,

Walter became Lord Bourchier and Earl of Essex. In celebration, on 4 May 1572 the queen held a formal ceremony at Greenwich Palace. The *State Papers* describe Walter's attire, 'a kirtle of crimson velvet and having on his Robe of State of crimson velvet ... a deep cape of ermine of three rows and a hood of crimson velvet'. He was 'led from the closet where the chaplains remain to the queen's presence between the Earl of Sussex on the right hand and the Earl of Huntington on the left hand, they also having on their Robes of State'. [39] Although Lettice was not recorded as being there to see her husband dubbed the Earl of Essex, she must have felt a great sense of pride and triumph for her husband, as well as for herself; she was now the Countess of Essex.

Understandably, it was around this time that Walter had his portrait painted. Several versions of this portrait have survived but the two main ones are at Ipswich Museum and at Ulster Museum. In it, we can see Walter wearing black armour, his dark helmet placed to one side with his hand resting upon it. The armour is trimmed in red and gold. An inscription within the painting reads VIRTUTIS COMES INVIDIA, 'envy is the companion of excellence.'

At this point Walter must have felt that his life was set. He was a Knight of the Garter, the Earl of Essex, he had married well, and his wife had provided him with four surviving children. However, Walter wanted more, and to do that he turned his attention to Ireland. This was a dangerous action to take, many people before Walter had tried and failed to rule this land. Being an ever-loyal servant to the queen, Walter wanted to rid her of the problem. Sir Henry Sidney, a member of the family, had been serving as Lord Deputy of Ireland for many years, but in 1571 he was replaced by Sir William Fitzwilliam, Sir Henry's brother-in-law. The fight against the Irish was long-running and resources from England were limited, England needed new people to take up the struggle.

Walter had basically put his hand up in the Elizabethan classroom to get himself noticed.

It is suggested that Robert Dudley didn't argue with this turn of events because he wanted Walter out of the way to spend time with Walter's wife. However, it could also be said that at this time Robert's attentions were still focused on the queen. It was thought by some that Lettice pushed Walter to go: 'She encouraged her first husband in his Irish enterprise, in hopes of sharing in the fame and fortune to be won.'[40] Or perhaps she did so to further her relationship with Dudley. The queen accepted Walter's proposal in 1572 and lent him 10,000 pounds towards the Irish cause, but that was not enough, and Walter had to re-mortgage his own lands in Essex, Buckinghamshire and Wales. Lettice may well have had confidence in her husband, but now he was risking his own family's finances to complete his task.

On 20 June 1572, Walter left the English court, making his way to his home at Chartley to say goodbye to his family before heading towards Ireland via Liverpool, getting there by 16 August. With her husband gone and her children growing up fast, the care of Chartley must have played heavily on Lettice's mind. Walter was uneasy about Lettice's overprotective ways with their children, especially towards their eldest, Robert Devereux. He wrote to William Cecil asking whether Robert could be taken away from Lettice and into the care of Cecil himself, for Walter feared that Lettice's love, the love of an overbearing mother, would turn his child petulant and spoilt.[41] Walter would never see how close to the mark his fears were.

Walter would write to Cecil again, this time concerning his son's marriage and in thanks for Cecil's help with raising his child: 'The direction, education and marriage of my eldest son, whom if you can like to match with your daughter, I will presently assure him 2000 marks by the year in England, besides my houses, domains and parks.'[42] Walter was proposing that his eldest son Robert marry Cecil's daughter. This would mean a family connection with one of the most powerful men in the Elizabethan court. It is not difficult to imagine Lettice being angered at this turn, a decision apparently made without her involvement. But the match was never made.[43]

While her husband was away, in the summer of 1574 Lettice travelled to Buxton in Derbyshire. Buxton was a spa resort, many of the nobility travelled there, including Mary, Queen of Scots in the previous year. So it is possible Lettice went there simply for the healing waters, but according to a letter sent to the Earl of Shrewsbury by his servant, Thomas Gieves, among 'the strangers which be at Buxton at this present time' were Lady Essex, Lady Norris, Lady Mildmay, Lady Gresham and Margaret, the Earl of Bedford's daughter, so it could well be that Lettice went to Buxton to be with friends.[44] While at Buxton, Lettice stayed at the Old Hall, a place that had been built for the Earl of Shrewsbury's friends whenever they stayed in town. While Lettice's husband was away, an affair with Robert Dudley could have begun, but on 7 August 1574 some news would prove that Robert's attention had not been fully focussed on Lettice at this time. Robert had become a father. He had not remarried after the death of his first wife, Amy. He had begun an affair with Lady Douglas Sheffield, who was one of the queen's ladies.[45] If Lettice had any feelings about this news, we do not know of them, however we do know that the queen was displeased. Though she probably didn't feel that Lady Douglas was a threat to her close relationship with Robert as she was unusually tolerant over the affair. It is worth noting the difference in the queen's behaviour with Lady Douglas Sheffield and her future dealings with Lettice. Lady Douglas, like Lettice, was related to the queen, being the daughter of William Howard. Lady Douglas was also roughly the same age as Lettice, both being younger than the queen. But the queen's reactions to their actions were very different.

How long Robert's relationship lasted with Lady Douglas is unknown, but for several years it was court gossip. It seemed as if Lady Douglas had fallen for Robert a lot more than Robert had fallen for her. She wanted more out of the relationship than Robert was prepared to give.[46] Their child was called Robert Sheffield. Robert Dudley accepted him as his own and was ready to make provisions for his son to leave his mother's side by the age of two to live with a relation of Robert's, John Dudley. At the age of fourteen, the child entered Christchurch, Oxford.[47]

In January 1575, Lettice was staying at Durham Place in London when she sent the queen a New Year's gift of 'a waistcoat of white satin all over, embroidered with Venice Gold and Silver'. Lettice received one in return, 'three gilt bowls with a cover'.[48] On 6 August 1575, the queen would make Lettice's home at Chartley a stop on her summer progress. During this visit the queen saw Lettice's children perhaps for the first time. It was probably then that Lettice learned the queen had given her husband a promotion, creating him the Earl Marshal of Ireland.[49] Lettice was probably also told that her husband would be returning home by October, by which time she would not have seen him for two years.

Walter landed in South Wales from Ireland and stayed in Lamphey to recover from the journey.[50] From there he presumably travelled home to see his wife and children at Chartley, but he was also eager to return to court in London. Walter must have felt depressed about his efforts in Ireland; two years away, nothing much had changed and now he was heavily in debt. He needed to see the queen as fast as he could to explain himself. His worries must have eased somewhat when the queen wrote to him that she was 'glad of his arrival and was well pleased that he should repair to the court, with condition that with over much haste he did not distemper his body'.[51] He took his wife and possibly his children, too. They spent Christmas in London, most likely at Durham Place. Walter wrote to the queen from there on 13 January 1576, describing his situation; he was seriously in debt and needed the queen's financial help.[52] He received no answer from the queen, nor from the queen's Privy Council, which must have made things feel even more stressful. The queen eventually made offers to Walter but he declined them all, which upset the queen and he was forced to write back to her explaining his refusal. He explained that he was a proud man and did not like the idea of grovelling for money.[53] This strong-willed response was not the wisest action for Walter to have taken, but perhaps it was the strain of indebtedness, the years spent away from his wife and children, and quite possibly feeling tired and ill that made Walter write that response. A few days later Walter seemed to have put his diplomatic head back on again as when he and Lettice were preparing to leave London on 5 January 1577, he wrote another letter to the queen which he had handed to Sir Francis Walsingham to give to her: 'I will ever be ready to adventure my life and to spend in her majesty's service everything that her highness shall think good to bestow on me.'[54]

The queen replied quickly and Walter must have been hoping for some sort of payment, but what he actually got was an order to return to his post in Ireland. At least he was not going alone, the queen was sending 300 men with him.[55] Lettice might have been alarmed that her husband was risking his life yet again – or relieved that the debt her husband had incurred might well be expunged.

Leicester's Commonwealth, a document that tends to show Robert Dudley in the worst light, states that when Walter left for the second time for Ireland, Lettice's relationship with Robert was a full-blown affair. There is no evidence to support this notion, and it is also difficult to accept that Lettice would risk losing her high standing at court at that time, especially as Robert Dudley's relationship with Lady Douglas was still in people's minds.

Walter left his family in the middle of July, landing in Dublin on 23 July, where he received a warm welcome from the people there.[56] All seemed to be well but just over a month later on 30 August, Walter's servant Edward Waterhouse writes that Walter was 'seized with a flux', a bad case of diarrhoea.[57] Walter was also moving around the country quickly so the full extent of his illness was not known until he returned to Dublin once again. Now Walter's servant writes in more detail; Walter was passing stools twenty to thirty times a day and he had been given a 'unicorn's horn' to purify the water he drank to help his recovery, but it had 'made him vomit many times'.[58] Walter made plans to return home to recover, but he only made it as far as Lamphey in Wales before he knew he was dying. He wrote to the queen to tell her of this and to ask her if she would be 'as a mother to his children'.[59] Walter also wrote to William Cecil to ask whether he could take Robert Devereux under his wing.[60] If Walter did write to Lettice, the letter has not survived.

At eleven o'clock on 22 September 1576 Walter died inside Dublin Castle, aged thirty-seven. There were later rumours that Walter had been poisoned, both by his wife and by Robert Dudley.[61] Once again these rumours were reported by the hostile *Leicester's Commonwealth*, published years after the death. At the time, nobody was suggesting that Lettice was a murderess. But as Dwight Peck points out in his introduction to his annotated edition of *Leicester's Commonwealth*, 'Examples of anti-Leicestrian gossip could be multiplied indefinitely.'

The inventory of Leicester House includes a portrait of Lettice dressed in mourning.[62]

After Walter's post-mortem was completed, which stated Walter had died of natural causes, his body travelled to Carmarthen where Walter had been born. On 26 November 1576, Walter was laid to rest in the chapel of St Peter's Church. Lettice did not attend the funeral and nor did Walter's heir, Robert Devereux, who was ill at the time. Walter's grave is unmarked.[63]

Lettice was now a thirty-three-year-old widow with four children and debts. Walter's will expresses the greatest concern over Robert's welfare. Walter suggested that responsibility for his son would be better placed with Walter's lawyer, Richard Broughton, rather than with his mother.[64] Walter also wrote of his hopes for his eldest daughter Penelope to marry the poet Sir Philip Sidney, however this was not to be. Penelope would inspire his 1580s sonnet sequence, *Astrophel and Stella*. Sonnet 37 is significant as the first poem in the sequence that actually refers to Penelope Rich née Devereux:

Toward Aurora's court a nymph doth dwell,
Rich in all beauties which man's eye can see…
Rich in those gifts which give th'eternal crown;
Who though most rich in these and every part,
Which make the patents of true worldly bliss,
Hath no misfortune, but that Rich she is.

A nymph (Penelope Rich) lives where the sun rises (in Essex, the east)
Rich in all the beauties a man's eye can see…
Rich in those (spiritual) gifts that grant an eternal crown:
Who though she is rich in these things and everything
Which constitutes true bliss in this world,
Has only one misfortune, that she is (married to Lord) Rich.

Although Walter mentions Lettice only a few times in his will, some affection for her remained. He calls her his 'right well-beloved wife' before listing out the properties and estates that she could call her own.[65] Lettice received the manors in Hertford, Pembroke, Brecknock and Gloucester. She also gained the manor and park of Benington, which she was to use later in her life. This gave Lettice a reasonable sum of money for a lady of her status and Walter had also left her goods, jewels and plate. Although she would later complain that it was not enough, Walter obviously provided for his wife in his will; does this mean he did not know of any affair with Dudley?[66]

Lettice still had to leave her family home of Chartley, as Walter had given it over to his son. This must have been a sad prospect for her, as she had spent many years there and it was where she had brought up her children, but go she must, after being allowed to spend her last Christmas there by her son's guardian, William Cecil. After that Christmas Lettice had to return to her parent's home of Greys Court, taking her daughters and younger son, Walter, with her. But if Lettice thought that she would be safe from her husband's creditors at her parent's home, she would be mistaken. Not only did Lettice have to deal with losing her husband, she had lost her home, she had lost her eldest son, whom she held dear, to Cecil, and now she was burdened with her deceased husband's debts. Walter owed the queen 6,190 pounds, plus debts to others.[67] Being in this situation might have driven many to despair, but Lettice was a Boleyn, and as we have seen, Boleyn family members did not give up if they felt entitled to more. Lettice wrote a letter to William Cecil and the council to ask for more money.[68] She claimed that her income did not provide enough for her to live on. She felt that she was entitled to at least a third of the revenues from what had been Walter's lands and refers to the debts her son Robert would inherit. While she waited for an answer, Lettice took herself off to the Elizabethan court, which at the time was at Hampton Court Palace[69] and although she seems to have enjoyed herself there, by the end of February her problems had not been solved and she had to go back to Greys Court. Lettice does not give up and writes to Cecil again, asking for financial help.[70] Her request for a third of Walter's revenue was declined, but she was given an extra sixty pounds per year and a life interest in the Manor of Benington.

In 1577 Lettice moved out of her father's home to live with her friends the Digbys at Coleshill in Warwickshire. She only had her daughters with her; as per Walter's last instructions in his will, Walter fils was taken into the household of Henry Hastings, the third Earl of Huntingdon, Walter's cousin.[71] Coleshill was ten miles from Kenilworth, Robert Dudley's home. Lettice would have had opportunities to meet with Robert during the many hunting parties that took place there. It may be that from June 1577 Lettice and Robert's relationship became more intimate. It would have been nine months after the death of Walter and witnesses later stated that Robert was talking of marrying Lettice for at least a year before he actually did, in September 1578.[72] Though their actions were conducted in secret and were a surprise to everyone, so it is hard to know for sure when the relationship started. Secrecy would have been essential for both of them. Lettice would have still been in mourning for her husband and Robert was the queen's favourite: both of them would have known only too well that the queen did not share her favourites.

For the rest of 1577, Lettice moved around with her two daughters and by late October the family were living in London, perhaps in Hackney with the queen's cousin Lady Margaret Lennox.[73] Lady Margaret was also the mother of Henry Darnley, making her the grandmother of King James I – and a friend of Robert Dudley's. By December 1577 Lettice and her daughters had moved once again, this time to Bedford House on the Strand, the place where Robert Dudley's brother Ambrose would pass away. Lettice and her daughters would spend the New Year there. After the New Year's celebrations were over, Lettice had to say goodbye to her two daughters as they had come of age and, as per their father's last wishes, they were to join their younger brother Walter in the Earl of Huntingdon's household. Henry Hastings and his wife, Katherine, Robert Dudley's sister, had no children of their own but oversaw many noble families' children's welfare and education. Penelope and Dorothy were sent north to King's Manor in York, now part of the university (which, among other subjects, houses the department of medieval studies). The two young women would soon fall in line with their guardian's strict moral code, and it would be Henry Hastings who would choose their husbands for them. So it was that at the beginning of 1578 Lettice was without any children, which must have felt strange to her. However, she finally moved on with her own life by moving into Benington Manor, a place to finally call her own.

Family trees often seem to reveal traits down the generations, and situations repeat themselves in the same family, too. For example, just as Anne Boleyn had seen how Henry had thrown aside her own sister, Mary, making Anne determined not to be treated the same way, Lettice had seen how Robert Dudley had thrown aside Lady Douglas Sheffield. Lettice would not have wanted to be treated the same way by Robert. That Lettice had fallen in love with Robert Dudley and he with her by 1578 is speculative; however, for both of them to risk so much, both knowing the dangers of getting married without the permission of the queen, does suggest that they were in love with one another.

As they married secretly, the date of their wedding day is not known, but it is believed it was shortly after Lettice's sister's wedding to Thomas Leighton on 10 May 1578. The location may well have been Kenilworth, Robert Dudley's home. This did not go down well with Lettice's strictly religious father, Francis Knollys, who was disturbed that no witnesses were present, so another wedding had to be held. This took place on 21 September 1578 at Wanstead House, the home of Lord Rich. This time, the marriage was witnessed, by Lettice's father, Robert's brother Ambrose, and Henry Herbert, the Earl of Pembroke, among other guests. Two years after the death of Walter Devereux, his widow had remarried, perhaps for love.

Rather like a plot device to ratchet up the tension, the queen was making her way to Wanstead as a part of her summer progress. She had no idea of what had happened there just two days before. When the queen arrived, a hearty feast was laid out and as Elizabeth ate, she had no idea her favourite, sitting beside her, was a married man again.

However, the secret would not remain so for long, within weeks there was gossip at court and by November 1578, the Earl of Sussex had told the French ambassador, Michel de Castelnau, that Robert had married Lettice. Sussex disliked Dudley and used this piece of court gossip to harm him. Eventually, even the incarcerated Mary, Queen of Scots had heard about the marriage – it seemed the only one who didn't know was Elizabeth. But who was going to tell the queen?

An enemy of Robert Dudley's would deliver the shocking news to the queen in the end. This was Monsieur Jean de Sumier, who had arrived in England on 5 January 1579 with orders to persuade the queen to marry the Duc d'Anjou. Robert was not keen on this suggestion and made his opinions on the match known. And after an attempt on Sumier's life, which he thought Robert had ordered, the news of Robert's marriage was relayed to the queen. She felt betrayed by the months of lying and by the fact that he had not asked her permission. The realisation that she wasn't the only woman in her favourite's life came as a huge shock to her. She had long ago given up any thought of marrying Robert, but she may have thought that he still loved her, and Robert certainly played up to that role. Elizabeth certainly had her insecurities, and not only had Robert married one of her ladies but also a relation, so close a relation that the woman looked very much like a younger version of herself.

Robert was sent away from court, while Lettice was to endure the full wrath of the queen. However, perhaps Elizabeth had forgotten at that moment that her fire and strength did not just come from her father, it also came from her mother – and there was before her 'a Boleyn girl', who had a strength and determination to rival her own. Lettice did not beg for mercy but was instead defiant. Although neither she nor Robert had asked permission from the queen to marry, they had not actually broken any laws. Lettice had spent a respectable two years a widow. She did not feel she had done anything wrong. The two Boleyn girls apparently came to blows within the Palace of Whitehall. 'Her majesty, after Sundry admonitions told her (Lettice) as but one Sun lightened the earth, she would have but one Queen of England, boxed her ears and forbade her from court.'[74] The fact that the queen had turned to violence does seem to suggest that she felt more threatened by Lettice than any other of Robert's potential partners. Lettice was no threat to the queen, but she had hurt her personally, her inner self that Elizabeth had trouble showing, which was one reason she had kept the Boleyn side of her family close to her.

Lettice soon left London, realising her presence might damage her new husband's position. Where she went is not recorded, however, a year later, awaiting the birth of her next child, Lettice was at her childhood home of Rotherfield Greys with her father. Although Robert had been accepted back into the court, it was made clear that Lettice should remain in the background, much like Robert's previous wife, Amy. Robert allowed Lettice to stay at his London home at Leicester House in the spring of 1581 to have the child. Lettice had given birth before, but the last time was over ten years earlier and that child had not survived. She was now thirty-seven years old and the risks of Tudor childbirth were higher as a woman got older, as they are today. However, being in London, where midwives and doctors would have been available, may have eased her worries.

Lettice went into confinement with her two maids, Bridget Fettiplace and Lettice Barrett, at Leicester House. Lettice would not only share the same name as her maid, but in later years they would become relations after the maid married Lettice's younger brother, Francis. Lettice gave birth to a healthy boy on 6 June 1581, to be called Robert after his father. The child was later given the title of Lord Denbigh. True to Lettice's known behaviour, she, as well as Robert, doted on the child. Nothing would be too much for this much wanted son. An expensive cradle was made for the boy, covered in crimson velvet.[75]

As Lettice cared for her fifth child, plans for the marriage of her daughter Penelope were laid. Lettice, even if she wanted to, could not do anything about the match, as her father had given that responsibility over to Penelope's guardian, the Earl of Huntingdon. Perhaps sensing Lettice's attention was elsewhere, the earl worked quickly. Just eleven days after his father had died and the title of lord passed to him, Lord Rich is mentioned in a letter from the earl to Francis Walsingham as 'one in years very fit for my lady Penelope Devereux'.[76] The queen gave her blessing to the match between Lord Rich and Penelope Devereux. We don't know how Lettice felt about the union, but we do know how Penelope felt. This was very much a forced marriage and Penelope was not happy with it. She showed some of her Boleyn spirit. She was meant to have just accepted her match gratefully; with her father dead and her mother still banished from court, a match to Lord Rich was a better one than she could have hoped. Penelope thought differently, and even voiced her objections at the altar on her wedding day. Nevertheless, the marriage went ahead on 1 November 1581.[77]

Although Penelope had married Lord Rich, she had made it clear that she did not wish to spend any time with him, choosing instead to spend more time with her own family while she was at court. Thoughts now turned to Lettice's other daughter, Dorothy and perhaps not wanting the same unhappy marriage as Penelope's, Robert Dudley mentions Dorothy in his will, written in January 1582. History was repeating itself inasmuch as Lettice and her first husband wanted Sir Philip Sidney to marry Penelope earlier, and now Lettice and her second husband wanted Dorothy to marry him. At this point, Dorothy was seventeen years old and had joined the queen's household. Robert Dudley writes in his will that there had been 'some talk of marriage between my well-beloved nephew Philip Sidney and Lady Dorothy Devereux'.[78] However, once again Lettice's hopes for her children are dashed as Sidney actually marries another member of the family. Remarkably, another suitor was put forward for Dorothy's hand, someone far higher in social status than Sir Philip Sidney: King James VI of Scotland, later to become James I of England. It was no doubt a proud moment for Lettice when the Scottish ambassador, Robert Bowes, suggested such a match.[79] However, it must have also not helped relations with Queen Elizabeth.

There was one thing they had all overlooked: Dorothy, too, was her mother's child. she also had the Boleyn spirit within her, and she took the matter of her marriage into her own hands when she met Sir Thomas Perrot. Perrot had attracted Dorothy's attention in an unusual way. He had written to Dorothy's sister Penelope and asked her to sing his praises.[80] Dorothy accepted his proposal and decided to follow in her mother's footsteps and not ask the queen's permission but instead elope with her new husband to Broxbourne in Hertfordshire.

Lettice did not approve. Perhaps she had been overwhelmed by the thought that she could have been the grandmother of royal children if Dorothy had married King James or she foresaw the problems Dorothy was making for herself by not asking permission. For years there had been a portrait at Syon House thought to be of Lettice, but because there is a parrot in the painting, it is now believed to be of Dorothy instead, the parrot being a play on her husband's name. The fact that for so long this portrait, painted around 1600, was thought to be of her mother, suggests that Dorothy had looked very much like her.

When the queen learned of this marriage between Dorothy and Sir Thomas, once again she flew into a rage and banished Dorothy from court, but unlike her mother's husband, Sir Thomas also paid the price for not asking permission – he was sent to Fleet Prison. Sir Thomas was helped by William Cecil who pushed for his release, but the pair were never to be in the queen's good graces again and were forced to retire to Sir Thomas's family home of Carelo Castle in Pembrokeshire.

Researching Lettice's married life with Robert Dudley is difficult as only two out of the ten years in which they were married survive in account form, and although Lettice does appear in Dudley's accounts from time to time, it is not as often as you might think. That, of course, is not to say that she did not enjoy the items bought for the household recorded, only that her name does not appear in connection with them. When she does get a mention, it normally concerns her travel expenses. On 26 September 1585 Lettice travelled to Baynard's Castle, the home of the Earl of Pembroke who had been at Lettice's wedding.[81] Lettice and Robert had an impressive 150 members of staff at Wanstead and Leicester House, which included gardeners, musicians and even their own fishermen. Lettice had her own footman.[82] So the pair lived a life of luxury, surrounded by silver and gold pieces, Venetian glass and many tapestries. A tapestry hanging in the Victoria and Albert Museum, London, today, probably belonged to Lettice and Robert. It had hung inside the banqueting room at Leicester House.[83]

Lettice and Robert's child, Lord Denbigh, like Dorothy, was linked to a royal match in Arbella Stuart, the great-great-granddaughter of King Henry VII. Her grandmother was the Countess of Shrewsbury and she was the daughter of Charles Stuart, brother to Mary, Queen of Scots' husband and grandson to Margaret Tudor, Henry VIII's sister. This match was not to be, but Arbella Stuart will still play a part in this story later on.[84]

Even Mary, Queen of Scots writes of this proposed marriage between Arbella and Lord Denbigh musing on 'settling the crown of England on the head of her (the Countess of Shrewsbury's) little girl, Arbella and this by means of marrying her to the son of the Earl of Leicester'.[85] Although she was banished from the English court, two of Lettice's children came close to the English throne.

On 19 July 1584, Robert Lord Denbigh died at Wanstead. He had only just had his third birthday and Lettice was alone with her son as he passed, as Robert Dudley was with the English court at Nonsuch Palace. It is often said that in times of crisis, the true nature of a person is revealed. With the news of the death of his child, Robert Dudley's first thought was of Lettice, not the queen. Although Robert was playing the role of the queen's favourite, perhaps communicating that although he had married, the queen was the first woman he actually cared about, when the news broke Robert dropped the pretence and left the court without asking permission. He did manage to tell Sir Christopher Hatton what had happened, who informed the queen. Robert Dudley raced home to Wanstead to comfort his wife in her grief. When the queen was told of the news, she wrote a letter of condolence to Robert, not to Lettice. Hatton and the queen were there as Robert's support network, but it would seem at first that nobody was there for Lettice,[86] who had now lost two sons.

However, William Cecil, a man who had already been an important figure in Lettice's life since he assumed responsibility for her eldest child, stood up for her at this low point. Cecil did this by writing to her, offering his condolences and even suggested the couple go to his own home for them to grieve together in peace. This thoughtful gesture was not missed by Robert Dudley, as he writes to Cecil thanking him for his 'kindness towards his poor wife, who is hardly dealt with. God only must help it with her Majesty'.[87] He appreciated the queen's words of comfort to him, but he felt the same attention should have been given to his wife, no matter how wronged the queen might have felt. Lettice and Robert took Cecil up on his offer and visited Theobalds Manor, but in a letter written to Cecil, Robert suggests that the trip did little to lighten their spirits before their son's funeral.[88] The funeral was held on 1 August 1584 and the body was buried at St Mary's Church, Warwick, in the Beauchamp Chapel. His tomb was decorated with a life-sized effigy of the small boy and the words,

> Here resteth the body of the noble imp Robert Dudley, Baron of Denbigh, son of Robert Earl of Leicester, nephew and heir unto Ambrose Dudley, Earl of Warwick, brethren, both sons of the mighty Prince John late Duke of Northumberland, herein interred, a child of great parentage but far greater hope and towardness, taken from this transitory world unto everlasting life, in his

tender age at Wanstead in Essex on Sunday 19th July in the year of our Lord God 1584 and in this place laid up among his noble ancestors, in assured hope of the general resurrection.[89]

The rest of 1584 was a quiet one for Lettice and Robert, Robert accompanying his wife as they visited friends and family. By the end of 1584, Lettice had turned her attention to her eldest child Robert Devereux, who had spent most of his recent time in idleness. Although Lettice was a doting mother, she could also lay down the law if need be and in the following year, with help from his stepfather, Robert Devereux became a courtier. Lettice's eldest child made an impression, as we shall see.

1585 saw both Lettice and her husband at Greys Court, where Robert lost money gambling at dice.[90] They then travelled around Oxfordshire making their way to Robert's London home, Leicester House. When Robert returned to court, he offered to lead Elizabeth's army to fight the Spanish. He was certainly not the first person the privy councillors would have thought of, so while he waited for their decision he returned home to be with his wife again, and it was not long before the couple were travelling once more, to Kenilworth.[91] This trip would be a short one as by the end of August Robert received news that his request to lead the queen's army was successful. Robert left Lettice at Kenilworth while he travelled back to London. However, Lettice soon travelled back to London as well, much to the queen's anger, as she believed Lettice might try to travel with her husband abroad.[92] Lettice and Robert had been married for seven years at this point, but the queen still held a grudge.

As Robert got ready for his mission, he sat for a portrait[93] and in December he received his instructions and bade his wife goodbye. Not only was her husband going to war, but he was taking Lettice's son and brothers with him. She must have waited anxiously for any news, but sadly, no letters sent between the two survive from this time.

On 15 January 1586, Robert accepted the position of Governor General of the Netherlands. Elizabeth was incensed and Robert tried to explain his actions in letters that he hoped would be passed to the queen. It seemed as if his words did nothing to help him this time, as the queen wrote back to him on 10 February 1586: 'How contemptuously we conceive ourself to have been used by you, you shall by this bearer understand, whom we have expressly sent unto to charge you withal' – and that was only the start of her raging letter.[94] This Robert might have known was not good news and with the suggestion that his wife, Lettice, might join him in the Netherlands, Queen Elizabeth was certainly not best pleased with the couple.[95] It would take until March for the queen to calm down, when she wrote to Robert in her normal manner: 'We think meet to forbear to dwell upon the matter wherein we ourselves do find so little comfort, assuring you that whoever professeth to love you best taketh not more comfort of your well doing, or discomfort of your evil doing, than ourself.'[96]

The war continued and on 22 September, one of Robert's men was injured. Sir Philip Sidney, the son-in-law of Francis Walsingham, had his horse shot from under him.[97] He was unhurt, so he mounted another horse, but as he did so he was 'shot into the thigh' by a musket ball.[98] At first it would seem that he would recover, Robert writing to Walsingham and describing him as 'well amending as ever any man hath done for so short time'.[99] However, gangrene had set in and on 17 October Sidney died at the age of thirty-one. Sir Philip had been Robert's heir before the birth of his child with Lettice and was again, after the sad death of that child.

At this time, Lettice did not just have her daughters close by her, she had also become a grandmother. Penelope had given birth to a daughter in late 1582 or early 1583 and this child was named after Lettice. As Lettice was known to be a doting mother, she surely became a doting grandmother, too, while her husband was away at war. At Christmas 1586 Robert would return home from war. He brought home the body of his nephew. Robert and his brother attended Sir Philip Sidney's funeral, a grand occasion, on 16 February 1587 at St Paul's Cathedral. One of the mourners was Lettice's son, Robert Devereux, Earl of Essex. Sir Philip left his 'best sword' to Robert.

In 1587 when Robert Dudley returned from the Netherlands he was worn out, his health had deteriorated, his gout was bothering him and there were mentions of a 'stone' in his stomach or some kidney problems. It must have been a shock to Lettice to see her husband this ill and perhaps they had discussed his retirement from public service. However ill Robert may have been, he still travelled with the queen to Tilbury, where in August 1587 she made her famous speech to the troops waiting for the Spanish invasion: 'I know I have but the body of a weak, feeble woman...'[100] He would also be with the queen as she celebrated the defeat of the Spanish Armada, but Robert's stay at court was brief, probably due to his health, and in the same month he left London. Robert and Lettice travelled to Buxton in order to find a cure for Robert's illness and had made plans to visit their home at Kenilworth, but instead they went to Rycote, the home of Sir Henry Norris, a good friend to Robert and Lettice. His father was the Henry Norris executed for his alleged adultery with Anne Boleyn. At Rycote Robert's health took a turn for the worse and the queen sent him some medicine. From Rycote they then travelled to Cornbury Park, a former royal hunting lodge where Robert died on 4 September 1588.[101] William Camden writes in his *Historie* that Robert had passed away with a 'continual fever'.

The sole executor of Robert's will was his 'most dear well-beloved wife'. Robert had left his widow very wealthy. All he left the queen was a gift of pearls.[102] These pearls may have been the ones Queen Elizabeth is wearing in her famous 'Armada Portrait'.[103] On 10 October 1588 Robert's funeral took place in Our Lady Chapel of St Mary's Church, Warwick, Robert being buried near his son, the 'noble imp'.

Lettice may have just got over the initial shock of losing a second husband when the queen delivered another shock. In the wording of his will, it seems that Robert did not know how much he actually owed the crown. The queen certainly seemed to know exactly how much Robert owed – 50,000 pounds, around 11 million pounds today. The queen took all the estates from Lettice to pay the debt. Lettice was powerless to stop the queen, but Lettice had been here before and again she wrote to William Cecil for him to act as a go-between. Lettice even gave the queen a valuable ship as a kind of mollifying gesture.

Although it might well be said that Robert Dudley was the love of Lettice's life, within ten months of his death, Lettice was married again for the third time. Sir Christopher Blount had been Robert's Master of Horse and he seemed to have been a favourite of Robert's, as his name and family appeared regularly within Robert's accounts, receiving gifts. It is not known if Christopher had any attraction towards Lettice when she was married to Robert, but we can surmise that she paid him little attention as he was twelve or thirteen years younger than her.

Although Christopher would not have been able to help much with Lettice's debts, having a husband itself meant that Lettice's position was stronger in Tudor society. Her son Robert Devereux frowned upon the match, describing it has an 'unhappy choice'.[104] He felt that Lettice had married below her social status; although Lettice was now technically Lady Blount, she was still being referred to as Countess of Leicester and she would sign her letters 'L. Leicester' for the rest of her life, which could suggest that she thought so, too.

Lettice and her third husband set up home mainly at Drayton Basset Manor, a place that Robert Dudley had bought in 1578, only twenty-five miles from Lettice's previous home at Chartley. Christopher started to try to ease Lettice's financial problems by selling off her jewellery to her own family members, but he may have sold it too cheaply as Lettice still owed a lot of money after this was done.[105] Christopher also put up for sale Lettice's estates and even sold some of Lettice's jewellery to the queen herself.[106] Finally, Lettice had paid back most of the money that her previous husband owed the crown.

Family tragedy hit Lettice in 1591. Her son Robert Devereux had been sent to Dieppe in France to help support King Henry IV against the Spanish troops. Robert took his younger brother Walter with him. Walter was shot and killed, close to his twenty-second birthday.[107] Lettice was a devoted mother to her children, perhaps even obsessively so, and this was the death of a third son.

Walter was laid to rest in the same church as his father in Carmarthen. More deaths would follow. Lettice lost her uncle, Henry Carey and her father, Francis Knollys, in the 1590s. Lettice arrived in London in January 1598 as she had been finally granted an audience with Queen Elizabeth. It looked as if the pair of them had realised that life was too short for feuds. Lettice had been away from the English court for almost twenty years. Sadly, if Lettice thought that this would be the end of their enmity, she would be mistaken, as at the last possible minute the queen changed her mind about granting Lettice an audience. This humiliated Lettice and showed the court that Lettice was still in disgrace, even after all this time.[108] When this happened a second time, Robert Devereux intervened on behalf of his mother.

Amazingly, Robert's words to the queen seemed to have some effect on her. Another meeting was arranged, which took place on 2 March. What was said at this meeting was sadly not recorded, but both Lettice and her son Robert left the meeting content, with hopes that this was the start of better things for them all.

As soon as Lettice left London, the queen returned to her normal attitude towards Lettice. The meeting had been a waste of time for both parties and when Lettice returned to her husband, she was a very disappointed wife. The disappointments did not stop there, next came the moment when her son lost favour with the queen. What must have Lettice thought at this point in her life? She had lost three sons and her daughter Dorothy was disgraced, as she herself was. She had gained power, status and money, only for it all to be taken away from her by the queen. She also took her son from her, too, on 25 February 1601, as described in the following chapter.

This would have been the fourth son Lettice had seen die before her, and just over three weeks later Lettice would be a widow again. On 18 March 1601 Sir Christopher Blount was executed on Tower Hill, also found guilty of being a traitor to the crown. The bodies of Robert and Christopher were interred in the Chapel of St Peter ad Vincula in the Tower of London, the same place where Lettice's great aunt Anne Boleyn and great uncle George Boleyn lay.

The death of Lettice's lifelong rival, Queen Elizabeth I in 1603 meant an end to the Tudor era and for Lettice it meant a fresh start. King James I was very generous towards Lettice, holding no ill will and cancelling all her debts to the crown. These debts had been hanging over Lettice since 1588. However, Lettice soon had another problem to worry about. Robin Sheffield, the son of Robert Dudley and Lady Douglas, reappeared. He claimed that because his mother and father had actually married, not only was

Robin Robert's only heir but Lettice's marriage to Robert was null and void. Lettice, showing her true Boleyn nature, stood her ground against these accusations and without her royal rival alive, Lettice had powerful friends. Robin was to leave England and live out his days in Florence, where he would die on 6 September 1649.

Lettice in her later years focused her cherishing nature on her grandchildren. She would go on to have nineteen grandchildren as well as a number of great-grandchildren. Many of these would visit her at Drayton Bassett Manor and family events were held there. For example, as described later, on 3 March 1617 Lettice hosted the wedding of Robert Devereux's daughter Frances to William Seymour. Two years later, Lettice's last remaining child, Dorothy, died at Syon, where she was buried without a memorial stone.

As well as outliving her children and three husbands, Lettice also outlived another monarch; James I died at Theobalds on 27 March 1625. Lettice was then eighty-three years old. She would live another eight years before passing away on Christmas Day 1634. She was given an elaborate tomb and lies next to the love of her life, Robert Dudley, and near to their son, 'the noble imp', in the church of St Mary's in Warwick. Her epitaph was written by Gervais Clifton, the husband of Lettice's granddaughter Penelope Rich:

> There you may see that face, that hand,
> Which once was the fairest in the land.
> She that in her young years,
> Matched with two great English peers.
> She that did supply the wars,
> With thunder and the court with stars.
> She that in her youth had been,

Darling to the maiden Queen.

Til she was content to quit,

Her favour, for her favourite.[109]

The last two lines would make any researcher of Lettice's life and times smile, if only for a second or two. From her joint tomb with Robert Dudley, it is tempting to infer that true love won the day in the end. Queen Elizabeth's last resting place is with her sister Mary at Westminster Abbey, while her love rival, her relation, her 'other Boleyn girl', lies with the man she loved and who may have truly loved her back.

Lettice had royal blood running through her veins and it was suggested that she could have been the illegitimate granddaughter of King Henry VIII. We have seen that Lettice seemed to have the Boleyn family nature in her, too, the good and the bad.

ROBERT DEVEREUX,
SECOND EARL OF ESSEX

Born on 10 November 1565, Robert was the first-born son of Lettice Knollys and Walter Devereux. Being the first-born of a noble family more or less guaranteed him a good education. Robert's first tutor was Thomas Ashton, a devout Protestant who started work for the Devereux family in 1571. Thomas had been appointed headmaster of Shrewsbury School ten years before he began working for the Devereux family. One of his pupils there was Sir Philip Sidney, who would play a part in Robert's life as a possible suitor for Robert's sisters, and as a friend. It may be through this friendship that Robert met his future wife.

Robert was an excellent pupil; his father's secretary, Edward Waterhouse, remarked to William Cecil that Robert 'can express his mind in Latin and French, as well as in English, very courteous and modest, rather disposed to hear than to answer, given greatly to learning, weak and tender, but very comely and bashful'.[1] However, his education was not to continue in the same way. The debts his father had left the family eventually meant that Robert as a ward of the crown entered the household of William Cecil, Lord Burghley, at a young age.

At the age of eleven, Robert went to study at Cambridge, gaining an MA in 1581 at sixteen.[2] After university, he went briefly into the household of the Earl of Huntingdon, like his sisters before him.[3] By 1585, the Earl of Leicester, Robert Dudley, showed signs that he wanted Robert Devereux to be his protégé.

As we have seen, Robert 's son with Lettice Knollys, had died and Robert Dudley surely saw in his wife's son a replacement.

Robert Dudley wanted the queen to notice this new Robert at court. However, despite what is depicted in historical television dramas, this did not happen straight away. Although Robert Devereux may have been deemed good looking in Tudor circles, the queen did not notice him all that much, or at least acknowledge his presence. There was a good reason for this: Robert was the son of Lettice Knollys, the woman, the rival, the relation who had been banished from court for hurting the feelings of the queen. The queen would naturally want nothing to do with Lettice's son, at first.

At the end of 1585, Robert travelled with his stepfather to fight against Spain in the Netherlands, where Robert was made Colonel General of the Cavalry. Robert was unsuited to the appointment, lacking in experience. He may well have been given the role because of his connections with the Earl of Leicester, his stepfather. It is very doubtful whether Robert actually saw much action in the field. He made a failed charge at the Battle of Zutphen in December 1586. Although this charge was reckless, Robert still gained a knighthood banneret for his efforts, the highest form of knighthood that a person could gain on the battlefield.[4] This was where Sir Philip Sidney was fatally wounded and as he lay dying, gave Robert 'his best sword', showing how genuine their friendship was. Robert took his friend's sword, but in the not too distant future, he would also take his friend's widow.

Robert returned to court a decorated war hero – and now the queen noticed him. It would only take Robert a few months to become the queen's main companion at court. Seeing this evolving, Robert Dudley helped his protégé further by resigning as Master of the Horse, but only if the role was given to Robert

Devereux. This new role must have helped the young Robert's financial problems, as did the queen's expensive New Year's gifts.

Robert was unhappy with not being the only male favourite of the queen and when Sir Charles Blount displayed a token of the queen's affections, a chess piece upon his arm, Robert became very jealous. He pushed Blount and even challenged him to a duel. However, when the queen found out, the two men quickly made up their differences and became friends for life. Nevertheless, Robert's jealousy did not go away and next he came to resent the presence of Henry Wriothesley, the third Earl of Southampton. Once again, the queen had to get involved and the two men became friends afterwards.

It wasn't so easy to organise a rapprochement when Walter Raleigh became a 'love rival'. He was a mirror image of Robert, dashing, athletic and handsome. Both also came from army backgrounds, and these similarities may have been the reason why their rivalry, above others, would last for many more years. It would seem from the fact that the queen gave more rewards to Robert than she did Walter that Robert held the upper hand in the queen's affections at this point.

The death of Robert's stepfather meant that Robert lost his patron in 1588, but Robert also gained from his demise. Robert Dudley had given Robert Devereux a farm that made and sold wine, and the earl's monopoly on sweet wines was transferred to him by the queen, which gave Robert an income that settled his debts. Later, he was able to gain possession of Dudley's home, Leicester House on the Strand, changing the name to Essex House.[5]

Although Robert desired to be the queen's one and only favourite, he was not prepared to be a courtier that danced around to win the queen's affections. He wanted to be a war hero. He was therefore dismayed when in the spring of 1589 the queen ordered that none of her favourites at court were to be involved in the battles with Spain and Portugal.[6] Acting against the queen, Robert managed to slip away from court on 3 April 1589 to fight with the English, taking part in the Drake-Norris Expedition, which sailed to Spain in an unsuccessful attempt to push further the English advantage following the defeat of the Spanish Armada. The queen flew into a rage over Robert's actions but by the time he returned home after a failed campaign, her temper had cooled.

Considering how badly Robert wanted to be the only favourite of the queen – and how the queen had reacted to his own mother when she did the same thing – it is pretty extraordinary that he married someone without the queen's permission. Did he really expect the queen to love him no matter what he did? In 1590, he married Frances Walsingham, widow of Sir Philip Sidney and daughter of Sir Francis Walsingham, Queen Elizabeth's famous spy master.

Francis Walsingham was a powerful man with powerful friends at court. He was the kind of man to see through Robert's pose as the charming war hero, so may have not wanted his only child to marry him, but in 1590, the year of Robert's marriage to his daughter, Francis died. This put his daughter in a better position than she had been in, as a widow with her past husband's debt hanging around her. On her father's death she now had enough money to pay off her debts and had more left over. Just a year after their marriage, in October 1591, Robert's mistress Elizabeth Southwell gave birth to their son, who they named after Robert's father, Walter Devereux.[7] Nevertheless, Robert and Francis had a number of children together during their marriage.

Robert had shown that he did not have any respect for the rules of court, or for the orders the queen herself had given him. How much did he really think he could get away with?

Although the queen was angry at first, it only took her a month to forgive his transgression once again. Robert's quest for glory was too strong for him to have learned from his mistakes, so he pushed the queen to send him with the army to help the French King, Henry IV take the town of Rouen. The queen refused him twice, even when he begged her on his knees for two hours to let him go.[8] It was only through the intercession of William Cecil and Christopher Hatton – and the fact that no one else really wanted the job – that the queen eventually gave in and gave him two months to complete the task as a general. [9] The queen sent advisors, such as Sir Thomas Leighton, with him, so she was still worried by Robert's youth and inexperience in such matters.

Her misgivings were reinforced when Robert failed to keep the queen informed about what was happening to her own army. The queen herself had to write to him to prompt him to do so.[10] It had been arranged that the French king would meet Robert in Dieppe, however Robert decided to abandon this plan and undertake the dangerous journey to the king through enemy lines. Even worse was the outcome of the meeting, whereby Robert agreed to attack the town of Rouen without the French king, against the queen's wishes. This time, the queen openly blamed Robert for his mistakes and after his two months were up, she called Robert and eventually, her army, home. [11] Robert's brother Walter Devereux had been killed in an ambush, and Robert himself was sick with a high fever; this and the queen's criticisms sent Robert into some kind of depression.[12]

On 11 January 1591 Robert had his first child with his wife Frances, Robert fils. He was born at his grandmother's home of Walsingham House in Seething Lane, London.[13] He enjoyed a fine education at Eton College and Merton College at Oxford, gaining an MA four years after his father's death, in

1605.[14] At the age of thirteen or fourteen, Robert was married to Frances Howard, a distant relation. The marriage was not a happy one. As soon as they were married Robert was sent on a European tour, probably not having consummated the marriage, returning with smallpox. His wife kept away from him and had an affair with King James's favourite, Robert Carr. She then tried to get her marriage to Robert annulled, claiming that Robert was impotent. Robert denied it, making the divorce a public spectacle. The annulment was eventually granted, but this would not be the last time his ex-wife would enter his life. After marrying her lover, Robert Carr, the couple would later be accused of the murder of Sir Thomas Overbury at the Tower of London by poison, and Robert would sit as a juror during their trial. Robert would press King James to send his ex-wife to the scaffold.[15] The couple were found guilty but escaped with their lives and were released in 1622 with a pardon. Four so-called 'accomplices' – who lacked any powerful supporters at court – were not so lucky and were hanged.

On 11 March 1630, Robert was to marry again, this time to Elizabeth Pawlett, daughter to Sir William Pawlett of Edington. A child was born to the couple on 5 November 1636 but would pass away a month later, probably a victim of the plague.[16] This marriage did not end well either. They separated a year later, and Robert would lose his father's London home, Essex House, to her.

Robert, the 3rd Earl of Essex would have a difficult career in the army during the first English Civil War, being made by Parliament 'Captain-General and Chief Commander of the Army appointed to be raised, and of all other Forces of the Kingdom' when a Parliamentarian army didn't actually exist. During the last years of his life he was given Somerhill House, near Tonbridge, in Kent. Robert passed away after a stroke while hunting in Windsor Forest in 1646 and he was buried in Westminster

Abbey. [17] Although Robert's mother and father would have more children together after him, infant deaths were to follow. Penelope Devereux, born in 1593, died on 27 June 1599.

To return to Robert père, with the death of Christopher Hatton, a place at the privy council had opened up and Robert Devereux was keen to fill it. He had time on his side as most other councillors were nearing the age of sixty. Robert tried to show himself in the best light, paying off his debts, behaving more maturely and even trying to win over his nemesis, Walter Raleigh. Raleigh was of course also a candidate for the role, but this was when Raleigh was caught out lying about his secret marriage and was banished from court. This meant that on 25 February 1593, Robert joined the privy council. [18]

In this new role, the normally impatient earl decided to wait for his moment to shine in the queen's eyes, for he must have sensed the near death of William Cecil. He, perhaps for the first time in his life, thought ahead. He made friends with the King of Scotland, James VI, who was the most likely to take over the English throne after the passing of Queen Elizabeth. Robert was setting himself up to be close to the future monarch. However, timing is everything in politics. William Cecil had his own plans and they would clash with Robert's, for William wanted his own son to take over from him in his close dealings with the queen.

Taking a leaf out of Cecil's book of skulduggery, in 1594 Robert accused the queen's doctor, Roderigo Lopez, of trying to poison the queen. Robert claimed he had used his own network of spies to learn of this. His accusation was provoked in part by the doctor talking of treating the earl for venereal diseases. Both the queen and Cecil laughed Robert literally out of court, not believing him for a second. This was not the response Robert wanted, but instead of letting the matter go,

Robert pushed on trying to prove his case and while on the rack, the doctor did eventually 'admit' that he had been paid by the Spanish to poison the queen. The doctor later claimed it was a lie to stop the torture, nevertheless he was still hanged in June 1594, just to be sure.[19]

A year later, Robert had another son named Henry, born in 1595, who died a year later on 7 May 1596. Frances's next two babies were stillborn in 1596 and in 1598.[20] Robert then spent the next few years trying to convince the queen to go to war with Spain. Robert suggested various ways of countering the Spanish threat, but the queen said no to all Robert's ideas until on 23 May 1595, the queen assented to the destruction of the Spanish fleet at Cadiz in Andalusia. Robert did not have complete control as General of the Army, he shared command with Lord Charles Howard of Effingham, the Admiral of her Fleet, who had led the victory over the Spanish Armada.[21]

This time, Robert completed his mission by destroying the Spanish fleet. However, in the course of this action Robert had again shown signs that he would have dismissed the orders of the queen if Howard hadn't been there to stop him. The queen objected to Robert claiming full credit for the success, let alone the fact that Robert had taken her army to Spain when she would have preferred it to be in Ireland. After all this, the queen decided to appoint William Cecil's son, Robert Cecil, to the role Robert Devereux most wanted.[22] Robert was feeling hard done by, believing that he should have been better treated by the queen, even though he had been rewarded. Robert did what he always had done, he threw a tantrum, left court and waited for an apology from the queen. The apology did not come. The queen was getting tired of him. When the Irish rebels came to the fore, Robert saw this as an opportunity to go back to war, but there was a problem. He had not been forgiven.

It was only when Robert became ill that the queen relented and allowed him back at court, where he went to a council meeting on 10 September 1598. Robert seemed to have believed the queen would grant him the Office of Master of the Court of Ward, but the grant was denied, the queen even letting it be known that she would let the role be unfilled or even abolish it rather than assign it to Robert.[23] So he could attend court but was not in the queen's good offices. Robert felt humiliated and it was around this time it is suggested that during an argument with Robert Cecil over the problems in Ireland in a Privy Council meeting, the queen tried to quiet them. In the heat of the moment, Robert was said to have pulled his sword on the queen herself.[24] He subsequently talked himself into the post of Lord Lieutenant of Ireland, something of a poisoned chalice, as indicated by the experience of his own father. However, Robert genuinely thought he could make the role his own, that he could do a better job. On 27 March 1599, Robert left court and his then pregnant wife, for Ireland, taking with him an army of 16,000-17,000 men.

Robert was preternaturally paranoid, he hated losing control and being away from the court and the queen for very long. This made him believe others were poisoning the queen against him, as they gained promotions. He also blamed his enemies for his problems and mistakes in Ireland. In truth, Robert did not help matters when he once again ignored the queen's orders and promoted Southampton to General of the Horse. Then for three whole months he did not attack Hugh O'Neil of Tyrone in Ulster. This was what the queen had commanded. Instead, Robert travelled down to Munster. Although Robert's actions did bring peace to Ireland temporarily, once again, he had not followed orders.[25]

Throughout his campaigns Robert, in a sense, paid for the loyalty of his officers by giving many of them knighthoods and by the end of his time in Ireland more than half the knights in England owed their elevation to him. Robert also made use of his time in Ireland by becoming the second Chancellor of Trinity College, Dublin, serving in that role from 1598 to 1601. Although Robert had brought a temporary peace in the south of Ireland by establishing garrisons, the effort – and disease – had thinned the ranks. So, when Robert eventually got around to doing what the queen had originally ordered him to do, his army was small and weak. This made Robert decide it would be better to avoid another clash and make a truce with the Chieftain, which he did on 7 September.

The queen was furious, Robert had gone too far and she forbade him to return to England. However, this was Robert Devereux, the Earl of Essex, and as we have seen on countless occasions, he does not follow orders, he does not listen to his queen. He wanted to explain to her that there was no other action he could have taken but to make a truce with the enemy. He must have believed that stating this to the queen face-to-face, he would be able to win the queen over once more. So, on 28 September at ten a.m., Robert arrived at Nonsuch Place, where the queen was staying at the time.

Without waiting to be announced, he barged straight into the queen's bedchamber, where the queen was getting dressed. The queen, who at this point was losing her looks and was trying her best to hide it from her courtiers, was now seen unadorned by Robert, of all people; a man she was close to, a man with whom she had played the game of courtly love. This could not end well – but the queen did not react at first. After gaining some composure, the queen asked Robert to leave the room for an hour and then she would speak to him. When the queen was ready, she listened to what Robert had to say, quietly and calmly. Robert may have thought that he had won over the queen easily this time. However, after lunch, it was then the queen's turn to speak. She accused him of insubordination and sent for her privy councillors to interrogate him. Robert would not know it then, but he would never see the queen again.[26]

On that day, the Privy Council met three times. It would have seemed from the outset that his disobedience might go unpunished, even though the queen had confined him to his rooms, stating that 'an unruly beast must be stopped of his provender.' On 29 September 1600, Robert was before the full Privy Council for five hours, and one notable member of the council was Robert's uncle, William Knollys, the first Earl of Banbury. Robert tried once again to explain his actions, stating a truce was the only way out of the situation that he had found himself in at the time. The council thought that the truce was indefensible and Robert's flight from Ireland tantamount to a desertion of his duty. Robert was charged with six offences and was put into the care of the Lord Keeper at York House. It was here that Robert grew ill. His family and friends tried to tell the queen of this, but it was only when Robert was close to death that she relented temporarily, sending her own doctors to his side. When he recovered, she went back to her earlier rejection of him.[27] While Robert was under the care of the Lord Keeper at York, Frances gave birth to a healthy girl named Frances Devereux, born on 30 September 1599. The younger Frances's story is told in the following chapter.

In 1600 Robert was allowed to go home to Essex House, and his wife Frances became pregnant again. Dorothy Devereux was born to Robert and his wife on 20 December that year; she would be the last child. She was born just a few months before her father's death so would not have known him at all.

It wasn't until 5 June that year that the Royal Commission decided to hear his case. Robert denied his disloyalty but at the same time admitted to some of his errors and perhaps most surprisingly, Robert accepted the guilty verdict of gross disobedience without demur. His punishment was to be suspended from office and banished from court; it could have been so much worse.[28] Robert may well have thought nothing much of his punishment, believing that he would be able to pick up his career where he left it, once the queen had passed and Robert's friend King James assumed the English throne. But the queen was not done with her former favourite.

On 30 October 1600, the queen did not renew his wine monopoly, making him nearly bankrupt. Robert believed members of the Elizabethan court were against him because of his relationship with the King of Scotland. He thought that some were trying to convince the queen to back a Spanish succession instead of a Scottish one. Although his paranoia on this point was misplaced, Robert was right to believe he had enemies at court. Powerful men like William Cecil, Buckhurst, Raleigh, Cobham, and Nottingham were all at this point looking for reasons to get rid of Robert before the queen passed away. If the queen died and King James took over, they were right to fear that Robert might gain more power.[29]

Robert played into the councillor's hands, taking action against them owing to his belief in conspiracies. This eventually led to Robert being charged with treason, the punishment for which was death. First of all, the councillors noticed many men were gathering at Robert's home and on Saturday 7 February 1601, he was ordered to attend the council again the next day to explain what he was up to. Robert panicked at the thought that people were gathering evidence against him, so he initiated a premature and doomed uprising against the queen and her council.

That very night Robert's house was fortified. On 8 February, four lords came to take Robert to the meeting, who were held hostage. Robert left Essex House with roughly two dozen men and paraded along the streets of London, claiming that councillors like William Cecil were trying to kill him. Amazingly, Robert's pantomime convinced some and he gathered 300 men to his side. Ultimately of course, Robert had delivered himself to his enemies. His actions were clear treason.

On Wednesday 25 February 1601 at eight o'clock in the morning, the Earl of Essex, dressed all in black apart from a bright red waistcoat, climbed the scaffold. The waistcoat would have had the most impact on the hundreds of spectators, as red was a sign of martyrdom. When he reached the block, he gave a speech in which he asked for forgiveness for his sins when he was young and asked to the world to think kindly upon him. He took off his ruff and gown. He knelt and placed his head on the block. Tilting his head to one side, he spoke the words of a Psalm while he waited for the sweep of the axe.[30] Robert Devereux was executed on Tower Green, the same ending in the same place as his relation, Anne Boleyn, sixty-five years before.

Robert's crime of treason meant that his earldom was forfeited and his son did not, at first, inherit his father's title. However, after Queen Elizabeth's death, King James I reinstated the disinherited son to the earldom as the third Earl of Essex. Robert's wife married again for the third time, to Richard De Burgh, Earl of St Albans and Clanricarde, two years after Robert's death, in 1603. She died in 1632 and was buried at St Peter and St Paul Church in Tonbridge, Kent.[31]

Although the queen had flirted with Robert at court, this was not the same relationship the queen had had with Robert Dudley. Robert Devereux was attractive, talented and certainly later on, a celebrated man at Elizabeth's court. He lent the court some kind of powerful magic. However, the idea that the queen actually loved him seems doubtful. She was angry that he had married without her permission, but this anger did not last as long as her anger towards other men at court who had done the same thing. She didn't seem to be terribly upset when Robert left court and she did not hesitate to sign his death warrant. As for Robert's side of the relationship, there didn't seem to be much real love for the queen, beyond the *courtoisie*, the love play, which an Elizabethan courtier was required to enact.[32]

Robert fought the queen over every political decision, believing she was not 'man enough' to do her job. He told the French envoy that the queen's council 'laboured under two things at court, delay and inconstancy, which proceeded chiefly from the sex of the Queen'.[33] Their relationship was not simply an unfulfilled romance, it was a power struggle between two strong-willed people. Perhaps Robert's downfall can be attributed to the fact that he did not fully understand he needed a good relationship not only with the queen, but with the men close to her, men that Robert did nothing to cultivate.

FRANCES SEYMOUR, DUCHESS OF SOMERSET, AND LADY JANE BOYLE

Frances Devereux was born on 30 September 1599 to Robert Devereux and his wife, Frances, at a time of crisis in her family. Two years after her birth her father was executed as a traitor at the Tower of London.

Frances was born at Walsingham House in Seething Lane, the home of her mother's family, so perhaps although she was a Devereux by name she might have grown up knowing more of her mother's side of the family, the famous Walsinghams. At the age of seventeen, she married William Seymour at the home of her grandmother on her father's side, Lettice Knollys, at Drayton Bassett Manor. William was almost ten years older than Frances and had been married before – a marriage that had caused quite a scandal – to Arbella Stuart in 1610.

As her surname suggests, Arbella was of the blood royal. She was the great-great-granddaughter of Henry VII, so in line to the English throne after Queen Elizabeth I had passed away. She was also the cousin of King James I, so had a double claim. Being fourth in line to the throne, Arbella was carefully watched by the English government and when she married William, who was sixth in line to the throne as the grandson of Lady Katherine Grey, the granddaughter of Henry VIII's sister, Mary, King James feared the marriage was an attempt to steal the throne away from him.

They had married on 22 June at Greenwich Palace, the place where Frances's distant relation, Mary Boleyn, had married ninety years before. William and Arbella were imprisoned under the pretext of their not asking permission from the king to marry. Arbella was placed under the watchful eye of Sir Thomas Perry at his home in Lambeth, while William was sent to the Tower.

The couple planned an escape. Arbella feigned illness to delay her move to Durham House, then dressed as a man to flee from her keepers to meet up with William at Lee in Kent. William had first won the 'liberty of the Tower', the freedom to move around within the walls. He was then moved from the lieutenant's rooms to his own rooms situated above what is now called the Traitors' Gate. After eleven months studying the routine of the Tower's tradesmen with their carts of hay, William simply followed the carts out in disguise and headed towards St Katharine's Dock, where his friends were waiting for him with a boat to take him to Lee to meet up with his wife.

However, probably sensing capture, Arbella had already moved on from Lee and was making her way to France, even though the weather in the English Channel was poor. Her ship was overtaken by the king's men, never reaching the shores of Calais. Arbella was sent straight to the Tower of London, never to see her husband again. Arbella refused to eat and on 25 September 1615 she died, aged thirty-nine. She was buried in the same vault as her aunt and the king's mother, Mary, Queen of Scots, in Westminster Abbey.

Meanwhile, William took the next ship to France and managed to dodge the king's men by doing so and reached the safety of the town of Ostend. Just twenty-five weeks after the death of William's first wife, William marries Frances Devereux. With the death of Arbella, the threat William posed to the throne faded away, as shown by his becoming a Knight of the Bath in November 1616.[1]

Two years later Frances and William had their first child together, named after her mother.[2] Lady Frances Seymour junior would marry three times, firstly to Richard Molyneux, the second Viscount Molyneux.[3] Like Frances's father, William Seymour, Richard played a role in the English Civil War. He raised two regiments, one of horse, the other of foot, placed under the command of the Earl of Derby, James Stanley.[4] Richard was at the Siege of Manchester in September 1642 and nearly a decade later he marched with King Charles II to Worcester. The battle there, like most other battles that Richard was involved in, ended in defeat, and Richard escaped by the skin of his teeth. He passed away shortly after the battle in 1654.[5] Frances and Richard had no children and on 7 May 1659, Frances married Thomas Wriothesley, the Earl of Southampton.

In 1660, after Charles II was restored to the throne, Thomas rose to become Lord High Treasurer. Among his many friends he could name the famous diarist, Samuel Pepys. Frances was Thomas's third wife, none of whom had children with him. Thomas passed away on 16 May 1667 at the age of sixty at his home in Bloomsbury and was buried at St Peter's Church, Titchfield, Fareham Borough, Hampshire. His red marble tomb dominates the chapel on the south side of the chancel. The chapel later became a mausoleum for all the Earls of Southampton.[6] Two years after the death of her second husband, Frances married for the third and final time, to Conyers Darcy, the Earl of Holderness.[7] Conyers was a political man and became a peer of the realm. Frances was Conyers' third wife; he had actually been married to a distant relation of hers before. Frances died at the age of sixty-two and was buried in Westminster Abbey on 5 January 1681.[8] Her family line ends with her.

In December 1620, William Seymour was elected MP for Marlborough in Wiltshire, but in the following year he gave up the role to take his grandfather's place in the Houses of Lords. Also in 1621, his first son with Frances was born; they named him William after his father. The younger William was to pass away in his early twenties, predeceasing both of his parents, on 16 June 1642. The next child was Robert Seymour, born in 1622. His life was cut short too, as he died four years after his elder brother in 1646.

The fourth child was a daughter called Judith Ann. She was to marry Peter Ramsone in 1637 at the age of fourteen. Peter was an American and the couple married in Virginia. This was only seventeen years after the *Mayflower* had taken the first pilgrims from Plymouth to the New World. Such a journey and such a life might once again suggest that the old Boleyn spirit was alive and well. Judith would spend the rest of her short life in Virginia; after having six children, Judith was to pass away at the age of nineteen.[9]

The next child was a son named Henry Seymour, born in 1626. He would be the one to take on his father's titles. On 28 June 1648 Henry married Mary Capell at her family home in Hadham, Hertfordshire.[10] Mary was a well-known botanist and one of the earliest distinguished female gardeners, writing many journals on the matter and finally giving her *Herbarium* of twelve volumes to Sir Hans Sloane, which became part of the Natural History Museum collection.[11] Henry and Mary would have two children, William Seymour, the third Duke of Somerset, born in 1654, and Lady Elizabeth Seymour, born in 1655. Elizabeth would not meet her father. Henry was imprisoned in the Tower from 9 April to 9 September 1651 as a supporter of Charles I. He was released on the payment of 10,000 pounds[12] and three-and-a-half years later he died on 14 March 1654, being buried in the village of Great Bedwyn in Wilshire.

William, Henry's father, originally sided with the Parliamentarians, signing his name to the Petition of Right, 1628. The petition sent to the king sought recognition of four principles: no taxation without the consent of Parliament, no imprisonment without cause, no quartering of soldiers on subjects, and no martial law in peacetime. To many, this document stands alongside Magna Carta and the Bill of Rights of 1689 in political importance. William soon changed his mind and rallied to the king's standard, who rewarded him by making him the Marquess of Hereford.

At this point Frances and William may have had a son called Edward, who passes away in early childhood, but nothing is known about this child. In 1637 Frances and William have two children, the first Mary Seymour, who would marry Heneage Finch, the Earl of Winchelsea, in 1650. Among other titles, Heneage was the Governor of Dover Castle and Lord Warden of the Cinque Ports, the same position George Boleyn once held. Mary and Heneage had four children. Mary passed away on 10 April 1673. The second child born that year was Lady Jane Seymour. We shall return to her later.

After the king's reconciliation in 1641, where a list of grievances was presented to Charles I by Parliament, William was made a privy councillor, becoming the governor of the Prince of Wales, the future King Charles II, in August the same year. William was to stay with the king while in York in April 1642, even though Parliament was ordering him to return to London. This act of loyalty raised him higher in the affections of the king, so that when the Civil War broke in the August of that year, William was made Commissioner of Array for Somerset and the Lieutenant-General of the king's forces.

Frances and William were to have their final child in 1646, named John. He eventually married Sarah Alston, becoming a Member of Parliament for Marlborough. John passed away in 1675 without having any children and was buried in Salisbury Cathedral.[13]

In 1647, the king was imprisoned within the walls and gardens of Hampton Court, with William in attendance. William was one of the peers who advised the king over the failed Treaty of

Newport, an attempt to in autumn 1648 to reconcile Parliament and monarch and stayed with the king throughout the king's trial in 1649. When all attempts to save the king's life failed and the day came when England beheaded its own monarch, William, together with the Duke of Richmond, the Earl of Southampton and the Earl of Lindsey, arranged the king's funeral. They were the four pallbearers at Windsor's St George's Chapel.[14]

How did the death of Charles I affect the Seymour family? They had chosen the losing side of course, but through the years that William had stayed by the king's side, a strong friendship may have been formed, so there might very well have been a genuine feeling of grief on his part. Though Frances and William would not have run the risk of expressing such grief for the king for fear of repercussions, so we cannot know if this is true. William would not have wanted to return to the Tower after being lucky to escape from it the first time. Perhaps Frances saw that history was echoing itself, if only faintly. She was related to Mary Boleyn, who, through the death of her sister, a *queen* of England, saw her family's lives turned upside down; so now with the death of a *king* of England, what would change for Frances and her family?

William moved away from politics, perhaps reasoning that he should not bring attention to himself – but always believing the monarchy would be restored one day. This meant William lost all his titles during the interregnum, which surely meant financial difficulty. It is a wonder that throughout this time of unrest for the country, William and Frances still managed to have seven more children. Fortune's wheel would turn for this Boleyn relation when Charles II took the throne, William regained all of his titles and positions that he had lost under the rule of Oliver Cromwell. He also became the Duke of Somerset.

William was one of those who met Charles II at Dover in May 1660 on his return. This meeting did mean an end to the family's worries and proved that William had been right that the monarchy would be restored, but this was also a meeting of friends. William had been the Prince of Wales's governor and this meeting must have been an emotional one. The good times were not to last, as by this time William's health was failing and in the October of that year William died at Essex House, a place with many Boleyn connections.[15] Frances's husband was buried on 1 November 1660 in the church of St Mary's in Great Bedwyn, Wiltshire. Fourteen years later his wife joined him there. Frances Seymour passed away on 24 April 1674, aged seventy-four. In the church is a memorial for Thomas Seymour, grandfather to King Edward VI and father of Queen Jane Seymour, the lady who replaced Anne Boleyn in Henry VIII's affections.

Frances's part of this family story does not end here. Upon the death of a lady of means, there is a will to think about, and Frances's caused a scandal. By the time of her death, she had outlived her husband and all but one of her children, so she did not have many family members to pass estates on to. It should be noted that at the time of her death Frances may not have been of sound mind. A year before her death, Frances had turned to her granddaughter Frances's husband, Thomas Thynne, to draw up this most important of documents. This sounds a natural thing for Frances to have done, but Thomas Thynne was constantly feuding with Frances's remaining child, John. Just four days before she died, on 21 April 1674, a change was made to her will by which Thomas gained more lands, estates and substantially more money. It looked suspicious to John and a case was brought against Thomas.

It was claimed that Thomas had made sure that Frances would be on her own when the change in the will was made, that it was Thomas who wrote the change in her will, and that he did not read the change out to her as he should have done. It was stated that she needed Thomas's physical help to sign the change, and that she could not remember how to spell her own name, so Thomas had to guide her hand to form the letters. Finally, it was stated that when she was asked to seal the new will, she was unable to complete the task herself. It is heart-breaking to think that this woman might have been treated so badly by a family member at the end of her life.

Thomas was one of the three executors. One passed away shortly after Frances's death, then by a stroke of extraordinary good luck for Thomas, John died. Thomas won his case and Frances's lands, estates and money made Thomas one of the richest men in the country. He also received many documents from Frances's side of the family and many paintings, such as the painting of Lady Arbella Stuart, Frances's husband's first wife, that still hangs upon the walls of Longleat, his home, today. It is even suggested that one of the shirts worn by King Charles I on that cold January day when he was executed, which Frances's husband held in safekeeping, ended up at Longleat.

Whether through pangs of guilt or genuine admiration, Thomas paid for a bust of Frances to be made and placed in Great Bedwyn church.[16]

Lady Jane Boyle

Born to Frances and William Seymour in 1637, Jane Seymour was baptised on 6 July 1637 at Amesbury, Wiltshire.[17] She married Charles Boyle, the third Viscount Dunganian, on 7 May 1661. Charles was the son of Richard Boyle and his wife, Elizabeth Clifford. He would eventually follow in his father's footsteps by buying property in the capital. His father, Richard Boyle, the Earl of Burlington, had bought an incomplete house and lands in 1667 that became the family home when the family stayed in London. The name was changed to reflect its new owners, a name that is still recognisable in the streets of Piccadilly today, Burlington House.[18]

A year after their marriage, Jane and Charles had their first child in 1662, Elizabeth. She would marry her second cousin, James Barry, the fourth Earl of Barrymore. James was an Irish soldier and politician, choosing to fight for William of Orange rather than James II. William appointed James Lieutenant Colonel of his army. Elizabeth Boyle was James's first wife. They had three children before she passed away in 1702. He married twice more and had seven more children before dying in 1748.[19]

Two years after the birth of their first child, Jane and Charles Boyle had another daughter, in 1664, Mary Boyle. She would go on to marry the second Duke of Queensbury, James Douglas. He became the Lord High Treasurer of Scotland in 1693, the keeper of the Privy Seal of Scotland in 1695 and a year later became the Extraordinary Lord of Session. In 1700, he became the Lord High Commissioner to the Parliament of Scotland and a year later a Knight of the Garter. In 1702, after the succession of Queen Anne, Mary's husband was appointed Secretary of State in Scotland.[20] Mary and James were to have three children before she passed away in 1709. James died two years after Mary, and they were both buried in an elaborate tomb in the Church of Durisdeer in Dumfries. The tomb has marble representations of the pair, Mary recumbent and James leaning on his arm lying on his side.

In 1669, Jane and Charles were to have their third child, named Charles after the father. We will leave Charles Junior here for the moment. In 1669, Jane and Charles have their fourth child, they name him Henry Boyle, born on 12 July. Henry would become a politician. He sat in the Irish House of Commons and also the British House of Commons, becoming the Chancellor of the Exchequer and the Secretary of State. He deserted the army of King James II in favour of William of Orange and would pass away on 31 March 1725, aged fifty-five, leaving behind no children.

Jane and Charles were to have one more child, Arabella Boyle, born in 1671. She would marry the first Earl of Selbourne, Henry Petty, a member of the Irish Houses of Commons from 1715 to 1727. Arabella and Henry would have no children and Arabella died in October 1740 at High Wycombe, aged sixty-one. On 23 November 1679, Jane passed away at the age forty-one. She was buried in Westminster Abbey, like so many of her relations.

Although Burlington House was the family's main residence, the Boyles were rich enough to buy a summer retreat, too. Charles bought the original Chiswick House, again a name we recognise today, in 1682. The Jacobean house was once owned by Sir Edward Wardour, the Member of Parliament for Malmesbury, whose father was said to have been the original architect of the place, building it in 1610.[21] It was no country cottage. We know this because the building was later sold to the Earl of Somerset, Robert Carr, at the time of the Hearth Tax. It was thought it would be easier to count the number of hearths there were in any property rather than the number of residents.[22] The 1664 Hearth Tax documents for Chiswick House record that the residence had thirty-three fireplaces.[23]

Charles Boyle bought Chiswick House from the Earl of Somerset, Robert Carr, James I's favourite and purported lover, the husband of a distant relation of Charles Boyle's wife. Robert Carr had married Frances Howard, the ex-wife of Robert Devereux, the third Earl of Essex and son of Robert Devereux and Frances Walsingham.

In 1689, Jane's husband Charles gained the Barony of Londesborough following his father's death and two years later the Barony of Clifford after the death of his mother. Both titles would eventually be passed on to Jane and Charles's eldest child. Charles Boyle died on 12 October 1694, aged fifty-four. He was buried at All Saints Church at Londesborough.[24]

CHARLES BOYLE, SECOND EARL OF BURLINGTON AND RICHARD BOYLE, THIRD EARL OF BURLINGTON

Born in 1669 to Jane and Charles Boyle, Charles was their first male heir to carry on the family name from Charles's grandfather. At the age of nineteen Charles married Juliana Noel at Ely House on 26 January 1688.[1] She was the only daughter of the Honourable Henry Noel. He had inherited Luffenham Hall in Rutland from his uncle, who had died as a prisoner of the Parliamentarians.[2] Henry, meanwhile, was to become a Knight of the Royal Oak at the Restoration, a reward for loyalty to Charles II while he was in exile. Henry was also given 1000 pounds per year.[3]

Two years after their marriage, Charles and Juliana had their first child, Elizabeth. She would marry Sir Henry Ardell Bedingfeld in 1719. Henry was born on 13 April 1689 in Bow Street, London and he, too, would 'have history' with the Parliamentarians. Henry's grandfather, also named Henry, had been captured by the Parliamentary forces and imprisoned in the Tower of London for supporting Charles I. He had to pay to get back all of his sequestrated property, and in addition was fined 20,000 pounds. He had hoped that after the Restoration his family would be compensated, but all they actually gained was a baronetcy. The anger Henry and his family felt led them to retreat from society and stay away from court. They instead spent most of their time at the family home of Oxburgh Hall, which is now run by the National Trust. This was where Sir Henry Ardell Bedingfeld took his new bride, Elizabeth Boyle. We know this because Sir Henry's letters, held at the British Museum today, mention his wife and are from Oxburgh.

However, no matter how Sir Henry felt about the betrayal his family had previously suffered, his sympathy for the royal family did not waver, mainly owing to the fact that, like the royal family, Sir Henry was Catholic. It is interesting to note that although Sir Henry must have felt very strongly about his religion, having previously signed away his property under the penal laws for his Catholic beliefs,[4] he does not seem to have pushed his wife to think the same way, as a letter from Sir Henry to the Duke of Newcastle suggests:

It would besides be verry (sic) hard that Lady Betty should be deprived of horses to carry her to church or to visit her neighbours at a distance and not in a manor suitable to her quality.

So Sir Henry did not stop his wife worshipping in a Protestant church, and made sure she arrived there in style.[5] Elizabeth and Henry would have seven children, Elizabeth passing away on 25 November 1751, at the age of sixty.[6]

In the same year that Charles and Juliana had their first child together, Charles was made a Member of Parliament for Appleby and a year later, in 1691, Charles was also made Governor of the County Cork. This post he only held for three years because when his father died in 1694, Charles gained his father's titles of Viscount Dungarvan, Baron Clifford and Baron Clifford of Londesborough. The year 1694 saw life as well as death. Charles's first-born son, Richard Boyle, arrived. His life is examined in the following chapter.

A year after the birth of Richard, Charles was appointed Lord High Treasurer for Ireland. Three years later Charles and Juliana had another child, named after the mother. This Juliana would marry Charles Bruce, the third Earl of Aylesbury, in 1717. After the passing of Charles Bruce's first wife, Charles had started his career in the House of Commons before he accepted his peerage and sat in the House of Lords. Juliana did not have any children and she passed away in 1739.

In 1698, Charles Boyle became the Earl of Burlington and Earl of Cork, titles which had originally belonged to Charles's grandfather. At the same time Charles was appointed a gentleman of the bedchamber, bringing Charles close to William III, assisting the king with dressing, serving his food and guarding the king's bedchamber. Charles Boyle and his family were certainly prominent members of the court.

In 1699, Charles was promoted to Lieutenant of the West Riding of Yorkshire and his wife gave birth to another child. This Boyle would pass away unmarried. Charles and Juliana have another child in 1701, Henrietta Boyle. She would marry Henry Boyle and as his surname suggests, he was Henrietta's distant cousin, Henry would later be the Chancellor of the Irish Exchequer. Henrietta died in 1746. Charles Boyle would pass away in 1704, all his titles passing on to his son, the 'Architect Earl', Richard Boyle.

Richard Boyle, the Third Earl of Burlington

Richard was born to Charles and Juliana Boyle on 25 April 1694. At the time, the family were living mainly in Yorkshire. At the age of just nine, Richard lost his father, Charles. The child Richard had gained his father's titles and eventually would hold his father's lands, too. Because of his age, these lands remained under the control of his mother and guardian, Dowager Countess Juliana Boyle.[7]

In Richard's early childhood he had showed signs of following a career in music rather than becoming a famous architect. For example, in 1719 he was one of the main subscribers of the Royal Academy of Music[8] and as much as Richard Boyle loved music, it would seem that music loved him back. While staying with the Boyle family at Burlington House, George Frederic Handel dedicated two of his operas, *Teseo* and *Amadigidi Gaula* to Richard, and Handel was not the only one to do this. Francesco Barsanti dedicated his six recorder sonatas of OP.1 to Richard as well.[9]

When Richard was nineteen and again when he was twenty-four, he made Grand Tours to Italy, visiting places such as Venice, Florence and Rome, and he also travelled to Paris. This inspired Richard to think his career belonged in architecture. The Palladian designs of these European cities helped Richard to gain confidence in his own work. This confidence grew to such an extent that when he was twenty-four, he dismissed the well-known Baroque architect James Gibbs, who had been redesigning his family home at Burlington House, in favour of the Scottish architect Colen Campbell. Colen would become a mentor to Richard and his work for a short time, before Richard's confidence in his own ideas grew further.

It was in 1716 when Richard and Colen first worked together on a small project, designing a garden at Richard's family retreat at Chiswick House. It is presumed because there is no documentation of Richard putting pencil to paper before this date, that the small garden project was the first work Richard took on as an architect.[10]

Richard and Colen worked together on the outside of his family home at Burlington House while the painter and designer William Kent would plan the inside of the building. His relationship with William Kent would continue until Richard's death and we could even say for a little while afterwards, as Kent would teach Richard's widow how to draw.

The first part of Burlington House that Richard and Colen worked on together was the now well-known courtyard at the front of the building. The courtyard features in the 1979 film *Murder by Decree*. In this Jack the Ripper tale, Sherlock Holmes tries to solve the case and the courtyard of Burlington House stood in for the entrance of the Royal Opera House. That the family home of the music-loving Richard Boyle, who personally designed the courtyard, becomes part of the Royal Opera House in a film made 226 years after his death, is satisfying.

The partnership between Richard and Colen did not last, however, and by the 1720s, Colen had been replaced by Henry Flitcroft. Born in 1697, Henry was only three years younger than Richard. Their backgrounds could not have been more different. Henry's father was a labourer at Hampton Court Palace in the reign of William III. Being a joiner by trade, Henry first began working as a carpenter on Burlington House. However, by the time he suffered an accident there when he fell off a scaffold, breaking his leg, Richard had noticed Henry's skill in drawing. From that moment on Henry became Richard's draughtsman and general assistant, not just at Richard's home at Burlington but also on other projects. Working regularly with Richard Boyle gained Henry the nickname of 'Burlington Harry'.[11]

Richard married Dorothy Savile on 21 March 1720. Dorothy was the daughter of William Savile, the second Marquess of Halifax, and his wife Lady Mary Finch. Through Dorothy's mother, Dorothy and Richard were distantly related. Dorothy's mother, Mary, was the daughter of Lady Essex Rich, she in turn was daughter to Anne Cheeke, who was the daughter of Lady Essex Rich. This Lady Essex Rich was the daughter of Penelope Devereux. Penelope Devereux was of course the granddaughter of

Lettice Knollys, and to take us right back to the start of this book, Lettice Knollys was the granddaughter of Mary Boleyn. What helped to cement the couple's relationship was their shared love of music.[12]

A year after his marriage, Richard began his designs for Tottenham House in Wiltshire. Now Grade II listed, Tottenham House was once owned by a relation of Richard's, Thomas Bruce, the second Earl of Aylesbury. Thomas was the great-grandson of William Seymour, through William's son Henry, while Richard was also the great-grandson of William Seymour, but through William's daughter Jane. However, this was not the only family connection Thomas Bruce had to Richard; a link that was a little closer to home was the fact that Thomas and Richard were brothers-in-law. Thomas had married Richard's sister, Lady Juliana Boyle. It was probably around the time of his sister's marriage to Thomas that Richard worked on Tottenham Lodge within the grounds of his brother-in-law's estate at Tottenham House.[13]

In 1722, Richard was commissioned to design the dormitory at Westminster School. This was Richard's first public commission from outside his own family, and he beat Sir Christopher Wren to get it. Richard winning the commission at the expense of Sir Christopher was a sign that English tastes in architecture were changing – and Richard Boyle was in the right place at the right time. It took nine years before the scholars at Westminster School could move into their new dormitory.[14] Without the intercession of Queen Elizabeth I, a Boleyn and a distant relation of Richard's, who re-founded the school in 1560, Richard would not have won the commission in the first place.

In 1724, Richard and Dorothy have their first child, named after the mother, Lady Dorothy Boyle. This Dorothy would marry George Fitzroy, the Earl of Euston. Also in 1724, Richard was commissioned by his friend and headteacher, Elijah Frenton, to redesign the school building at Sevenoaks. It took eight years to complete the building to Richard's designs. A year after, Richard was commissioned to design the Belvedere Tower in Waldershare Park, Dover. This tower has long been thought of as Colen Campbell's work, but a drawing of the Belvedere Tower was recently found among Richard's draughts now held at Chatsworth. The Belvedere Tower was designed for the owner of the park, Sir Henry Furnese, as a folly. Richard designed – if indeed he was the architect – a towering three-storey building of redbrick with white Portland stone detailing. It has a large semi-circular doorway and Venetian window surrounded by three keystones. The cost of this design was 1,703 pounds seven shillings and four pence[15] and although it may look a little sorry for itself today, with most of the detailing lost, it is one of the last remaining designs of Richard Boyle's work that survive (again, if the attribution is correct).

Richard and Dorothy's second child came along in 1727, Lady Julianna Boyle. By the time of her birth, her father was becoming more and more popular as an architect. Horace Walpole, the writer, art historian, politician and son of the first British Prime Minster, described Richard as 'the Apollo of Arts'.[16] In that year Richard began working full-time on his family's summer retreat, Chiswick House. Chiswick House was one of the earliest Neo-Palladian villas in England. At first, the brilliant white building we see today stood beside the old family home that Richard's grandfather and father would have known, however this became impractical for the family's requirements, so in 1732 a connection was built between the two. Full of artworks and inspirations taken from William Kent and with beautifully maintained gardens, there are many reasons to visit Chiswick House today. One of the reasons is to see the bedchamber and closet situated to the right of the Green Velvet Room. This was where Richard's wife was to pass away.

The entrance to Chiswick House would have looked slightly different. The main road was a lot closer to the house in Richard's time than it is today and there were, to match the three others within the gardens, statues of two sphinxes placed upon the entrance pillars. The originals are in Green Park in London today, replaced at Chiswick House by impressive replicas. Of course, with the Palladian design being derived from the Classical, sphinxes are not out of place and sphinxes are guardians, so it would naturally make sense to have them at the entrance. However, what if they were to symbolise something else?

The sphinx guarded the entrance to the Greek city of Thebes. To enter the city the visitor had to answer the sphinx's riddle: 'Which is the creature that has one voice, but has four feet in the morning, two feet in the afternoon, and three feet at night?' A wrong answer left the sphinx with apparently no option but to strangle the visitor for their failure. Oedipus answers the riddle: Man. When we are born, we walk on all fours, in adulthood we walk on two and in old age we walk with a stick, so three legs. The sphinx was so surprised that a human could work out its riddle that it chose to self-destruct. So, sphinxes were guardians, but they were also riddle makers.

Do the sphinxes at Chiswick House point to a secret that only the architect would know? It has been claimed that Chiswick House was a secret Freemason temple. Apparently, there are clues to this, if you know where to look and know what to look for. From 1736 Richard was listed in the *Freemason's Pocket Companion,* so we know that he was a Freemason from then, but he may well have been a Freemason before that date, a member of his Grand Lodge at its formation in 1717,[17] when he was twenty-three years old.

Richard also did work on the lawns to the west of Chiswick House. Richard widened and deepened the Bollo Brook there and decided to open up the space within the gardens nearby, adding Roman statues. Richard was given the Inigo Jones gateway that stands at the entrance to these gardens by Sir Hans Sloane when he was rebuilding Beaufort House in Chelsea. There was originally a paddock for deer and a deer house to the north end, designed by Richard himself. When in 1727 Richard bought the property of Sutton Court to add to his lands at Chiswick, his deer park was redesigned as an orangery.

In 1731, Richard and Dorothy had their last child, Lady Charlotte Elizabeth, the subject of the next chapter. Richard's reputation as an architect was growing. He even produced designs for the new Houses of Parliament. The idea to rebuild Westminster was not new, it had first been debated in 1712 and was brought up again in 1718, when Colen Campbell, Richard's mentor, and William Benson laid out designs. In 1732, Nicholas Hawksmoor did the same. Richard Boyle offered his Palladian design in 1735. The Houses of Parliament would have looked like the British Museum or the National Art Gallery if Richard's designs had been accepted.[18]

In 1739, Richard became the governor of the Foundling Hospital charity. This was a charity set up by philanthropist Thomas Coram in that year. Thomas Coram had returned to London from America and had campaigned for seventeen years to get a Royal Charter from George II to establish a foundling hospital. Many of Richard's friends were involved in the charity, including George Handel and by 1741, the first babies were admitted. Over time the Foundling Hospital took in 25,000 babies.[19]

Richard died on 4 December 1753 at the age of fifty-nine at Chiswick and was buried in the family vault on his Yorkshire estate at the church of Londesborough. His estates eventually went to the Devonshire family, as Richard's daughter, Lady Charlotte Boyle, married the Marquis of Hartington, the fourth Duke of Devonshire. This is why many of Richard's drawings were found at the Devonshire's family home of Chatsworth. With his death, the Earldom of Cork was given to his cousin, John Boyle, but the title of Earl of Burlington fell into disuse until 1831, when Richard's grandson George Cavendish assumed it.

CHARLOTTE CAVENDISH, MARCHIONESS OF HARTINGTON, AND HER DAUGHTER DOROTHY, DUCHESS OF PORTLAND

Born on 27 October 1731 to Richard and Dorothy Boyle, Charlotte received all the Burlington family estates, Burlington and Chiswick Houses, the estates of Bolton Abbey, Londesborough Hall in Yorkshire where her parents were buried, and Lismore Castle in County Waterford, Ireland. On 28 March 1748, when Charlotte was sixteen years old, she married William Cavendish. William, who was eleven years Charlotte's senior, was at the time the Marquess of Harington and had been the MP for Derbyshire from 1741 until a year before his marriage.[1] They married at Charlotte's family home in Pall Mall, St James's, Westminster.

This was a match made in Charlotte and William's childhoods, and it was not liked by everyone. William's mother, Catherine Cavendish, did not like the fact that Charlotte would one day take over her role as Lady of Chatsworth House. Catherine even went as far as to leave her husband when he agreed to the match.[2] William as the 4th duke decided the famous gardens of the family home at Chatsworth were to be designed by the royal favourite, Capability Brown. William hired James Payne, a well-known architect inspired by Charlotte's father, Richard Boyle, to design the stables.

Marriage seemed to suit the couple as they were devoted to each other from the very start. Lady Mary Wortley Montagu found in William 'so great a vocation for matrimony that I verily believe if it had not been established before this time, he would have had the glory of the invention'.[3] Charlotte and William had four children, the first born in 1748 and named William after his father. This William would marry Georgiana Spencer in 1774, the great-great-great-great aunt of Diana, Princess of Wales. Like her future relation, Georgiana was very popular with most who knew her and her fashion set trends. Georgiana used this power and fame to highlight women's rights more than a century before suffragism was to take form. She was very much a heavyweight in political circles and was also an author, her works include *Emma; or The Unfortunate Attachment: A Sentimental Novel*, and *The Sylph*, published anonymously, which included autobiographical elements, the story of an aristocratic bride who has been corrupted. Georgiana started to become ill in her forties and it was thought that she was suffering from an abscess on her liver. She passed away on 30 March 1806 at the age of forty-eight.

Georgiana has two links to Sir Arthur Conan Doyle's Sherlock Holmes, created eighty-one years after her death. Chatsworth House was used in two episodes of Granada's *Sherlock Holmes* starring Jeremy Brett as the detective. And it is suggested that the inspiration behind Sherlock Holmes's nemesis, Moriarty, was the real-life criminal Adam Worth. However, instead of stealing the Mona Lisa as Moriarty does,[4] Worth stole a portrait by Thomas Gainsborough, which stayed with Adam for a number of years because he liked the look of the sitter so much. The sitter was none other than Georgiana, and this portrait is now hanging in Chatsworth House.

William had married Georgiana on 7 June 1774 at Wimbledon Parish Church.[5] William would later become famous for having his wife and his mistress Lady Elizabeth Foster under the same roof for more than twenty years. William became the Lord Treasurer of Ireland before passing away on 29 July 1811, aged sixty-two.

William's father was well known within the political world at this point and was even given the opportunity to be the governor of the Prince of Wales, the future King George II, but William could afford to turn down this prized role.[6]

On 27 August 1750, Charlotte gave birth to her second child, Dorothy Cavendish, whose story comes later. Charlotte gave birth to another child on 19 June 1752. They named him Richard, after his architect grandfather. Richard was to go on to study at Trinity College, Cambridge[7] before entering into the House of Commons as MP for Lancaster in 1773. At this time Richard moved into Number 1 Savile Row, which meant he was living in a street with family connections to himself through his grandmother, Dorothy Savile. It also placed him in an area of London that had many streets named after his family. There was New Burlington Street, Old Burlington Street, Clifford Street, Cork Street and of course Boyle Street. Richard moved out in 1781, when he went to Italy in hopes that the trip would improve his health, however, this wasn't to be and he died, having not married, in Naples on 7 September that year.[8]

On 31 March 1754, Charlotte and William have their last child, George Augustus Henry Cavendish, who takes his grandfather's title as the Earl of Burlington. George would not have known his mother as she was to pass away by the end of the same year. George was a Member of Parliament for Knaresborough for five years from 1775 to 1780 and then became MP for Derbyshire from 1797 to 1831, until he gained a peerage and became Baron Cavendish of Keighley.[9] In 1815, George bought back his distant ancestral home of Burlington House from his nephew, the 6th Duke of Devonshire, and with the help of Samuel Ware, a well-known architect who worked for the family, built the famous Burlington Arcade on the west side of Burlington House. Burlington Arcade is a nineteenth-century version of a shopping centre that opened on 20 March 1819, a place 'for sale of jewellery and fancy articles of fashionable demand, for the gratification of the public'.[10] George probably designed it in part so his wife could shop safely, away from the busy, dirty streets of the capital.[11]

At the beginning of the arcade's life, it was a single, well-lit walkway with seventy-two small two-storey units. The sculptures within it were carved by the Professor of Sculpture at the Royal College of Art, Benjamin Clemens, but these were added in 1911. The arcade was patrolled by paid 'beadles' who wore top hats and frockcoats, an early form of the police force. They were former members of George's regiment, the 10th Royal Hussars, who were involved in the Napoleonic Wars, later they would be renamed 10th (The Prince of Wales Own) Royal Hussars. Burlington Arcade was set on fire in 1836, was looted in 1871 and again in 1936, and was bombed in the Second World War.

George married Lady Elizabeth Compton on 27 February 1782. Elizabeth was the only daughter of Charles Compton, the seventh Earl of Northampton and Lady Ann Somerset. Working as the Ambassador Extraordinary and Plenipotentiary to the Republic of Venice, Charles was the Bearer of the Ivory Rod with the Dove at the coronation of King George III.[12] George and Elizabeth had eleven children in total together, including Lady Anne Cavendish, born at Hardwick Hall on 11 November 1787, who later married Lord Charles Fitzroy. Lord Charles had assumed the title of Earl of Burlington after the original line of descent of the title in his wife's family had ceased. George and Elizabeth also had Lady Caroline Cavendish, born on 5 April 1797. She was to pass away on 9 January 1867, aged sixty-nine and is buried at St Andrews Churchyard, Funtington, West Sussex.[13]

On 8 December 1754, Charlotte died at Uppingham, Rutland, being buried at All Saints Church in Derby on Christmas Eve 1754, after catching smallpox.[14] She was only twenty-three years old, but in that short life she had seen her family estates grow through her union with her husband, who would later become Prime Minister. It was said when Charlotte passed away her husband was inconsolable.[15] William was appointed Master of the Horse; he held this post until 1755 when he was given the title of Baron and left the House of Commons for the House of Lords. It was also in 1755 that William's father died and William became the Duke of Devonshire.

A year later, the Seven Years' War broke out, a complex and bloody global conflict. Partly a continuation of Prussia's rise to power following the War of the Austrian Succession of 1740, it was also a struggle between Britain and France for dominance, especially in North America. In October 1756, the war was going badly for the British under the Duke of Newcastle. King George II asked William Cavendish to take over the duke's role. William agreed to do this but only until the end of the Parliamentary Session.[16] William was appointed First Lord of the Treasury. At this point he became de facto Prime Minister. He found the funds to send the army to America.[17] William began to work together with the Duke of Newcastle to end the war and their relationship was vital in doing this, and both were highly praised by their peers. However, when King George II died and King George III took over, the new king was suspicious of the close friendship between William and the Duke of Newcastle, believing that they were trying to undermine him. When the Duke of Newcastle retired in May 1762, William, in an act of defiance towards the king and loyalty to his friend, said that he would rarely attend

Lord Bute's councils. Lord Bute was John Stuart, the third Earl of Bute, the first ever Scottish-born British Prime Minster and the king's favourite.

In October 1762, the king requested William to attend a cabinet meeting, but William stood his ground and declined by claiming that he had inadequate knowledge to help in the meeting.[18] On 28 October, while William was travelling from Kew to London, the king's carriage overtook him. The king believed that William intended to resign without the king being present. When William arrived, the king refused to see him. George struck William's name off the list of privy councillors, which was seen at the time as petulant; William was well liked by most in the council.[19] However, the bitterness the king showed towards William actually helped his decision to resign from his post as Lord Lieutenant of Derbyshire.

For a long time, William was very ill and ended his days in 1764 in the Netherlands, where he had gone to take the waters at Spa. This makes William the shortest-lived British Prime Minster at 44, and he is buried at Derby Cathedral.[20]

Dorothy Bentinck, Duchess of Portland

Born on 27 August 1750 to William and Charlotte Cavendish, at the age of sixteen Dorothy was married off to William Cavendish-Bentinck, the third Duke of Portland, on 8 November 1766. Her husband was the eldest son of William Bentinck, the second Duke of Portland and his wife, Margaret Cavendish-Harley. It would be from his mother's side of the family, that he would later inherit many of his lands. His grandmother was the widow of John Holles, the first Duke of Newcastle.[21]

William was educated at Westminster School, no doubt using the dormitory that his future wife's relation had designed. He gained his Masters in 1757 at Christchurch College Oxford.[22]

Four years later, William was elected to parliament as MP for Weobley, Herefordshire. This was only for a short time before he entered the House of Lords. Between 1765 and 1766, he served as Lord Chamberlain of the Household belonging to Lord Rockingham's Whig's government.[23]

Two years into their marriage, Dorothy and William have their first child. On 24 June 1768 William Henry Cavendish Bentinck was born. He was educated in Ealing, studying under Samuel Goodenough. Samuel was a classical tutor, but he had a love of anything botanical. A famous collector of plants, he had species named after him such as Goodenia, and even an Australian bird, the red-capped robin, Petroica Goodenovii.

William junior left Ealing in 1774 before attending Westminster School like his father before him, and then again like his father, he went to Oxford.[24] In 1786, his father sent William to the Hague, the seat of government for the Netherlands, for experience. William returned three years later in 1789[25] and went back to Oxford to become a Doctor of Civil Law in 1793.[26] William also became a trustee of the British Museum, lending it the Portland Vase, a Roman cameo glass vase, the best known of its kind, dated between AD1 to AD25.[27] William became a Member of Parliament in 1790 for Petersfield and then for Buckinghamshire from 1791 to 1809,[28] and in between he worked under his father as Lord of the Treasury in March and September 1807. He was appointed Lord Privy Seal in 1827 by his brother-in-law, George Canning, the Prime Minister, and joined the Privy Council in the same year.

William married Henrietta Scott, the daughter of Major-General John Scott of Fife and his second wife, Margaret Dundas, on 4 August 1795. At the time of his marriage, William obtained a royal licence to take the name and arms of his wife's family of Scott in addition to his name of Cavendish-Bentick. They had nine children before his wife passed away on 24 April 1844.[29] William died ten years later, aged eighty-five. He wanted to be buried in the churchyard closest to Bolsover Castle, his family seat, but instead he was interred in the Cavendish vault in London.

Dorothy and William have another child on 1 July 1770, The Right Honourable Lord Charles William Cavendish Bentinck, however he was to pass away within the month.[30] In the *Newcastle Chronicle* on 7 September 1771 it states that Dorothy had 'safe delivery of a son, at his Grace's house in Charles Street, Berkeley Square' on 25 August 1771. However no more is known about this child, which sadly suggests an early demise.

Next came William Henry Cavendish Bentinck. Born on 14 September 1774, at the age of just nine he was given the sinecure of Clerk of the Pipe for life. This defunct role once recorded the government's income and expenditure.[31] He, also, was educated at Westminster School.[32] At the age of sixteen, he joined the Coldstream Guards after paying for an ensign commission.[33] He was promoted to Captain-Lieutenant in the Second Regiment of Dragoons on 4 August 1792[34] and then promoted to Captain in the 11th Regiment of the Light Dragoons on 6 April 1793.[35] William also gets promoted to Major in the 28th Foot in 1794[36] and to Lieutenant-Colonel in the 24th Dragoons in the same year.[37] He gets promoted again on 9 January 1798 to Colonel.[38] In 1803 he was appointed Governor of Madras and promoted to Major-General on 1 January 1805.[39]

William provoked the Vellore Mutiny of 1806 by ordering the native troops not to wear their traditional attire. After some serious violence and William agreeing to cancel that order, he was allowed to come back in 1807. Later, he was given British troops to command in Sicily and became a Lieutenant-General on 3 March 1811.

William was very opinionated in his role, even if those opinions went against the policies of his country. In 1814, for example, he landed at Genoa with British and Sialia troops and started to make liberal proclamations of a new order in Italy. This embarrassed the British government, which had intended that Italy be ruled by Austria, and this led once again to William being recalled in 1815. Famously, William was known in his role as the First Governor General of India to be a cost cutter. He cut the wages of military men, which won him no friends. He prohibited female infanticide, made *Sati* illegal and he removed flogging as a punishment within the Indian Army.[40] Oddly, some thought, when William returned to England in 1835 he refused a peerage. There were two reasons for this: the first was because he had no children to pass the peerage onto and the second because he wanted to stand for Parliament again.

William married Lady Mary Acheson, daughter of the Earl of Gosford, Arthur Acheson, on 18 February 1803.[41] He was married for thirty-six years before he died on 17 June 1839, in Paris. His wife died four years later. Both are buried in the family vault in St Marylebone Parish Church, London.[42]

The next child that Dorothy and William were to have was Lady Charlotte Cavendish Bentinck, born on 3 October 1775. She was to marry Charles Greville, the MP for Petersfield and the Under-secretary of State for the Home Office. They were to have four children before Charlotte died on 28 July 1862. Lady Mary Cavendish Bentinck came next on 13 March 1778, passing away in the November of 1843. Dorothy and William have their seventh child on 3 October 1780, Lord Charles Cavendish Bentinck, whose life is examined later.

The eighth child was Lord Frederick Cavendish Bentinck, born on 2 November 1781. He went on to marry Mary Lowther and have one child, named George Cavendish Bentinck. George would become a British barrister and Conservative politician, serving under Benjamin Disraeli. In 1889, George was involved in a scandal that shocked the public and press at the time, named by the rent boy, John Saul, in his list of the clientele of the infamous male brothel at Cleveland Street. This scandal would even touch the royal family.[43] He passed away at his home at Branksea Castle on Brownsea Island in 1891, aged sixty-nine.[44]

When Lord Rockingham entered his second government term, in 1782, William was given the role of Lord Lieutenant of Ireland. In this role, William found himself facing pressure to do something about the heavy taxation imposed on the people because of the American War of Independence.[45] William fought his case and won, going against Lord Shelburne, the then Home Secretary. The issues between these two men continued and when Lord Rockingham died, William decided to resign from his post rather than to carry on under Shelburne. William was not alone in this action, as many resigned in support of the Whig statesman, Charles James Fox.[46]

In April of 1783, William became Prime Minister in a coalition government with Charles James Fox and Lord North. On his watch the American Revolutionary War ended with the signing of the Treaty of Paris. He also served as the First Lord of the Treasury in this term until December of the same year, when the government lost a vote in the House of Lords on reform of the East India Company.[47] In 1789 William became the vice president of the London's Foundling Hospital charity. Fifty years earlier, William's father had been one of its founding members. Four years later, William became its president, taking over from Lord North.

Although William had been a supporter of Charles Fox, he was deeply concerned by Fox's enthusiasm for the French Revolution and broke with Charles over the matter. He then joined Pitt's government as Secretary of State for the Home Office in 1794. This was an important role at the time, as he oversaw the secret accounts to secure the 1800 Acts of Union, to create the United Kingdom of Great Britain and Ireland.[48]

Dorothy Bentinck died on 3 June 1794. She had been unwell for some time with some kind of intestinal problem, but it was after an unrelated short illness that she passed away at her family home of Burlington House.[49] William stayed in service after Pitt's death in 1806 as Lord President of the Council and then as Minister without portfolio.[50] In 1807, William becomes the Prime Minister again. The Peninsular War had begun, Spain and Portugal fighting against the invading French army. Two years later, on 30 October 1809, William passed away at his wife's family home of Burlington House after an operation to remove a stone. He was buried alongside his wife at St Marylebone Parish Church in London, where a memorial stone stands at his family's vault. He died owing £52,000. This debt was paid off by his family selling property. Today there is a parish in Jamaica named after William and in London, Great Portland Street and Portland Place remind us that these were areas he once owned.

LORD WILLIAM CHARLES AUGUSTUS CAVENDISH BENTINCK AND THE REVEREND CHARLES CAVENDISH BENTINCK

Although mainly known as Charles Bentinck, following the family tradition of naming their children William, this man's full name was actually William Charles Augustus Cavendish Bentinck. He preferred Charles.

Like many of his relations before him, including his brothers, Charles was sent to Westminster School. At the age of sixteen, Charles joined the Coldstream Guards, and again like many of his relations, Charles seemed to move effortlessly up through the army ranks. However, perhaps rather like his Boleyn family relations before him, Charles preferred the life of a courtier instead, being a regular visitor to Harriette Wilson, a very famous courtesan. This was actually quite a dangerous indulgence for Charles and indeed his brother, Frederick, as Harriette was a known blackmailer of gentlemen with titles. Men at risk on her list included the Duke of Wellington and the Prince Regent.[1]

Although Charles was a friend of the Prince Regent, the future King George IV, this friendship was put to the test when Charles married Georgiana Seymour in 1808 as this marriage could have made Charles a relation of the prince. Georgiana's mother was Grace Dalrymple Elliott, the famous eighteenth-century courtesan, who did not know who the father was. Grace had probably been born in Edinburgh around 1754.² Her parents, Grisel Brown and Hew Dalrymple, had separated at the time of Grace's birth, and she was probably brought up by her grandparents.³ After an education in a French convent, she returned to Scotland and to Scottish society. She married John Elliott, a physician, on 19 October 1771 when she was seventeen years old. The couple grew apart and by 1774, Grace had fallen for Lord Valentia, with whom she started an affair. Her husband found out and eventually brought a Criminal Conversation case against Lord Valentia for £12,000, before divorcing Grace. Following the case her reputation was of course damaged, and it can be argued that she had no practical alternative to becoming a professional mistress. She began relationships with Lord Cholmondeley and the Prince of Wales at the same time and gave birth to Georgiana Augusta Frederica Seymour on 30 March 1782 without knowing who the father was.

Georgiana was given the female versions of those royal male names to suggest she was the child of the Prince of Wales. When it came to her christening, she was baptised under the surname of Elliott, her mother's married name, at the church where her future husband would have a family vault, St Marylebone Parish Church. Georgiana's father could have been Lord Cholmondeley and not the Prince, but either way, Georgiana was brought up well after her mother left for France. Georgiana was also blessed with good looks, this, plus her known possible links to royalty made her a good if potentially dangerous catch. She made an impression on Charles. Both families did not like the idea, but this coupling was very much a love match rather than for money or status. A wedding was hastily arranged at Chester, the original plan of their being married at Cholmondeley Castle changed at the last minute.

After being sent to the Peninsular War and returning, Charles decided to end his career in the army and enter politics.

This did not go well and his only means of support came from his connections with the royal family and the income set by his brother, once he became the Duke of Portland.

Their first-born passed away within hours of its birth. The second child, a female, survived and was given, as her mother before her, a string of royal names: Georgiana Augusta Frederica Henrietta (Cavendish) Bentinck was born on 21 August 1811.[4] Charles's marriage to Georgiana had allowed him, through the social circles it opened up to him, to become Treasurer of the Household in 1812, a role he was able to keep even after the divorce scandal that would consume the remaining years of his life.[5]

On 10 December 1813, Georgiana, Charles's wife, passed away and with his daughter being sent to be raised by Lord Cholmondeley, the child's possible grandfather, at Cholmondeley Castle, Charles was all of a sudden alone. However, through the many social gatherings Charles's role took him to, he would not be alone for long. Soon Charles was to meet Lady Anne Abdy.

Lady Anne Abdy née Wellesley was the daughter of Richard Colley Wellesley, the second Earl of Mornington and first Marquess Wellesley of Norragh, making her the niece of Arthur Wellesley, Duke of Wellington. Her mother was Hyacinthe Gabrielle Rolland, a French opera dancer and singer who had met her husband while he was on a trip to Paris and who had instantly fallen in love with her. Lady Anne had married a man that her parents approved of – Sir William Abdy had given their daughter status, wealth and a title. However, there was a problem. William seemed dull to his wife to the point of stupidity. They lived together in a mansion just off Park Lane and Hyde Park, on the corner of Hill Street at Number 20B. As the word 'mansion' might suggest, the Abdy's family home was large. Three storeys high, it was much larger than that of most houses along the same street. Number 20B was so large in fact that later it would become numbers 42 and 44 Hill Street.[6]

Although from the outside Lady Anne's life may well have seemed complete, she felt that she was lacking emotional support from her husband and went looking for it from someone else. This was when she met Lord Charles, a thirty-four-year-old widower with a four-year-old daughter. He was close to the Prince Regent and being retired from the army meant he had many stories to tell. He delighted the ladies at the ballroom parties, he was handsome, charming and stood out in a crowd. For Lady Anne, who had no children of her own, the thought of a four-year-old girl without her mother may have been an added attraction towards Charles. Their close friendship soon became something more serious.

Lady Anne came from a family that believed in falling in love for its sake alone, not for status or for wealth. Her father Richard Wellesley had fallen head over heels in love with Mademoiselle Hyacinth Gabrielle Rolland, who had no social status. This might have been where their daughter had got her belief in love; and she was certainly not in love with her husband. Lord Charles must have seemed like a dream to her – so much so that on a whim, Lady Anne left her home with nothing but her pet dog to be with Charles. She took no money, jewels or clothes – and fled with such haste that she left behind all her love letters from Charles, to be found by her husband's mother and sister.

Although Lady Anne seems to have regretted her decision at first, writing letters to her husband asking him to take her back, the deed was done, Lady Anne had chosen Charles over her husband, and she would have to live with that choice and the scandal it would cause. Charles and Lady Anne stayed at a house in Crooms Hill, Greenwich Park undetected while the gossip pages of the newspapers were filled with the scandal. In the days and weeks afterwards, there were a lot of questions to be answered. Would Lady Anne now stay with her lover, or go back to her husband? Would her husband take her back or would he want a divorce?

The answers to these questions were made for them when Lady Anne discovered that she was pregnant with Charles's child. On 1 December 1815, the case was brought before the Sheriff's Court, with Lady Anne's husband claiming £30,000 in damages for losing his wife.[7] This sum was reduced to £7,000 by the end of the court case, a sum that Charles never got around to paying. After the case, Charles joined Lady Anne in Paris and it was in May 1816 that Lady Anne's divorce proceedings were heard in the Consistory Court at the Doctor's Commons on Paternoster Row, near St Paul's Cathedral. This was settled and then it was a matter of establishing whether Lady Anne and Lord William would be allowed to remarry. The decision had to go through the House of Lords. The divorce bill was committed with the newspapers reporting that 'the allowance to the adulteress was fixed at £400 a year.'[8] On 10 June 1816, the divorce bill had its second reading in the House of Lords, when it was stated that William was happy for Anne to keep the money that she had brought into their relationship; and by the third reading it was consented that William and Anne were free to marry again, if they chose to. This came just in time, as Lady Anne was coming close to term with her first child.

In a rush to make this child legitimate, a marriage licence was obtained for Lady Anne Wellesley, who was described as 'single' on the marriage register, to marry Lord Charles Bentinck in the church of St Martin in the Fields, Westminster, on 23 July 1816. One week and two days later, Lady Anne gave birth to her and Lord Charles's first child. The child was named after its mother and grandmother, the Honourable Anne Hyacinthe Cavendish Bentinck.

Money was tight for the couple at first. Lady Anne's mother died shortly after the birth of this child and she had in the past written Anne out of her will, not getting around to changing this. This was probably because at the time of writing of her first will, Anne's ex-husband may have had a chance to claim on Anne's estates; perhaps her mother had plans to change it back once everything was settled but caught a cold and died so suddenly that she could not do so. Lady Anne's ex-husband had held back on paying the £400 a year that he was meant to have provided for her, as her new husband had paid none of the £7,000 that he owed in damages.

There was also another problem for the couple. While the divorce settlement was going through, Charles had been trying to get back his first daughter from his previous marriage. Although Georgiana came to stay with her father, Lord and Lady Cholmondeley, who had been looking after the child since the death of Charles's first wife, now wanted to adopt her. They had offered £15,000 for the child, but Lady Anne did not want to give her stepchild up. Months passed with the child caught between the two families. Finally, Lady Anne acquiesced, but only if the money went to her own child and any more children she was to have. Lord Cholmondeley was not happy about this and wanted to walk away from the whole business.

The 'business' of Charles's daughter was settled on 6 November 1817. Lord and Lady Cholmondeley adopted her and Charles and his future family received £10,000.[9] Lady Anne was soon pregnant again and gave birth to their first son in November 1817, William Charles Cavendish Bentinck, the full name of the father, and like his father, he would be known as Charles, not William.[10]

In 1819, in the same month as the birth of Princess Alexandra, the future Queen Victoria, Charles and Anne were to have another child, named Arthur, on 9 May 1819.[11] Anne falls pregnant yet again soon after and in April 1820 gives birth to Emily Cavendish Bentinck.[12] Emily would marry Henry Hopwood before passing away on 6 June 1850. Both of these children were born at Charles's Little Brompton Villa on Lillie Road, known as Hermitage.

When the Prince Regent became King George IV, he appointed Charles to the Privy Council and later he was made Treasurer of the Royal Household. Charles was at the funeral of King George III on 16 February 1820 at St George's Chapel, Windsor. He was able to trade up to live in Eaton Place in Pimlico. At the time it was part of Pimlico, but today Eaton Place is in Belgravia. Charles also took part in King George IV's coronation, giving out specially minted medals to the judges in accordance with his position as Treasurer of the Royal Household. Later that same day Charles took his place in the coronation procession from Westminster Hall to Westminster Abbey.

At the end of 1821, the Bentinck family moved once more, to Number 1 North Row, near Park Lane, now Number 138 Park Lane. The family also kept a country residence in Tunbridge Wells in Kent, an area that probably unbeknown to Charles had family connections. And Number 1 North Row was a short walk from the family home of a future relation of his, a queen of England. It was at this address that Lady Anne gave birth to her fifth child, Frederick William Cavendish Bentinck, on 14 November 1822. He died within a week of his birth.

Charles was spending more and more time with George IV. He was going on royal trips to Scotland rather than spending time with his wife. This caused tension between the couple, which only worsened when the courtesan Harriette Wilson entered the picture. In 1825, Harriette published her first volume of memoirs that featured famous people who had been her clients, including Charles, his brother Frederick – and Lady Anne's first husband, Lord William Abdy. The stress of being in not just one but two volumes of Harriette Wilson's memoirs, and therefore in the public eye again, probably added to Charles's health problems. He died of a heart attack at North Row, on 28 April 1826. He collapsed while undressing and was found by a footman.[13] He was only forty-five years old, leaving a wife and four children. He left no will. Lady Anne managed to continue to live in North Row for some time, with the help of her brother-in-law, the then Duke of Portland. Lady Anne was to pass away fifty years later, on 19 March 1875.

(William) Charles Bentinck Cavendish

At the time when his mother was travelling to and from the Continent with her daughters by her side during her widowhood, Charles was sent with his brother, Arthur, to Harrow School, one of the oldest schools in Britain. When Charles and Arthur joined the school, it had 200 pupils and was being run by Charles Longley, who would later become the Archbishop of York.

When it came to the school holidays, it seems that Charles did not find living with his mother all that agreeable, as he writes a letter to his uncle, the Reverend Henry Wellesley, begging to stay with him instead.[14] His wish was granted and Charles stayed with his uncle, his aunt, their son called Guy and their little dog, Snowball. He stayed at the Old Abbot's Hall in the grounds of Battle Abbey in Sussex, which is now the Battle Abbey School.[15] Perhaps this affection that Charles had for his uncle set Charles on a career in the Church.

On 1 June 1837 Charles entered Merton College at Oxford University. He was now nineteen years old. It was here that Charles met Sinnetta Lambourne, daughter to a gipsy mother also named Sinnetta, and James Lambourne, a horse dealer.

Perhaps following in his grandfather's footsteps, he fell head over heels in love with Sinnetta, a woman that his family would not have approved of. Charles proposed to Sinnetta and obtained a marriage licence. As Sinnetta was under the age of twenty-one, one person had to know that they were planning to get married and that was Sinnetta's father, James Lambourne. He gave his permission for his daughter to marry. He describes himself as an 'esquire' in the marriage record rather than a horse dealer.

The wedding took place the day after Charles had obtained the licence, on 26 September 1839, at St George's Church in Hanover Square. On the marriage register Charles gives his address as Brook Street and his new bride gave the address of her parents' house in Southwich Street in Paddington. The two witnesses were John Henry Cole, a greengrocer, and Mary Baldwin.

The newly married couple took up lodgings at Number 20 Pickering Terrace in Paddington, now a part of Porchester Road. There they had their first child, on 24 June 1840. They named him Charles William Cavendish Bentinck. He died with convulsions just three weeks later and was buried at All Souls Cemetery in Kensal Green. Not only had Sinnetta lost her first-born child, but it was also at this time that her father was admitted to Bethnal Green Asylum, situated where Bethnal Green Library is today. He, too, passed away, suffering from palsy, on 6 January 1841 at the asylum.

Sinnetta must have felt very lonely at this time, living in secret with her husband but only when he was in London, at other times using her maiden name and living at her aunt Nancy Drewitt's home.[16] To make matters worse, with her husband still studying at university, Sinnetta fell pregnant again. She was to give birth on 24 July 1841 and the couple decided to give the child the same name as their first, Charles William Cavendish Bentinck. Would such a thing help to ease the loss, or remind the couple of it?

Sadly, history was about to repeat itself. This child only lived for seven months. On 3 March 1842 he was buried with his older sibling at Kensal Green Cemetery. As much as this death must have affected the couple, life carried on and Charles returned to his education.

To fit in to her husband's social circles, Sinnetta resorted to desperate – not to say heartbreaking – measures. She was unhappy with the way she looked or felt her look caused problems for her husband. Sinnetta had toned skin and she started to use lead-based cosmetics to whiten it.[17] This was not only dangerous to her own health but potentially damaging for her unborn child, too, as Sinnetta was pregnant again. Sinnetta did not know of the danger, none of the women doing the same knew until much later.

At the age of twenty-seven, Charles gained his Bachelor of Arts. Charles was given a new place to live, Bothal in Northumberland, by the Duke of Portland. Now it was time for Charles to drop the bombshell on his family, to tell them that he was in fact married and would be bringing his wife with him to Bothal.

After researching the family that Charles had married into, finding them to be horse dealers and gipsies, the Duke of Portland did not want Charles to have Bothal after all. At first, the Duke also wanted to disinherit Charles. However, after many family discussions, it was finally agreed that Charles would get the sum of £6,000, and another £3,000 at a later date, with an annuity of £600.[18] This money would no doubt have felt like a godsend to the couple, as Sinnetta gave birth on 23 December 1845 to another boy. But yet again, the child was to die early, within four months. The death of this child happened at their new home at Hayes in Middlesex.

Charles became Deacon for St John the Evangelist Church in Westminster on 31 May 1846, then with the help of Charles's uncle, Henry Wellesley, Curate to the Reverend John Hodgen in the village of Lidlington in Bedfordshire. The couple moved to a house on Ampthill on Church Street in the village, where Charles entered the priesthood in August 1848. A year later Charles left Lidlington to work in Husborne, Crawley and Ridgemont, a post given to him by his new patron, the Duke of Bedford, who did not have a problem with Charles being married. This allowed the couple to move further along the road in Ampthill into a mansion house built in 1742.

In 1850 Charles's wife began to show signs that she was not well. With abdominal pains, and losing weight but with her stomach growing, perhaps Sinnetta and Charles thought that she was pregnant again. Then came the doctor's diagnosis that Sinnetta had mesenteric disease and that there was nothing that could be done to help her. At the age of thirty-two, Sinnetta died on 19 February 1850.

Charles had to move to a smaller place in Ridgemont and he threw himself into his work. He then met Caroline Louisa Burnaby, fifteen years younger than him. She was certainly someone that his family would approve of. Her father was Edwyn Burnaby, the Deputy Lieutenant and High Sheriff of Leicestershire and her mother, Anne, was the daughter of a solicitor. Two of her paintings are in the Royal Collection at Windsor. Caroline came from her family home of Baggrave Hall in South Croxton, Leicester, to marry Charles on 13 December 1859 at St Paul's. Marrying into the Burnaby family meant that through Charles's new father-in-law, he was introduced to Queen Victoria and Prince Albert at St James's Palace on 26 April 1860. Charles was certainly going up in the world.

While in London, the newly married couple lived at Caroline's parents' home at Number 50 Eaton Place in Belgravia, where they had their first child on 11 September 1862, named Cecilia Nina Cavendish Bentinck. The child was baptised in Ridgemont a month later. Charles and Caroline had two more daughters, twins, in 1864, Violet Anne and Hyacinthe Mary. Charles was not to enjoy his new fatherhood for long, as on 17 August 1865, at the age of forty-seven, he died with what was described at the time as a tumour and dropsy, oedema of the abdomen. He was buried at Croxton Church in Cambridgeshire on 22 August 1865 and has an ornate tomb there.

CECILIA BOWES-LYON, COUNTESS OF STRATHMORE AND KINGHORNE, AND LADY ELIZABETH ANGELA MARGUERITE BOWES-LYON, THE QUEEN MOTHER

Cecilia was born in Belgravia on 11 September 1862, the eldest child of Charles Cavendish Bentinck and his second wife, Caroline Louisa née Burnaby. Cecilia would have been just four years old when she lost her father, then it was her, her mother and her two siblings for the next five years, until her mother remarried. She married Harry Warren Scott, a wealthy Scotsman of Balgay and Logie, the son of Lieutenant Sir William Scott of Ancrum. Coincidentally, Harry was studying at Merton College at Oxford in 1852 and so could have heard about his wife's former husband's marriage to Sinnetta Lambourne and the 'scandal' it became.

At the time of his marriage to Caroline, Harry was a Justice of the Peace. This marriage never produced children, but being a private, kind man, Harry was a caring stepfather. The new family lived in a town house at Number 45 Grosvenor Place, as well as having a country house on Ham Common.[1]

On 16 July 1881, Cecilia married Lord Glamis, Claude Bowes-Lyon, at Petersham Church in Surrey.[2] This was a grand marriage and meant that Cecilia could add Glamis Castle to her family's estate as well as the estates of St Paul's Walden Bury in

Hertfordshire. Even though Cecilia had married, she still visited her mother and stepfather often, especially when they were staying in Florence in Italy, for her stepfather's health.

Cecilia's husband was the son of Claude Bowes-Lyon, the thirteenth Earl of Strathmore and Kinghorne and Frances Smith.[3] (His brother Patrick Bowes-Lyon was an 1887 Wimbledon doubles champion.) Cecilia's husband went from Eton to spend the next six years in the 2nd Life Guards. He was an active member of the Territorial Army and served as an honorary Colonel of the 4th and 5th Battalions of the Black Watch.[4]

On 16 February 1904, on his father's death, Claude became the Earl of Strathmore and Kinghorne, which meant that Cecilia had become a countess.[5] Although Claude had also become Lord Lieutenant of Angus at this time, he would give this title up once his daughter had assumed a higher rank.

On 17 April 1882, Cecilia gave birth to her first child. They named her Violet Hyacinth Bowes-Lyon. Sadly, she was to die on 17 October 1893 at the age of eleven from diphtheria. She was buried alongside her step-grandfather, Harry Warren Scott, at Ham Cemetery.[6]

A second daughter was born in Angus, Scotland, on 30 August 1883, Mary Frances Bowes-Lyon.[7] On 24 July 1910, Mary would marry Sidney Elphinstone, the 16th Lord Elphinstone. Mary's husband would fulfil many roles including Governor of the Bank of Scotland, Lord Clerk Register of Scotland, Keeper of the Signet and Lord High Commissioner of the Church of Scotland.[8] The couple would go on to have five children, most of whom would later undertake specific responsibilities regarding future royal weddings. In 1937, at the coronation of King George VI, Mary was sitting behind Princess Elizabeth, the future queen. Mary later becomes a President of the British Red Cross, before passing away on 8 February 1961 aged seventy-seven at Carberry Tower in Inveresk, Scotland.[9]

On 22 September 1883, Cecilia's son Patrick Bowes-Lyon was born. In the First World War he served in the Black Watch like his father before him, and he was appointed Lieutenant of Forfarshire.[10] Patrick married Lady Dorothy Beatrix Godolphin Osbourne, daughter of the 10th Duke of Leeds, on 21 November 1908 and the couple would have four children. Patrick passed away on 25 May 1949, aged sixty-four, in Angus.

On 1 April 1886, the fifth child, commonly known as 'Jock', although his name was John Herbert Bowes-Lyon, was born. He studied at Eton and Oxford[11] and was a keen sportsman, playing for the university cricket team. On 29 September 1914 he married the Honourable Fenella Hepburn-Stuart-Forbes-Trefusis, daughter of the 21st Baron Clinton and they would have five children. Two of them, it was later discovered, were placed in Earlswood Hospital for the mentally disabled in 1941, Nerissa and Katherine Bowes-Lyon. Although the 1963 *Burke's Peerage* stated that they had died in 1940 and 1941 respectively, Nerissa had actually passed away in 1986, being buried at Red Hill Cemetery. She now has a headstone to mark her grave. Katherine passed away in 2014.

John worked as a stockbroker in the City of London at the start of the First World War and although he had suffered from a nervous breakdown in 1912, in 1915 he went to war. He served, like his brother and father before him, in the Black Watch, where he accidentally shot himself in his left forefinger and had to have it amputated. (It is impossible not to wonder if this was a self-inflicted wound.) He returned to his job in the City after the war, dying on the morning of 7 February 1930 of pneumonia, aged just forty-four, at Glamis Castle.

On 14 April 1887, Cecilia gave birth to Alexander Francis Bowes-Lyon, known as Alec.[12] Sadly, he was to pass away at the age of twenty-four from a tumour at the base of the cerebrum. On 18 April 1889, Cecilia gave birth to another male, Fergus Bowes-Lyon. Fergus was born at the couple's country house in Ham and would be educated like his brothers at Eton College in Berkshire. Also like his siblings, he was a keen sportsman, mainly excelling at cricket.[13]

On 17 September 1914, Fergus married Lady Christian Norah Dawson-Damer, daughter of the fifth Earl of Port Arlington. They had one child, Rosemary Luísa Bowes-Lyon, born on 18 July 1915. She was only two months old when her father died on 29 September 1915. Fergus was killed at the Battle of Loos, attacking the German lines. His leg was blown off, and he fell back into his sergeant's arms. Bullets then hit him in the chest and shoulder, and he died on the battlefield.[14] He was buried in a quarry at Vermelles, although this quarry was later transformed into a war cemetery. The details of where Fergus was buried are still unknown. His name appears among the missing on the Loos Memorial; a Portland stone marker in Row A, Grave 15 reads: 'Buried Near this Spot, Captain, The Hon. F. Bowes-Lyon. The Black Watch. 27th September 1916, Aged 26'.

On 6 May 1890, Rose Constance Bowes-Lyon was born. She would marry William Leveson-Gower in 1916, becoming a countess once her husband took over his brother's titles in 1939.[15] The couple would have two children. Rose was given an honorary degree of Doctor of Laws by Queen's University, Belfast.[16] In 1953, the year of Elizabeth II's coronation, she was invested as a Dame Cross of the Royal Victorian Order.[17] She passed away on 17 November 1967, aged seventy-seven.

On 1 October 1893, Cecilia gave birth to Michael Claude Hamilton Bowes-Lyon, known as 'Mickie'. Like many of his family, he joined the war effort. He was incarcerated at the Holzminden prisoner-of-war camp in Lower Saxony.[18] He would go on to marry Elizabeth Cator in 1928, and they had at least two children before Michael passed away on 1 May 1953.

On 4 August 1900, Cecilia gave birth to another daughter, Elizabeth Angela Marguerite Bowes-Lyon, and on 2 May 1902, to David Bowes-Lyon, the last child. He would marry Rachel Clay in 1929 and together they had one child before David passed away on 13 September 1961, aged fifty-nine.

At Glamis Castle and elsewhere, Cecilia was known to be a great hostess. She was also an excellent piano player.[19] She was a meticulous overseer of the estates, as shown in her creation of the Italian Garden at Glamis to designs by Arthur Castings.[20] Understandably perhaps, knowing the career her father had, Cecilia was a deeply religious person and she, like her husband, preferred a quiet life. Perhaps this was because of the scandals both her grandfather and her father were involved in. Could this also be why, when their daughter eventually married, Cecilia and Claude were displeased at first? As much as the match meant a vertiginous elevation in social circles for the family, it could also mean a fall from a great height.

In the First World War, Glamis Castle opened its doors to serve as a hospital for the wounded and Cecilia helped out. This was until she was diagnosed with cancer and in October 1921 underwent a hysterectomy to remove it.[21] A year after her recovery, Cecilia and her husband saw their second youngest child, Elizabeth, become engaged to Prince Albert, Duke of York. Fifteen years later, Cecilia would suffer from a heart attack at the wedding of her granddaughter, Anne Bowes-Lyon, to Thomas Viscount Anson, in April 1938.[22] She passed away eight weeks later aged seventy-five at her home, 38 Cumberland Mansions, London. She was buried on 27 June 1938 at Glamis. Her husband passed away with bronchitis on 7 November 1944, aged eighty-nine, at Glamis Castle.[23]

Lady Elizabeth Angela Marguerite Bowes-Lyon, The Queen Mother

As described at the beginning of this story, Mary Boleyn's place of birth has been debated. Having descended the family tree through the centuries, remarkably enough we come across the same problem. Elizabeth Bowes-Lyon was born at her parent's home at Belgrave Mansions, Westminster – or at Forbes House in Ham, London, or at Glamis Castle, or even in a horse-drawn ambulance on the way to hospital![24] However, we do know Elizabeth's birth was registered at Hitchin in Hertfordshire,[25] near the family home in St Paul's Walden Bury. This would also be noted as Elizabeth's place of birth on the 1901 census. Born on 4 August 1900, Elizabeth Bowes-Lyon was a Victorian, but only just.

Elizabeth was christened on 23 September 1900 at the church of All Saints in the parish of St Paul's Walden Bury. Elizabeth spent much of her childhood between her parent's home there and the magnificent Glamis Castle, home of the Lyon family since the fourteenth century. Like her siblings before her, she was fond of sports and like her future daughter, she loved horses and dogs.[26] At first taught at home, she went to school in London at the age of eight. She then returned to private education under a German governess called Käthe Kübler and passed the Oxford Local Examination with a distinction at the age of thirteen.[27]

Elizabeth's fourteenth birthday fell on a significant date in Britain's history. To celebrate this birthday, her mother had organised a trip into the capital for her and members of her family to the famous London Coliseum, to watch a Vaudeville concert starring the Russian ballerina Sofia Fedorova. The London Coliseum was one of the first theatres to have electric lighting, it had the largest proscenium arch in London and the stage was eight feet wide, plenty of room for the ballerina's skills. We can quite easily imagine Elizabeth laughing with her family and having a wonderful time at this event. However, Elizabeth was not to know when she left the theatre that evening that a meeting was underway twenty minutes' walk away at a place that would be her future home, Buckingham Palace. This meeting was between the King George V, Elizabeth's future father-in-law, and his Privy Council. The outcome of this meeting would change Britain forever, and many, many lives. On this date, 4 August 1914, Britain entered the First World War.

On 26 April 1923 Elizabeth married Prince Albert, the Duke of York. This was a decision Elizabeth had taken with some trepidation. Her parents were not enamoured of high society with all its demands and pitfalls, something we can understand knowing the history of this fascinating family. When Prince Albert first asked Elizabeth to marry him, she turned him down, stating that if she were to marry him, she was 'afraid never, never again to be free to think, speak and act as I feel I really might do'.[28] Elizabeth may have thought this would be the last she would hear from the prince, and she turned to James Stuart, the Prince's equerry, instead.[29] However, what Elizabeth did not know was that the prince had told his mother that Elizabeth was the only woman for him. He proposed to her again in March 1922, and again Elizabeth said no.

In January 1923 – prefacing his question by saying it was the last time he would ask it – the prince proposed again. This time Elizabeth said yes. The wedding was at Westminster Abbey. As Elizabeth walked past the tomb of the Unknown Soldier, she made a gesture that was not part of the itinerary. In a ceremony that had everything timed to the second, Elizabeth suddenly stopped beside the tomb and placed her wedding bouquet on it, in memory of her brother Fergus, whose actual burial place was unknown.[30] By doing so, Elizabeth had unbeknown to her begun a royal tradition. Now every royal bride places her wedding bouquet, just as Elizabeth had done, on the tomb of the Unknown Soldier.

After the wedding, the couple honeymooned in Surrey and then visited Scotland, where Elizabeth suffered from whooping cough.[31] The first royal visit for the newly married couple was to Northern Ireland and because it was deemed a success, they were then sent to East Africa from December 1924 until April 1925.[32] However, the more official duties the couple undertook, the more the prince's stammer became noticeable. From October 1926, Elizabeth assisted him through the speech therapy devised by the Australian-born Lionel Logue over the next ten years.

In 1926, Elizabeth and Prince Albert have their first child, named after her mother, however the child would be forever known as 'Lilibet' by her parents. In 1930, Princess Margaret Rose was born. Six years later, the family's lives were turned upside down with the death of King George V on 20 January 1936. With his passing, Elizabeth's brother-in-law, David, ascended the throne as King Edward VIII. David, as everyone knows, wanted to marry an American divorcee, Wallis Simpson, and to do so he chose to abdicate. This meant the throne passed to Elizabeth's husband, Prince Albert. He became king on 11 December 1936 taking the regnal name of King George VI, and Elizabeth became Queen Consort of England when they were both crowned at Westminster Abbey on 12 May 1937.

While the new king and queen were on a state visit to France in 1938, Elizabeth learned of the death of her mother. Elizabeth immediately went into mourning. When the then Prime Minister Neville Chamberlain came up with the Munich Agreement that year, he was invited onto the now famous balcony of Buckingham

Palace with the king and queen.[33] This caused mixed feelings in the House of Commons. Just as some of Queen Victoria's actions seemed to suggest she preferred a certain political party over another, by allowing the Prime Minister on the royal balcony it felt to some as if the king and queen were not staying impartial. Others thought the king and queen were simply doing what they had been advised to do.[34]

In the early summer of 1939, the couple travelled to America, where they spent some time with the American President Roosevelt and his wife Lady Eleanor, who described Queen Elizabeth as 'perfect as a Queen, gracious, informed, saying the right thing and kind but a little self-consciously regal'.[35]

During the Second World War, Elizabeth kept herself in the public view as a sign of a united front. She visited the troops, factories, hospitals and parts of Britain that were bombed, including the East End of London. This at first did not seem to have the desired effect, as Elizabeth in all her finery encountered some hostility from the people of the East End who had lost everything; Elizabeth even had rubbish thrown at her.[36] When Buckingham Palace was bombed itself, Elizabeth was relieved: 'I am glad we've been bombed; it makes me feel I can look the East End in the face.'[37] She was described as 'the most dangerous woman in Europe' by none other than Adolf Hitler, proving just how powerful a unifying force her popularity was at this time of crisis.

From 1951 Elizabeth and her daughter started assuming more and more public duties as the king's health was failing him. Although he had undergone a successful operation to improve the circulation in his leg in 1949, this, with hindsight, was the beginning of the end. In September 1951, he was diagnosed with lung cancer.[38] Princess Elizabeth and her husband made a trip to Australia and New Zealand in his stead in January 1952.

The king passed away on 6 February 1952, when Princess Elizabeth was in Kenya. She was to return as the new Queen of England.

Soon after the death of the king and now knowing she was no longer queen, Elizabeth styled herself as Her Majesty Queen Elizabeth, The Queen Mother. This was to avoid confusion with her daughter. Her grief soon overcame her, and Elizabeth retired to Scotland, the area she knew so well from her childhood. The only person with enough sway to persuade her to return to her royal duties was the Prime Minister, Winston Churchill. He succeeded, and Elizabeth was soon back within the royal fold. She went on a state visit to the Federation of Rhodesia and Nyasaland with her daughter, Princess Margaret, laying the foundation stone at what is today the University of Zimbabwe. Elizabeth also at this time began acting as Counsellor of State and looking after her grandchildren, Charles and Anne, when Queen Elizabeth and Prince Philip were away on state visits themselves.[39] She oversaw the refurbishment of her Scottish retreat, the Castle of Mey. On the remote north coast of Scotland, Elizabeth felt she could use the castle as her bolthole, away from public duties.

In the 1960s, Elizabeth's health started to decline. In February 1964, she had to have an emergency appendectomy, and in December 1966, she had an operation to remove a tumour on her colon. Two years later, she was diagnosed with breast cancer and had a lump removed. None of these health problems were made public during Elizabeth's life, surely a prohibition demanded by Elizabeth herself – she was always going to fight another day. Dare we suggest that this was the fight of her ancestors maybe, the blood of the Boleyns in her veins?

In 1982, Elizabeth was rushed to hospital when a fishbone became stuck in her throat. Elizabeth had to have an operation to remove it. This happened again in 1986, when she was taken to Aberdeen Royal Infirmary for an overnight stay, though no operation was needed. Amazingly, this happened for a third time in 1993, when surgery was needed yet again. In later years, Elizabeth also had operations to remove a cataract and to replace her right, then her left hip, due to a fall she had at Sandringham stables.[40]

The celebrations for Elizabeth's one hundredth birthday included a parade in her honour and speeches made by such luminaries as Sir John Mills. She had a birthday lunch at the Guildhall in the City and her image appeared on the twenty-pound note of the Bank of Scotland. More than 40,000 well-wishers gathered in the Mall to watch the Queen Mother and her two daughters step on to the balcony of Buckingham Palace. They were joined by the rest of the family.

Sadly, her health problems were added to in her last years. In November 2000, she broke her collarbone from another fall and in August 2001 she suffered from heat exhaustion. Elizabeth nevertheless managed to stand outside her home at Clarence House to celebrate her 101st birthday, she even stood up when the National Anthem was played during the Memorial Service for her husband in February 2002, even though she had fractured her pelvis in a fall the year before.

On 30 March 2002, Queen Elizabeth, The Queen Mother passed away in her sleep at the Royal Lodge at Windsor. Her only surviving child, Queen Elizabeth II, was by her bedside, Princess Margaret having passed away in the February of that same year. Elizabeth lay in state at Westminster Hall for three days, during which time it is estimated that 200,000 paid their respects. On 9 April, her coffin travelled from Westminster Abbey to St George's Chapel in Windsor Castle. She was buried beside her daughter, Princess Margaret, and her husband, George VI.

The Queen Mother was buried near Henry VIII and his wife, Queen Consort Jane Seymour. Henry was the man who passed sentence on one of Elizabeth's distant relations, Queen Consort Anne Boleyn; and Jane Seymour was Anne's successor in both King Henry's affections and to the throne. However, Henry also looked after Queen Anne's sister and Elizabeth's relation, Mary Boleyn, in a number of ways. He made provisions for her and eventually handed over estates to her, he looked after her children at certain times, and it is from those children, travelling down a most extraordinary family tree, that we have arrived at Queen Elizabeth, the Queen Mother. So, in Elizabeth's last resting place near King Henry, we have come full circle, from the Tudors to the Windsors.

Epilogue

QUEEN ELIZABETH II

Young Elizabeth was just ten years old when her whole world changed. Her uncle, an uncle that she had held dear to her heart, abdicated on 10 December 1936. News of this had been passed to Elizabeth's family at their home at Number 145 Piccadilly, near Hyde Park. It meant that Elizabeth's father would now be King of England and she herself would be queen one day. One wonders what must have been running through this young girl's head at such a moment. It may be hard for us all to think of Queen Elizabeth II as a ten-year-old girl, accustomed as we are to Elizabeth in her role as queen, but the truth of the matter is that she was never prepared for the role, she was never meant to be the monarch. Much as it was for Queen Elizabeth I and Queen Victoria, the thought of becoming queen, of wearing a crown and sitting on the throne, must have been for her, as it is for many a young girl, a fantasy; but this fantasy became very real, very fast.

Elizabeth, her mother, the then Duchess of York, had wanted her first-born to be a daughter,[1] so when Elizabeth was born to the Duchess and Duke of York on 21 April 1926, both parents must have been delighted. The child, Elizabeth Alexandra Mary of York, arrived at twenty minutes to three in the morning after a caesarean operation. She was born at her maternal grandparents' home at Number 17 Bruton Street, Mayfair, London. Her name was not a reference to good Queen Bess, her distant relative. For although this new baby was third in line to the throne on the date of her birth, it was never expected that she would become queen. They simply liked the name, it hadn't been used in their family for a long time, and of course it was her mother's name. Young Elizabeth was christened in the chapel of Buckingham Palace, dressed in a robe of white satin, the same robe that Queen Victoria's child, Vicky, had worn on her Christening Day in 1841. Although Elizabeth was quite vocal at her christening, she was overall deemed a quiet and rather observant child.

Both parents doted on her, the Duke of York allowing his child to call him affectionally 'Big Ears'.[2] In January 1927, when Elizabeth was only nine months old, her parents had to do their royal duty and take a six-month tour of Australia and New Zealand. The duke was to open the Commonwealth Parliament in Canberra. Elizabeth did not go with them, her parents believing the importance of routines for the baby outweighed their missing their new-born, which they constantly did. After their trip and a holiday to Scotland, where Elizabeth learned to walk, the family moved to their new family home at 145 Piccadilly, a grand Georgian five-storey building with twenty-five bedrooms. Elizabeth and her nanny occupied the top floor.

At Christmas 1927, Lady Airlie, the Lady of the Bedchamber to Elizabeth's grandmother Queen Mary, gave Elizabeth a dustpan and brush for a present, suggesting perhaps that Elizabeth came across as a disciplined and possibly tidy child from early on, like her grandmother on her mother's side.[3] Gifts had improved somewhat by her fourth birthday; George V, Elizabeth's 'grandpa England' as she called him, gave her her first pony, Peggy.

In 1929, the king's health was poor and he was sent to Bognor to recuperate. Young Elizabeth went too, and she would go down to the beach with her grandfather to build sandcastles, an indication of their closeness. George was not always so indulgent of his family members. In the early 1930s, he thought that it was right that the royal family experienced at least a taste of the economic downturn the nation was suffering, so he cut the state support that the royal family received by £50,000. This meant that Elizabeth's father was to lose £10,000 per year and he had to sell his beloved horses, which must have hurt him as well as his horse-loving daughter. However, as some recompense for selling his horses and helping his father to save money, the duke and duchess were given the Royal Lodge in Windsor Great Park. Set in ninety acres, the Royal Lodge was in a run-down state when the Yorks obtained it. They got to work to restore their new retreat, painting the Grand Saloon green and hanging a portrait of King George IV inside. They installed a modern kitchen as well as bathrooms, and the outside was painted in a wash of rose pink, the duchess's favourite colour. It was here that the young Elizabeth learned to garden and was never happier than when she was covered in mud, helping her father weed and plant.[4]

By 1929, the duchess was pregnant again; this time the parents were hoping for a boy. The family travelled to Glamis Castle for the duchess to have the child and although the labour was long with the possibility of another operation on the horizon, the baby was delivered naturally in the evening of 21 August 1929. It was another girl. The public was delighted, fireworks were lit, bells were rung and at least 4,000 people rushed into the nearby village square. The parents wanted to name their new child Ann, but the king rejected the idea, so the name Margaret was chosen, after Margaret of Scotland. She was christened Margaret Rose in October 1929. The family moved back to their London residence, where it became clear that the two daughters were very different in character, even at this early stage. Elizabeth was reserved and dutiful while Margaret was more playful. From the moment of Margaret's birth, the Yorks began to call themselves 'we four', a sign of unity that would be needed soon.

Being second in line to the throne, the Yorks had more time to spend with their children as their duties were a lot less onerous than those of the Prince of Wales. Elizabeth as a toddler loved this, always rushing to be with her parents and sit on her father's knee.[5] Although the duke loved this caring side of his daughter Elizabeth, he was determined that his other daughter Margaret did not feel second best, as he had in his own childhood. This was the main reason the two princesses were dressed in the same way; however, the duke also saw the differences between his two daughters and even worked on enhancing them.

Oddly, following the birth of Margaret, focus actually turned more towards Elizabeth. At this point the duke and duchess were in their later thirties and would probably not have another child. The Prince of Wales was thirty-six with no signs of marrying. Could it be that Elizabeth was the most likely heir to the throne?

The Yorks turned their attention to finding a governess who would be different from the normal type assigned to royal children in the past. This was probably because the duke had bad memories of strict tutors who had done nothing to make his education a rewarding experience. Academic subjects were not a priority for the two daughters. Instead, the Yorks wanted a governess who would develop their daughters' personalities. They found one in Miss Marion Crawford. She was only twenty-two when she became Elizabeth's governess in 1933. Trained in Moray House College in Edinburgh, she had planned to become a child psychologist specialising in underprivileged children, but one does not say no to the royal family.

How the Yorks felt about education ultimately meant that lessons were short for Elizabeth, with the governess complaining that there were many distractions, making it hard to teach the child anything. These distractions came in the form of, say, hairdressers' appointments, and even from the duchess herself.

By the age of seven, Elizabeth was only having one-and-a-half hours of lessons a day, finding it all a little boring – except when it came to the subject of history, which she found thrilling.[6] Elizabeth liked to read, *Black Beauty*, *Dr Dolittle* and *Winnie the Pooh* were favourites, but she found *Alice in Wonderland* a little too odd for her liking.[7] Her future husband would know the words to that story pretty much off by heart.

Elizabeth was all about the animals and outdoor living, while Margaret was fond of music and the arts. However, one thing they both found difficult and boring was needlework, rather like Anne Boleyn! She could not make the king's shirts to the same standard as Katherine of Aragon.

Elizabeth was a very young girl when Mrs Wallis Simpson became a part of her family circle. Elizabeth was surely clever enough to notice something was amiss within her family before the news broke. Children are often more astute than their elders think, especially when it comes to family matters. Perhaps she sensed the tension in the air and noticed a change in her uncle. He had previously doted on his nieces and would often visit them, but now was distant, sometimes forgetting he had made plans with them and seeming distracted. If they noticed the change, they would look for what was new. What was new, was Mrs Wallis Simpson. Then another change: the death of her grandfather, George V. Although the younger Margaret could not fully comprehend what had happened and what it meant, Elizabeth was nine years old and might have understood the possible consequences.

Very soon after the death of her grandfather, the situation with Elizabeth's uncle and Wallis Simpson came to impinge on the family. There was no more time to play with her parents, her family home had become a command centre with various high-ranking people visiting – ministers, archbishops and the Prime

Minister, Stanley Baldwin. The governess did what she could to distract Elizabeth and Margaret away from the events that were unfolding, for example by taking them to learn to swim at the local baths.

The date that was originally set for the coronation of King Edward VIII saw the coronation of Elizabeth's father, George VI, instead: 12 May 1937. Elizabeth was now the heir to the throne and her 'cosy' little home at 145 Piccadilly was gone. They moved into Buckingham Palace a few weeks after George VI was crowned. Elizabeth had been taken there a number of times during those weeks to get used to her new home. Elizabeth's grandmother, Queen Mary, became an historical tour guide for the princesses. She took them to Hampton Court Palace, Kew, Greenwich Palace, and of course the Tower of London. Elizabeth's education was expanding, she visited Eton College twice a week in 1938 learning constitutional history. And back home the book of the week was changing, too. Out was A.A. Milne and in was P.G. Wodehouse. She became a Girl Guide at this time, cooking sausages on an open fire and 'trekking' in the grounds of Buckingham Palace.

The new king and queen travelled to the US in May 1939, to be entertained by President Roosevelt – and to prove they could do better than the Duke and Duchess of Windsor, Elizabeth's uncle and his new wife Wallis, who had recently taken a trip to America themselves. The king and queen didn't take the princesses as it was thought to be too taxing a trip for them. After the six-week tour, when the king and queen returned they noticed that Elizabeth had changed greatly in their absence. The thirteen-year-old princess was becoming an adult, ready to take on more duties.

In July 1939, the whole family visited the Royal Naval College and stayed on HMY *Victoria and Albert*. They were all meant to have gone to church nearby on the Sunday, but as two boys in the area had come down with the mumps, it was thought that the princesses should stay behind. They went to the house of the captain of the college instead, where Elizabeth and Philip, her future husband, played with trains until Philip suggested that the princesses and he should play a game of tennis. It was possibly even at this very early stage that Philip's uncle, much as 'Uncle Leopold' had done for Queen Victoria and Prince Albert, mooted the idea of a match between Elizabeth and Philip. The next day, Philip joined the royal family for lunch and went with them to the swimming pool. Elizabeth, who had not had many opportunities to talk with boys near her own age, was very interested in Philip and asked him lots of questions.[8]

As much as Philip would become an ideal suitor for Elizabeth, with his good looks, social grace and Greek royal blood, there were also some aspects that predicated against the union. Their meeting was at a time when Britain was on the cusp of war with Germany again. Philip's mother was German and four of his sisters had married Germans. Philip was born on 10 June 1921, making him five years older than Elizabeth, in Villa Mon Repos, a Greek royal home on Corfu. He was the only son of Prince Andrew and Princess Alice of Greece and Battenburg, putting him in line to the Greek throne. It was at the coronation of King Edward VII, Prince Andrew's uncle through marriage, that Prince Andrew met his future wife and mother to Prince Philip. She would sadly become ill in later years and was committed to an asylum in 1930 with schizophrenia.

Philip started his education in an American school before being sent to England to go to Cheam. By 1933, he was studying at Salem in Baden in Germany before returning once again to England to finish his education at Gordonstoun in Scotland, where he would later send his son, Charles. Philip thrived in the strict, exhausting routines of this school; his son, famously, would not.

On Sunday 3 September 1939 at 11.15 a.m., the Prime Minister announced that Britain was at war again; and within half an hour, an air raid test began. The king and queen went for the first time into their shelter in Buckingham Palace. The princesses at that moment were at the local church of the Birkhall estate, Aberdeenshire. The king and queen wanted their daughters to stay in Scotland with their governess for as long as possible, away from the potential dangers of the capital. The king and queen telephoned their daughters every day, and the queen visited them on 18 September 1939.

The princesses listened to the radio like everyone else for news of the war. Elizabeth was most shocked when hearing of the sinking of warships. From that point on, Elizabeth wanted to do her part for her country. There was, of course, a limit to what a princess would be allowed to do. It was not all doom and gloom for the princesses; with the help of a local who owned a projector, Elizabeth and Margaret watched Charlie Chaplin and Laurel and Hardy films. By the winter of 1939 the princesses were missing their parents terribly and were no doubt delighted to be catching the train back to London. From there they travelled to Sandringham for a family Christmas. The girls received diaries as gifts from the queen on Christmas Eve. It was from here that Elizabeth's father gave his first Christmas broadcast to the nation.

Although the king and queen would remain in London to face the Blitz, they sent the princesses away from danger. First, they were placed in their old family home of the Royal Lodge in Windsor Park and then in Windsor Castle itself, where they would stay for the rest of the war. Air raids were a constant, which meant broken sleep. The princesses had not known Windsor Castle itself all that well, so time was spent exploring it. It is said that while exploring the underground vaults of Windsor Castle the princesses found the Crown Jewels, which had been removed from the Tower and stored there for safekeeping. This might have been the first time the princesses had seen the jewels up close. Elizabeth would try a few on – later.

In 1940, the idea of Princess Elizabeth making her own broadcast on the radio arose for a second time. Earlier, there had been a request during National Children's Week in the US for the princess to speak on the radio to introduce the event, but this was denied. After the air raids it was thought that the public needed to hear from their princess – and reinforcing connections across 'the pond' was a sensible idea. On 13 October 1940, Princess Elizabeth's voice was on 'Children's Hour' on the BBC. She spoke to the children of her future realm, but her message of unity in adversity was aimed at the adults listening in. The 14-year-old Princess sent her best wishes to the children evacuated from Britain to America, Canada and elsewhere. Princess Margaret joined her to wish all children goodnight. Her broadcast was a success and was reported in all the newspapers. The king was delighted that she did not have his problem with speaking in public.

In an attempt to 'do their bit' within the strictures that royalty imposed, Margaret painted acorns, which were sold off, and Elizabeth knitted. Both were said to have given away half of their pocket money to causes that helped the war effort. Their clothes ration was the same as everyone else's, which meant one new outfit a year. At sixteen, Elizabeth wanted to join the war effort in earnest, but the king was not sure. He, like many fathers, wanted to protect his daughter from the horrors of the conflict. Nevertheless, in 1942 Elizabeth became an Honorary Colonel of the Grenadier Guards. On her sixteenth birthday she completed her first task in this role, inspecting the Grenadiers at Windsor with her father.

In the same year, Elizabeth and her younger sister had to deal with another death in their family. On 25 August 1942 word reached the king and his family that his brother, George, Duke of Kent, had died in a plane crash in Scotland. Elizabeth's uncle George was only thirty-nine. Elizabeth had been a bridesmaid at his wedding and had played with his children on a number of occasions.

Philip was still writing to Elizabeth at this time. In 1942, Philip was in the middle of 'a good war', distinguishing himself as a lieutenant and eventual Second in Command in the Royal Navy. Sometimes in company with his uncle Mountbatten, Philip was introduced to many women, but he chose to write to Elizabeth and no other, often absenting himself until he had completed the delicate task. At Christmas 1943, Elizabeth began openly to express her feelings towards Philip, and they seemed very close over the festivities. The king and queen seemed to be unaware of the situation, only realising when Philip's cousin, King George II of Greece, wrote to them on the subject. Elizabeth's parents' first response was that although they liked Philip, they thought Elizabeth was too young. It was true that Elizabeth was still being dressed in the same clothes as her sister, and even her governess was calling the sisters 'little girls', but Elizabeth was to turn eighteen in April 1944.

She was then allowed to move out of the 'nursery' and into her own suite of rooms and was given a small number of her own household staff. Other people could see that Elizabeth had grown into an adult, but the king still saw her as his own little princess. He did not grant her the title of Princess of Wales and it was only with much persuasion that he allowed her to become a Counsellor of State. (Today, by law, Counsellors of State include the Sovereign's spouse and the next four people in the line of succession who are over the age of 21. They are authorised to carry out some of the official duties of the sovereign, such as attending Privy Council meetings.) In this official role, on

23 May 1944 Elizabeth gave her first public speech at the Queen Elizabeth Hospital for Children. She launched her first ship, HMS *Vanguard*, and became the President of the National Society for the Prevention of Cruelty to Children. Her performance of her duties was exemplary, so finally in the early months of 1945 Elizabeth was allowed to join the Auxiliary Territorial Service as a trainee driver. Her number was 230873. Second Subaltern Elizabeth Alexandra Mary began her training at Aldershot. She learned how to drive and take an engine apart. This was great propaganda for the British and the princess was photographed constantly because of it.

Post-war, out went most of Elizabeth's lessons in favour of written correspondence and speaking to charities and other bodies. Elizabeth was now allowed adult clothes and she assumed a higher public profile. She opened a library at the Royal College of Nursing, inspected more battalions, and handed out prizes to schoolchildren and Girl Guides.

Philip returned home in 1946 from Japan at long last. He visited the royal family frequently and even went on outings to restaurants and dances with Elizabeth, but her parents were still not sure about the marriage, believing Elizabeth should wait until she was twenty-one. Finally, on 8 July 1947, the engagement was announced, infecting the country with royal wedding fever. The wedding was to be on 20 November 1947.

Some wartime limitations were still in evidence. Elizabeth's dress was made of material bought with clothing coupons. More than 3,000 women donated their own coupons, but they had to be returned as such a transfer was illegal. The designer Normal Hartnell's inspiration for Elizabeth's dress was Botticelli's *Primavera* (Spring) painting, using flowers that symbolised rebirth. This wedding was supposed to represent a new start after the sacrifices and suffering of the war. With embroidered crystals, pearls and a fifteen-foot train, the dress cost £1,200. One of the patterns on Elizabeth's dress featured the white rose of the House of York. This takes us right back to the mother of Henry VIII, who also happened to be named Elizabeth. With the young Elizabeth being a Princess of York, too, the past and the future met in the design of a dress.

On the morning of the wedding, Philip was created Duke of Edinburgh, a title that would pass to their son Edward in future years. He also became the Earl of Merioneth and Baron Greenwich, and of course assumed the title of 'His Royal Highness'. He also became a member of the Order of the Garter.

Elizabeth travelled with the king to Westminster Abbey in the Irish State Coach, her father wearing his Admiral of the Fleet uniform. As they walked up the aisle, Elizabeth's sister Margaret was behind them followed by seven other bridesmaids, each one carrying white roses. Behind them were two five-year-old boys, Prince Michael of Kent and Prince William of Gloucester, Elizabeth's cousins, page boys dressed in tartan. After the ceremony, 150 members of the party returned to Buckingham Palace to dine on 'Filet de Sole Mountbatten' and 'Bombe Glacée Princess Elizabeth'. The cakes, of which there were twelve, were sent as presents to relations and local hospitals; one was sent to Australia.

By the evening Princess Elizabeth, who had changed into an outfit of blue, ran out with Prince Philip into a blizzard of confetti before getting into their open landau. Crowds cheered them all the way to Victoria Station. Princess Elizabeth and Prince Philip honeymooned at Birkhall. By 14 December 1947, the newlyweds were back in London for the celebration of the king's fifty-second birthday, and almost instantly Princess Elizabeth was back into her role as a royal. She was more in demand and her work increased. This, plus living at Buckingham Palace with his royal in-laws, made Philip feel uncomfortable, that he was not being used to his full potential. The public's view of Elizabeth was changing, already seeing her as the future sovereign, even though her father was only fifty-two. His health probably accelerated this change; although Buckingham Palace did not publicly admit it, the king's health was getting worse.

Elizabeth was appointed her first private secretary, John Colville, at this time. He was very strong-willed and wished to educate the princess in the ways of politics. He even arranged for Foreign Office telegrams to be sent to Elizabeth, so that she could have a better idea of what was going on elsewhere. He also took the princess with Prince Philip to a debate in the House of Commons on foreign affairs.

In February 1948, a trip to Paris was arranged for the couple to attend the opening of the Exhibition of Eight Centuries of British Life at the Musée Galliera (now the Palais Galliera). Elizabeth was now a few months into her first pregnancy. Some noticed that the princess was looking tired and had requested more breaks, but her pregnancy was not officially announced until June 1948. In the spirit of recycling, the old pram that Elizabeth herself had been pushed in, as well as the family basket and cot, were brought out of storage and painted yellow, to avoid any display of gender preference. At the same time, the renovations budget for Clarence House, the home the couple had been given, was agreed by parliament. The figure was £50,000, which caused some grumbling in the newspapers. And as with most renovations, the couple went over budget, in this case by almost £30,000.

For many years it had been thought that Princess Elizabeth was not the heir apparent to the throne, as she was not male. This left the child she was carrying without a royal title. Suggestions for the child's title were the Earl of Merioneth for a boy, or Lady Mountbatten for a girl. This proved too much for the king, so even in his ill health he signed papers that confirmed the child would be either a prince or princess. By doing this, the king was finally accepting Elizabeth was his only heir, and therefore heir presumptive to the throne.

On the evening of 14 November 1948, Elizabeth went into labour. She was attended by four doctors and just after nine o'clock, weighing seven pounds six ounces, a boy was born. He was named Charles Philip Arthur George. Instantly, comparisons were made between his looks and those of his forebears. Some people thought the boy looked like his great-grandfather, George V, others thought he looked more like Prince Albert. Elizabeth nursed her own son for the first two months, but she then caught measles and had to stay away from her child. They did not know it then, but this would not be the only occasion when mother and son would be separated.

A month and a day after Charles's birth, he was christened in the Music Room at Buckingham Palace. Not only was this a happy occasion for the family, but it seemed to improve the health of the king for a short time, too. In March 1949, he would undergo a spinal operation to help with the blood circulation to his leg and although this seemed to have helped, it was only a small improvement, a pause on the road to invalidism. Perhaps still unaware of the seriousness of her father's illness, Elizabeth celebrated her twenty-third birthday at the Café de Paris, before going on to a London nightclub to party with Laurence Olivier.

By the summer, Elizabeth, Philip and baby Charles were set up in Clarence House, but in October the parents were on the move again. Philip was now First Lieutenant on the destroyer HMS *Chequers* of the Mediterranean Fleet, and he had to leave for Malta. Elizabeth soon joined him, leaving Charles at Clarence House with the nurse. While in Malta, the couple seemed a little more relaxed away from their royal duties and after five weeks,

Elizabeth returned to England refreshed and ready to get to work again, leaving Charles in the care of Elizabeth's mother and father at Sandringham.

In April 1949, it was announced that Elizabeth was pregnant again and on 15 August 1949, she gave birth to Anne Elizabeth Alice Louise. This time, Princess Elizabeth was quite ill after the birth and had to cancel many appointments leading up to Christmas that year. Elizabeth decided to spend Christmas with her husband in Malta, while Charles and Anne were sent to Sandringham to be with their grandparents. However, as the king's health declined, more pressure was put on Elizabeth to make up the shortfall. This meant a change for Philip, too, as he was now expected to be by Elizabeth's side rather than in the Navy. This was not a welcome development for Philip, but as Elizabeth took on more and more, no doubt he could see that her father's health had worsened and that this was the reason for his wife's heavy workload.

After exploratory surgery, it was confirmed that the king had lung cancer and he had part of his left lung removed. In October 1951, Elizabeth and Philip began a tour of the US and Canada. This trip had been planned before, but Philip had said no to it, believing that family and career should come first. Now that the former at least had come first, this trip could finally commence. It did not seem to be a happy experience for Elizabeth. Perhaps we could speculate with hindsight that the reason for this was that the health of her father was distracting her; the press at the time seemed to notice that she wasn't smiling a lot and wondered why. Philip tried to lighten her mood, but he, too, began to lose patience, perhaps dwelling upon what the death of Elizabeth's father could mean for them both.

While Elizabeth and Philip were away, Prince Charles turned three, the day celebrated at Buckingham Palace with a tea party.

The family were together for Christmas that year, but Elizabeth and Philip were on their travels again soon after, taking on the king's role once again. This time they went to Kenya, at the request of the Kenyan government. Prince Charles and Princess Anne were left with the nannies once more.

One of the saddest moments in the family's life so far was captured on film. The king travelled with Elizabeth and Philip to the airport to watch them leave for Kenya. The king kept watching until the plane was out of sight, probably knowing that he was to never see his daughter again. Did Elizabeth know this, too?

While Elizabeth settled into the start of her holiday by filming elephants, back in London, after a few episodes of renewed vigour, at half past seven in the morning of 6 February 1952 George VI died of a coronary thrombosis. Princess Elizabeth was probably the last in the family to know of her father's death. It was at least five hours before a message was passed to Philip and it was he who had to tell Elizabeth the sad news. Back to Britain they went, each knowing their lives had changed forever.

So began the reign of Queen Elizabeth II, the longest reigning monarch of the United Kingdom of Great Britain and Northern Ireland. Queen Elizabeth II is very much a Windsor, however, as we have seen, she has Boleyn blood running through her veins, no matter how distant that might seem. This is not from the famous Boleyn, Anne, it is from the other Boleyn sister, Mary.

Queen Elizabeth II has survived so much, something made even more remarkable when we consider that she was never expected to be queen. Mary Boleyn might not have been the Boleyn who was expected to survive out of her siblings; but survive she did. They both have had times when their actions were criticised. With Mary, it was mainly marrying for the second time without asking permission from her family first; for HRH Queen Elizabeth it could be said her most criticised moment was her slow reaction to the death of Diana Spencer, the previous Princess of Wales and the queen's ex-daughter-in-law.

However, they were and are very much loved. Henry gave Mary estates to live comfortably, something he did not have to do; was this ultimately out of love for Mary? She was loved by her second husband, William Stafford, too, so far as we can ascertain. The queen today is very much loved by her family, the vast majority of her subjects, and the press.

We may not immediately associate Queen Elizabeth II with her relation, Mary Boleyn. But time and time again we have witnessed the same strong, forceful nature, and the same indomitable spirit.

NOTES

'Letters and Papers, Foreign and Domestic' refers to *Letters and Papers, Foreign and Domestic, of the Reign of Henry VIII: preserved in the Public Record Office, the British Museum, and elsewhere in England*, a multi-volume edition of documents from the reign of Henry VIII. The series was edited by J.S. Brewer, James Gairdner and R.H. Brodie, and originally published between 1862 and 1932.

Introduction
1. 'Some notes on the Boleyn Family', Norfolk Archaeology Volume 25, W.L.E. Parsons.
2. Ibid
3. Extracts from the Household and Privy Purse Accounts of the Lestranges of Hunstanton from AD 1519 to AD 1578. 1833, D. Gurney
4. 'Some Notes on the Boleyn Family', Norfolk Archaeology Volume 25, W.L.E. Parsons.
5. Ibid
6. Ibid
7. Calendar of the Close Rolls of Richard II, Volume III p.140
8. Salle Court Records
9. The Story of a Norfolk Parish and its Church, Manors and People, W.L.E. Parsons.
10. 'Some Notes on the Boleyn Family', Norfolk Archaeology Volume 25, W.L.E. Parsons.

11. Ibid

12. Ibid

13. An essay Towards a Topographical History of the County of Norfolk Volume III, 1797.

14. The Visitation of the Archdeacon of Norfolk 1368-1420, W.L.E. Parsons

15. Some Notes on the Boleyn Family', Norfolk Archaeology Volume 25, W.L.E. Parsons

16. Court case: 1463

17. Biographical History of Gonville and Caius College, J. Venn.

18. The Warden's Account Book 1435 for the Mercers of London p.477.

19. The Warden's Account Book for the Mercers p.485

20. Calendar of Fine Rolls XVIII p.563

21. 'Some Notes on the Boleyn Family', Norfolk Archaeology Volume 25, W.L.E Parsons.

22. Calendar of Fine Rolls XIX p 195.

23. Testamenta Vetusta: Being illustrations from Wills, of Manners, Customs &c. As Well as of Descents and Possessions of Many Distinguished Families from the Reign of Henry the Second to the Accession of Queen Elizabeth, Volume 1 p.272. N.H. Nicolas. London 1826.

24. Daughters, Wives and Widows after the Black Death: Women in Sussex 1350–1535, M.E. Mate

25. Antiquarian researches in Gentleman's Magazine, 1855.

26. Paston Letters 182.

27. Geoffrey's will.

28. The Boleyns, David Loades. Amberley Publishing 2011

29. TNA PROB 11/18 Earl of Ormond's Will

30. Ibid

31. Grace's Annales Hiberniae p161

32. The Six Wives of Henry VIII, Alison Weir. Grove Press 1991

33. Ibid
34. Church records
35. Calendar of Fine Rolls XXII p.324
36. Calendar of the Patent Rolls 1476
37. Thomas Boleyn's Account November-December 1526: Letters and Papers.
38. Henry Howard, Earl of Surrey, E Casady
39. Accounts and Memoranda of Sir John Howard, First Duke of Norfolk AD 1462 to AD 1471, B. Botfield
40. Household Books of John Duke of Norfolk and Thomas Earl of Surrey 1481–1490, J.P.Coller
41. The Early Career of Thomas, Lord Howard, Earl of Surrey 1474–1525, S.E. Vokes
42. Ibid
43. Calendar of the Close Rolls Henry VII Volume II p.179
44. Calendar of Fine Rolls XXII
45. Letters and Papers, Foreign and Domestic XI 17
46. Hever Castle Guide Book, Hever Castle
47. Guide at Hever Castle, April 2019
48. Hever Castle Guide Book, Hever Castle
49. The Yeoman of the Guard and the Early Tudors: The Formation of a Royal Bodyguard, Anita Rosamund Hewerdine. I.B Tauris 2012
50. Letters and Papers, Foreign and Domestic, Ed J. S. Brewer. London 1920
51. The Household of Edward IV: The Black Book and the ordinance of 1478. Ed. Alec Reginald Myers. Manchester University Press, Manchester. 1959
52. List of opponents. Letters and Papers of Henry VIII 1 Appendix 9. Letters and Papers, Foreign and Domestic, Ed. J. S. Brewer. London 1920
53. Original Letters Illustrative of English History Volume Two, Henry Ellis. R. Bentley 1846, London

54. Letters and Papers of Henry VIII. 1, 707. Foreign and Domestic, Ed. J. S Brewer. London 1920

55. Letters and Papers of Henry VIII. II, 1573. Foreign and Domestic, Ed J. S. Brewer. London 1920

56. Letters and Papers, Foreign and Domestic I 3196, 3370 and 3460

57. Letters and Papers, Foreign and Domestic I 3370

58. Letters and Papers, Foreign and Domestic I 3402 (September 1512).

59. Letters and Papers, Foreign and Domestic I 4237 and 4307.

60. Boleyn, Thomas Earl of Wiltshire and Earl of Ormond, Courtier and Nobleman, Jonathan Hughes. Oxford Dictionary of National Biography. Oxford University Press 2004

61. Cavendish's Metrical Visions in Norton 2011a p.227

62. Annales rerum Anglicarum, et Hibernicarm, regnante Elizabetha, ad annum salutis, William Camden. EEBO Editions ProQuest, 2010

63. Letter to Anne's father, Norton p.25

64. Examination of Thomas Smyth July 1536: Letters and Papers XI 148

65. An Essay Towards a Topographical History of Norfolk Volume V.E. Blomefield

66. Family records

67. Lincolnshire Pedigrees III p.952

68. Letters and Papers, Foreign and Domestic I 82

69. Letters and Papers, Foreign and Domestic I 1549

70. Space, Time, and the Power of Aristocratic Wives in Yorkist and Early Tudor England 1450-1550, B.J. Harris

71. Letters and Papers, Foreign and Domestic

72. Anne Boleyn in her Own Words and the Words of Those Who Knew Her, E. Norton. Amberley 2011

73. President Address: The Tudor Government: The Points of Contact III, G.R. Elton

74. The Rise and Growth of the Anglican Schism, N. Sander. Facsimile TAN Books 1988

75. Lisle Letters, V, 1137. University of Chicago Press 1983

76. Ibid

Chapter One

1. Rise and growth of the Anglican Schism, N. Sander.

2. Ibid

3. Annales rerum Anglicarum et Hibernicarum Regnate Elizabetha, ad anum salutis MD LXXXIX, William Camden. EEBO Editions ProQuest 2010

4. The Life of Jane Dormer, Duchess of Feria, H. Clifford. Theclassics.us. 2013

5. Life of Queen Anne Boleigne, G. Wyatt. Richard and Arthur Taylor. 1817

6. The High and Puissant Princess Marguerite of Austria, Princess Dowager of Spain, Dowager of Savoy, Regent of the Netherlands, C. Have. Palala Press 2015

7. Lives of Four and Gallant Ladies, Seigneur de Brantome. Ed. Alfred Richard Allinson. Liveright Publishing Corporation, New York 1933

8. Rise and Growth of the Anglican Schism, N. Sander. TAN Books 1988

9. Lives of Four and Gallant Ladies Seigneur de Brantome. Ed. Alfred Richard Allinson. Liveright Publishing Corporation, New York 1933

10. The Early Life of Anne Boleyn, J.H Round. Endeavour Compass 2016

11. Ibid

12. 'Extracts from the life of the Virtuous Christian and Renowned Queen Anne Boleigne', George Wyatt. The Life of Cardinal Wolsey, W. Cavendish. Harding and Lepard, London 1641

13. The Life of Cardinal Wolsey, W. Cavendish. Harding and Lepard, London 1641

14. 'Extracts from the life of the Virtuous Christian and Renowned Queen Anne Boleigne', G. Wyatt. The Life of Cardinal Wolsey. W. Cavendish. Harding and Lepard, London 1641

15. The History of Parliament: The House of Commons 1509–1558, Ed. S.T. Bindoff: Wyatt, Sir Thomas of Allington Castle, Kent, Helen Miller

16. The Mistresses of Henry VIII, Kelly Hart. The History Press 2009

17. The Poetical Works of Sir Thomas Wyatt, Ed. J. Nichol. James Nisbet and Company, Edinburgh 1858

18. The Rise and Fall of Anne Boleyn, Retha Warnicke. Cambridge University Press 2017

19. 'Extracts from the life of the virtuous Christian Renowned Queen Anne Boleigne', George Wyatt. The Life of Cardinal Wolsey, W. Cavendish. Harding and Lepard, London 1641

20. Letters from Chapuys to Charles V on the 1st January 1530. Letters and Papers, Foreign and Domestic, Henry VIII, Volume 5. Stationery Office, London 1880

21. Jean Du Bellay: 9th November 1528. Letters and Papers, Foreign and Domestic, Henry VIII, Volume 5. Stationery Office, London 1880

22. Health, Medicine and Mortality in the Sixteenth Century, Patricia Allderidge. Cambridge University Press, Cambridge 1979

23. Letters from Chapuys to Charles V: 10th May 1530. Letters and Papers, Foreign and Domestic, Henry VIII, Volume 5. Stationery Office, London 1880

24. Letters from Chapuys to Charles V: 1st October 1532. Letters and Papers, Foreign and Domestic, Henry VIII, Volume 5. Stationery Office, London 1880

25. The Life and Death of Anne Boleyn, Eric Ives. Wiley/ Blackwell 1986

26. The Life and Death of Anne Boleyn: 'The Most Happy', Eric Ives. Oxford 2005

27. King Henry cancelled a jousting event he had arranged to celebrate the birth of what he thought would be his son and heir

28. Letters from Chapuys to Charles V: 10th February 1536. Letters and Papers, Foreign and Domestic, Henry VIII, Volume 5. Stationery Office, London 1880

29. Letter from Chapuys to Charles V: 1536. Letters and Papers, Foreign and Domestic, Henry VIII, Volume 5. Stationery Office, London 1880

30. 'Extracts from the Life of the Virtuous Queen Anne Boleigne', G. Wyatt. The Life of Cardinal Wolsey, W. Cavendish. Harding and Lepard, London 1641

31. Labelled A true and Exact Draught of the Tower Liberties Survey'd in the year of 1597, Gulielmus Haiward and J. Gascoyne

32. A Chronicle of England during the Reigns of the Tudors from AD 1485 to 1559, Volume One, Charles Wriothesley. Printed for the Camden Society 1875

33. The Union of the Two Noble and Illustrate Famelies of Lancastre and Yorke (Hall's Chronicle), Edward Hall. Published by Richard Grafton, 1548

34. The Lady in the Tower: The Fall of Anne Boleyn, Alison Weir. Jonathan Cape 200

35. Her Last Days, blog by Amanda Harvey Purse. Wordpress.com

36. Macaulay's History of England, Vol. I, pp 628-9, quoted in Notices of the Historic Persons Buried in the Chapel of St Peter ad Vincula in the Tower of London, With an Account of the Discovery of the Supposed Remains of Anne Boleyn, Doyne C Bell, 1877

37. Ibid

38. Ibid
39. Ibid
40. Ibid
41. Divorced, Beheaded, Survived: A Feminist Reinterpretation of the Wives of Henry VIII, Karen Lindsey. Perseus Books, Reading 1995
42. The Life and Death of Anne Boleyn: 'The Most Happy', Eric Ives. Oxford 2005
43. Metrical Visions, George Cavendish. South Carolina Press 1980
44. Letters and Papers II, Revel Accounts. Letters and Papers, Foreign and Domestic, Henry VIII, Volume 5. Stationery Office, London 1880
45. Ibid
46. Letters and Papers, Foreign and Domestic, IV 1939, Henry VIII. Stationery Office, London 1880
47. Ibid
48. New Hall School website
49. Ibid
50. The History of Bethlem, Jonathan Andrews. Routledge. London 1997
51. The Politics of Committal to Early Modem Bethlem, Jonathan Andrews in Medicine in the Enlightenment, Roy Porter. Rodopi. Atlanta 1995
52. Du Bellay's Correspondence September 1527–February 1529. Jean Du Bellay: Ambassades en Angleterre de Jean Du Bellay – La Premiere Ambassade. Paris 1905
53. Ibid
54. The Spanish Calendar IV 265. Calendar of State Papers, Spain. Her Majesty's Stationery Office, London, 1888
55. Spanish Calendar IV, ii, 1056. Calendar of State Papers, Spain. Her Majesty's Stationery Office, London, 1888
56. Ibid

57. Letters and Papers, Foreign and Domestic VI, 1481
58. Reformation Parliament, Lehimberg Stanford. Cambridge University Press. Cambridge. 1960
59. Ibid
60. Letters and Papers, Foreign and Domestic VI 954
61. State Papers VII 565, National Archives, Kew, London
62. Ibid
63. Letters and Papers, Foreign and Domestic VI, 1111
64. Metrical Visions p.20, George Cavendish. South Carolina Press. Columbia 1980
65. The firste volume of the chronicles of England, Scotlande and Irelande, Raphael Holinshed. London 1577
66. Catalogue of Royal and Noble Authors of England, Scotland and Ireland, Horace Walpole. John Scott. London 1806
67. Ibid
68. Specimens of Early Elizabeth Poets to Which is Prefixed, an Historical Sketch of the Rise and Progress of English Poetry and Language, George Ellis. Bulmer and Co. London 1803
69. Catalogue of Royal and Noble Authors of England, Scotland and Ireland, Horace Walpole. John Scott. London 1806
70. The Constables and Wardens: Dover Archives Online
71. Ibid
72. Letters and Papers, Foreign and Domestic, VIII, 760, Henry VIII, Stationery Office, London 1880
73. Ibid
74. Ibid
75. Ibid
76. The Constables and Wardens: Dover Archives Online
77. Ibid
78. The Spanish Calendar V, ii, 9. Calendar of State Papers, Spain. Stationery Office, London, 1888.

79. Letters and Papers, Foreign and Domestic X 141, Henry VIII, Stationery Office, London 1880

80. The Spanish Calendar V, ii, 39. Calendar of State Papers, Spain. Stationery Office, London, 1888

81. Ibid

82. Ibid

83. Ibid

84. Letters and Papers, Foreign and Domestic X 876

85. Ibid

86. Ibid

87. The Spanish Calendar V ii 55. Calendar of State Papers, Spain. Stationery Office, London, 1888

88. Ibid

89. Clonony Castle, Banagher, A Brief History, Banagher Parish Council, June 1951

90. Ibid

91. Ibid

92. Jane Boleyn: The True Story of the Infamous Lady Rochford, Julia Fox. Ballantine Books 2009

93. Boleyn, George, Stanford Lehmberg. Oxford Dictionary of National Biography. Oxford University Press

94. Ibid

95. The Privy Purse: 'Expenses of King Henry the Eighth, from November 1529 to December 1532'. Letters and Papers, Foreign and Domestic X 876, Henry VIII, Stationery Office, London 1880

96. Ibid

Chapter Two

1. Royal Sex: Mistresses and Lovers of the British Royal Family, Roger Powell. Amberley Publishing 2010

2. The Rutland Papers: Original documents, illustrative of the courts and times of Henry VII and Henry VIII, John Henry Manners Rutland. Printed for the Camden Society by J. B. Nichols and Son 1842

3. Calendar of the Close Rolls Henry VII 1485–1500. K.H. Ledward, 1955. British History Online

4. Blickling Estate, Anna Groves. National Trust 2017

5. Ibid

6. Ibid

7. Ibid

8. Ibid

9. Letters and Papers, Foreign and Domestic

10. Ibid

11. Spanish Calendar: Calendar of Letters, Despatches and State Papers, relating to Negotiations between England and Spain: Archives at Simancas. Public Record Office, London 1862

12. Ibid

13. Katherine Howard: The Story of Henry VIII's Fifth Queen, Michael Glenne. John Murray 2016

14. All Colour Book of Henry VIII, John Walder. Octopus Books 1973

15. Her Majesty: The Romance of the Queen of England 1066–1910, Elsie Thornton Cook. E. P. Dutton, New York 1927

16. The Life and Death of Anne Boleyn: 'The Most Happy', Eric Ives. Oxford 2004

17. Calendar of State Papers and Manuscripts: Archives of Milan 1385–1618, Ed. Allen B Hinds. Stationery Office, London 1912. British History Online

18. Spanish Calendar: Calendar of Letters, Despatches and State Papers, relating to Negotiations between England and Spain: Archives at Simancas. Public Record Office, London 1862

19. Letters and Papers, Foreign and Domestic
20. The Rise and Fall of Anne Boleyn: Family Politics at the Court of Henry VIII, Retha M. Warnicke. Cambridge University Press 1991
21. Letters and Papers, Foreign and Domestic
22. Ibid
23. The Visitor Information Centre at Greenwich
24. Ibid
25. Ibid
26. Ibid
27. Ibid
28. A Guide to All Saints Church, Clovelly, William Griggs. Church publication
29. Mary Boleyn: The True Story of Henry VIII's Favourite Mistress, Josephine Wilkinson. Amberley Publishing 2009
30. Letters and Papers, Foreign and Domestic
31. Henry VIII: The Politics of Tyranny, Jasper Ridley. Fromm International 1986
32. Six Wives: The Queens of Henry VIII, Dr David Starkey. Vintage 2004. The Early Loves of Anne Boleyn, Josephine Wilkinson. Amberley Publishing 2009
33. Letters and Papers, Foreign and Domestic
34. Ibid
35. Ibid
36. This was later published without the Cardinal's permission, entitled *Pro ecclesiasticae unitatis defensione,* In Defence of Ecclesiastical Unity. It was a document the Cardinal used to justify his objections the King's marriage to Anne. Rome 1536. Lambeth Palace Library
37. Letters and Papers, Foreign and Domestic
38. Six Wives: The Queens of Henry VIII, Dr David Starkey. Vintage 2004

39. The Other Tudors: Henry VIII's Mistresses and Bastards, Philippa Jones. New Holland Australia 2009

40. Venetian Calendar: Calendar of State Papers and Manuscripts relating to English Affairs in the Archives of Venice 1531

41. Letters and Papers, Foreign and Domestic

42. Ibid

43. The Triumphant Reign of King Henry the Eighth, Edward Hall. Published by Richard Grafton, London 1547

44. Letters and Papers, Foreign and Domestic

45. Ibid

46. Ibid

47. Mary became Lady Mary Carey from 1529, when her father was given the titles of Earl of Wiltshire and Earl of Ormond

48. A Popular History of the Reformation, Philip Hughes p.177. Hanover House 1957

49. Reconstructing the Word: The Political Prophecies of Elizabeth Barton, Diane Watt. Renaissance Quarterly 50 1997

50. The Angel of Syon: The Life of Martyrdom of Blessed Richard Reynolds, Adam Hamilton p.26. Sands and Co, London 1905

51. Reconstructing the Word: The Political Prophecies of Elizabeth Barton, Diane Watt. Renaissance Quarterly 50 1997

52. Dover Archives Online.

53. Ibid

54. Dover Castle: Historicengland.org.uk

55. Calendar of State Papers and Manuscripts in the Archives and Collections of Milan: October 1532

56. Letters and Papers, Foreign and Domestic

57. Spanish Calendar in the Archives in Simancas, Spain 1532

58. Collected Works of Erasmus. Letter 1341A Volume 9. Toronto University Press, Canada

59. Letters and Papers, Foreign and Domestic

60. Oxford Dictionary of National Biography online. DOI: 10.1093/ref:odnb/69753 Simon Adams 2006

61. Spanish Calendar in the Archives in Simancas, Spain 1534

62. Magna Carta Ancestry: A Study in Colonial and Medieval Families IV, Douglas Richardson. Salt Lake City 2011

63. History of Parliament, Sir John Fogge

64. The History and Topographical Survey of the County of Kent: Volume 8, Edward Hasted. Canterbury 1799

65. The Historical Literature of the Jack Cade Rebellion, Alexander Kaufman. Routledge 2009

66. Ibid

67. 2022's Sheriff of Kent is Russell Race

68. Elizabeth, England's Slandered Queen, Arlene Okerlund The History Press 2006

69. Henry VI died on 21 May 1471; some say on the orders of Edward IV.

70. Richard III, Paul Murray Kendall. Norton 2002

71. Letters and Papers, Foreign and Domestic

72. Ibid

73. Spanish Calendar in the Archives in Simancas, Spain 1534

74. Letters and Papers, Foreign and Domestic

75. The Triumphant Reign of King Henry the Eighth, Edward Hall

76. All Colour Book of Henry VIII, John Walder. Octopus Books 1973

77. Ladies of the Bedchamber: The Role of the Royal Mistress, Dennis Friedman. Peter Owen Publishers 2003

78. Rochford Hall: The History of a Tudor House and Biographies of its Owners, Dr Michael Clark. Alan Sutton 1990

79. Spanish Calendar in the Archives in Simancas, Spain 1534
80. Letters and Papers, Foreign and Domestic
81. The Chronicle of Calais: In the reigns of Henry VII and Henry VIII to the year 1540, John Gough Nichols. Scholar's Choice 2015
82. Letters and Papers, Foreign and Domestic
83. Ibid
84. The Manor of Great Bounds was given to Mary's son Henry Carey after her death. He built the Bound Lodge, which can see be seen on the London Road between Tonbridge and Southborough today. Before the manor was owned by the Boleyns, it was owned by the 3rd Duke of Buckingham, Edward Stafford. After his execution at the Tower of London, Henry gave the house first to Thomas Boleyn, with George Boleyn gaining 'lordship' of it. After their deaths, the king gave the estate and lands to Mary Boleyn
85. History of Acts and Monuments of the Church, John Foxe. John Day 1563
86. The Chronicle of Calais: In the reigns of Henry VII and Henry VIII to the year 1540, John Gough Nichols. Scholar's Choice 2015
87. Letters and Papers, Foreign and Domestic
88. The Chronicle of Calais: In the reigns of Henry VII and Henry VIII to the year 1540, John Gough Nichols. Scholar's Choice 2015
89. Letters and Papers, Foreign and Domestic
90. Reference to this grand manor exists today in Great Bounds Drive, close by
91. Letters and Papers, Foreign and Domestic
92. Ibid
93. Ibid
94. Ibid

95. Her post-mortem records at the National Archives, Kew

96. Rochford Hall: The History of a Tudor House and Biographies of its Owners, Dr Michael Clark. Alan Sutton 1990

97. Southborough Conservation Area Appraisal 2003

98. Ibid

99. The author would like to thank Roger Evernden for his information about the area surrounding St Thomas's church, and for introducing her to Fiona Woodfield, a local historian. The information Fiona passed on corresponded to what the author already had on the subject, and in sharing her knowledge Fiona confirmed that the author was on the right track

100. Kent: With her Cities and Earles Described and Observed by Cartographer John Speed, 1614

101. Letters and Papers, Foreign and Domestic

102. Ibid

103. Ibid

104. Ibid

105. Lady Stafford: Oxford Dictionary of National Biography. DOI: 10.1093/ref:odnb/69753, Simon Adams 2006

106. William Stafford: Oxford Dictionary of National Biography online, Peter Holmes. Oxford University Press

107. A Survey of the Cities of London and Westminster, John Stow 1598.

108. Rochford Hall: The History of a Tudor House and Biographies of its Owners, Dr Michael Clark. Alan Sutton 1990

109. The House of Commons 1509–1558, S.T. Bindoff. Boydell and Brewer, London. 1982

110. Right Royal Bastards: The Fruits of Passion, Peter Beauclerk-Dewar and Roger Powell. Burke's Peerage and Gentry 2006

111. Rochford Hall: The History of a Tudor House and Biographies of its Owners, Dr Michael Clark. Alan Sutton 1990

112. Ibid

113. Household Expenses of the Princess Elizabeth during her residence at Hatfield October 1, 1551 to September 30, 1552, Percy Smythe. Forgotten Books 2018

114. Mary Stafford: Oxford Dictionary of National Biography online, Jonathan Hughes. Oxford University Press

115. The Complete Peerage, G.E. Cokayne. George Bell and Sons. London 1887

116. Calendar of Letters and State Papers at the Archives of Simancas

117. The Elizabethan Renaissance: The Life of the Society, A.L. Rowse. First published 1971. Ivan R. Dee 2000

118. Henry Carey: Dictionary of National Biography, Leslie Stephen. Smith, Elder and Company. London 1887

119. Ibid

120. Ibid

121. The Herald and Genealogist, Volume 4, Ed. John Gough Nichols. Printers to the Society of Antiquaries. London 1867

122. Information from Devon County Council

123. Elizabeth's Tilbury speech, www.bl.uk.The British Library

124. Shadowplay: The Hidden Beliefs and Coded Politics of William Shakespeare, Clare Asquith. Public Affairs. 2005

125. Ibid

126. Fragmenta Regalia, Sir Robert Naunton. Folger Shakespeare Library. 1985

127. Rochford Hall: The History of a Tudor House and Biographies of its Owners, Dr Michael Clark. Alan Sutton 1990

128. With thanks to Alison Weir for allowing the author to quote her on the subject of the 2020 findings concerning Mary Boleyn's portrait.

129. With thanks to Justin Davies for details of the findings.

Chapter Three

1. Letters and Papers, Foreign and Domestic
2. In the Tudor period only royal births were recorded, not even noble births were noted.
3. Hence why the author has spelt Katherine's name with a 'K'.
4. Letters and Papers, Foreign and Domestic
5. Sir Francis Knollys's Latin Dictionary: New Evidence for Katherine Carey, Historical Research Vol 80, Sally Varlow. August 2007
6. Ibid
7. Letters and Papers, Foreign and Domestic 4 4408
8. History of Parliament Online
9. Letters and Papers, Foreign and Domestic 14 572
10. Letters and Papers, Foreign and Domestic
11. The Marrying of Anne of Cleves: Royal Protocol in Tudor England, Retha M Warnicke, Cambridge University Press 2000
12. Letters and Papers, Foreign and Domestic November 1539
13. Letters and Papers, Foreign and Domestic XIV C67
14. Letters and Papers, Foreign and Domestic XV III pt1 275
15. Dictionary of National Biography Volume XXXI, G.C. Boasle
16. The Marian Exiles: A Study in the Origins of Elizabethan Puritanism, Christina Hallowell Garrett. London 1966
17. Mary Queen of Scots, Antonia Fraser. Phoenix Press 2003
18. Ibid
19. Calendar of State Papers, Scott II p.428
20. Calendar of State Papers, Scott II
21. Mary Queen of Scots, Antonia Fraser. Phoenix Press 2003
22. Ibid
23. Cecil Papers Volume 1 739 at Hatfield House. British History online

24. Miscellanies of the Philobiblon Society Volume XIV
25. Cecil Papers Volume 1 772 at Hatfield House. British History online.
26. Ibid
27. Miscellanies of the Philobiblon Society Volume XIV
28. She died on 15 January 1569 at Hampton Court Palace
29. Cecil Papers Volume 3 963 at Hatfield House. British History online
30. History of Parliament Online
31. Ibid
32. Sex in Elizabethan England, Alan Haynes. The History Press 1997
33. Shakespeare A to Z, Charles Boyce. Facts on File 1990
34. History of Parliament Online
35. He died on 26 May 1632
36. History of Parliament Online
37. Ibid
38. Ibid
39. Ibid
40. Ibid
41. Cecil Papers Volume 1 1314 at Hatfield House. British History online
42. Westminsterabbey.org

Chapter Four

1. Sir Francis Knollys and Family, F.J. Maipas. Reading. 1993
2. The Acts and Monuments of John Foxe. London 1838.
3. Dudley and Devereux papers originally held at Longleat House
4. Calendar of State Papers Scotland 1563–1569 ii (811)
5. The Marian Exiles: A Study in the Origins of Elizabethan Puritanism, Christina Hallowell Garrett. London 1966

6. Letters of Royal and Illustrious Ladies III, Mae Wood. London 1846
7. The Marian Exiles: A Study in the Origins of Elizabethan Puritanism, Christina Hallowell Garrett. London 1966
8. Elizabeth's Women: The Hidden Story of the Virgin Queen, Tracey Borman. London 2009
9. Ibid
10. Ibid
11. Lives and Letters of the Devereux Earls of Essex: In the Reigns of Elizabeth, James I and Charles I 1540–1646, Walter Bourchier Devereux Volume 1. John Murray 1853
12. The Tower of London Prisoner Book: A Complete Chronology of the Persons Known to have been Detained at their Majesties' Pleasure 1100–1941, B A Harrison. Leeds 2004
13. Devereux Papers originally held at Longleat House V, F, 22. In the funeral charges for Walter it states that his body was returned to 'the castle of Carmarthen where he was born'
14. The Complete Peerage, Cokayne 1887
15. Tailor Accounts in the Devereux Papers Volume III originally held at Longleat House
16. TNA LRL/B7 f8or National Archives
17. Lives and Letters of the Devereux Earls of Essex: In the Reigns of Elizabeth, James I and Charles I 1540-1646, Walter Bourchier Devereux Volume 1. John Murray 1853
18. Elizabeth and Leicester, Sarah Gristwood. London 2007.
19. Robert Dudley, Earl of Leicester, Elizabeth Goldring. Yale University Press. 2014
20. The Elizabethan New Year's Gift Exchanges, J.A. Lawson. Oxford 2013.
21. Ibid
22. Devereux Papers originally held at Longleat House

23. Calendar of State Papers, Spanish: Elizabeth 1558-1567
24. Calendar of State Papers, Spanish: p.472
25. Calendar of State Papers, Spanish: Elizabeth 1558-1567
26. Robert, Earl of Essex: An Elizabethan Icarus, Robert Lacey. Weidenfeld and Nicolson 1971
27. Warwickshire County Record Office. MI 229
28. British Library: Landsdowne MS 24 f 208
29. The Elizabethan New Year's Gift Exchanges, J.A. Lawson. Oxford 2013
30. Historical Manuscripts Commission: Salisbury III 435
31. Historical Manuscripts Commission: Salisbury I 1343
32. Ibid
33. Lives and Letters of the Devereux Earls of Essex: In the Reigns of Elizabeth, James I and Charles I 1540-1646, Walter Bourchier Devereux Volume 1. John Murray 1853
34. Ibid
35. Ibid
36. Ibid
37. The Complete Peerage, Cokayne 1887
38. Calendar of State Papers: Spanish. Elizabeth 1568–1579
39. State Papers 86f 163-4
40. Poor Penelope: Lady Penelope Rich, An Elizabethan Woman, Sylvia Freedman. Kensal Press 1983
41. Lives and Letters of the Devereux Earls of Essex: In the Reigns of Elizabeth, James I and Charles I 1540-1646, Walter Bourchier Devereux Volume 1. John Murray 1853
42. Ibid
43. Ibid
44. 3 August 1574 Historical Manuscripts Commission: Bath V
45. Letters of Thomas Wood, Puritan 1566–1577, P. Collinson. London 1960
46. Elizabeth and Leicester, Elizabeth Jenkins. Phoenix 1961

47. Alumni Oxonienses 1500–1714, Joseph Foster. Oxford. 1891

48. The Elizabethan New Year's Gift Exchanges, J.A. Lawson. Oxford 2013

49. Calendar of the Carew Manuscripts, John Brewer and William Bullen. Lambeth Palace Library 1867

50. Annales rerum Anglicarum et Hibernicarum regnante Elizabetha, ad annum salutis M.D. LXXXIX, William Camden. London 1607

51. Lives and Letters of the Devereux Earls of Essex: In the Reigns of Elizabeth, James I and Charles I 1540-1646, Walter Bourchier Devereux Volume 1. John Murray 1853

52. Ibid

53. Ibid

54. Ibid

55. Historical Manuscripts Commission: De L'Isle

56. Lives and Letters of the Devereux Earls of Essex: In the Reigns of Elizabeth, James I and Charles I 1540-1646, Walter Bourchier Devereux Volume 1. John Murray 1853

57. Ibid

58. Ibid

59. A collection of State Papers relating to Affairs in the Reign of Queen Elizabeth from year 1571 to 1576, W. Murdin. London 1759

60. Historical Manuscripts Commission: Salisbury II

61. Annales rerum Anglicarum et Hibernicarum regnante Elizabetha, ad annum salutis M.D. LXXXIX, William Camden. London 1607. Leicester's Commonwealth 1584, Ed. D. C. Peck. Ohio University Press. London

62. Robert Dudley, Earl of Leicester, and the World of Elizabethan Art, Elizabeth Goldring. Yale University Press. 2014

63. The Death and Burial of Walter Devereux, E.J. Jones article in The Carmarthen Antiquary I 1941
64. The Essex Inheritance, H.A. Lloyd in the Welsh History Review 1974
65. PROB 11/58/438 f248
66. Ibid
67. Devereux Papers originally held at Longleat House
68. Landowne MS 24f 26
69. Ibid
70. Ibid
71. PROB 11/58/438 f248
72. State Papers 12/148 f83
73. The Lady Penelope: The Lost Tales of Love and Politics in the Court of Elizabeth I, S. Varlow. Andre Deutsch 2007
74. Leicester's Commonwealth 1584, Ed. D. C. Peck. Ohio University Press. London
75. Elizabeth and Leicester, Elizabeth Jenkins. Phoenix 1961
76. Landowne MS 31 f105
77. Ibid
78. Poor Penelope: Lady Penelope Rich, An Elizabethan Woman, Sylvia Freedman. Kensal Press 1983
79. Calendar of State Papers Spanish: Elizabeth 1580–1586 III
80. Dudley Papers X f 41
81. Household Accounts and Disbursement Books of Robert Dudley, Simon Adams. Cambridge University Press 1995
82. Ibid
83. Ibid
84. Calendar of State Papers: Spanish. Elizabeth 1580–1586 III
85. Sweet Robin: A Biography of Robert Dudley, Earl of Leicester 1533–1588, Derek Wilson. Allison and Busby 1981
86. Memoirs of the Life and Times of Sir Christopher Hatton, H. Nicholas. London 1847.

87. Calendar of State Papers: Domestic Series. Elizabeth 1581–1590 172

88. Ibid

89. St Mary's Church, Warwick

90. Household Accounts and Disbursement Books of Robert Dudley, Simon Adams. Cambridge University Press 1995

91. Ibid

92. Calendar of State Papers: September 1585–May 1586

93. Dudley Papers VI

94. Letters of Queen Elizabeth, G.B. Harrison. Greenwood Press 1981

95. Correspondence of Robert Dudley, Earl of Leycester, Ed. John Bruce. Printed for the Camden Society by J. B. Nichols and Son, 1844

96. Cotton MS Galba Cix f179

97. A Summarie of the Chronicles of England, Diligently Collected, Abridged and Continued unto this Present Year of Christ 1604 by John Stow, Ed. B.L. Beer. Edwin Mellen Press Ltd 2008

98. Annales rerum Anglicarum et Hibernicarum regnante Elizabetha, ad annum salutis M.D. LXXXIX, William Camden. London 1607

99. Correspondence of Robert Dudley, Earl of Leycester, Ed. John Bruce. Printed for the Camden Society 1844

100. Harley 6798 f87

101. Annales rerum Anglicarum et Hibernicarum regnante Elizabetha, ad annum salutis M.D. LXXXIX, William Camden. London 1607

102. PROB 1/1.

103. Elizabeth the Queen, Alison Weir. Vintage 1998

104. Landowne MS 62 f78r

105. Cornbury and the Forest Wychwood. Cited in V.J. Watney. London 1910

106. Ibid
107. The Memoirs of Robert Carey, F.H. Mares. Oxford University Press 1972
108. Letters and Memorials of State, Arthur Collins, 1746
109. Thank you to all of the staff of St Mary's Church in Warwick for the care they take over of the tomb of Lettice Knollys, Robert Dudley, and their son

Chapter Five

1. Lives and Letters of the Devereux, Earls of Essex, Walter Bourchier Devereux
2. Folger Shakespeare Library: La 37
3. British Library: Landsdowne 36 Fo 37
4. The Polarisation of Elizabeth Politics: The Political Career of Robert Devereux, Second Earl of Essex, Paul E.J. Hammer. Cambridge University Press 1999
5. Ibid
6. Annales rerum Anglicarum et Hibernicarum regnante Elizabetha, ad annum salutis M.D. LXXXIX Volume 2, William Camden 1589
7. Love, Lust, and License in Early Modern England. Illicit Sex and the Nobility, Johanna Rickman. Aldershot 2008
8. Illustrations iii 31–2 of Illustrations of British History, Biography and Manners in the Reigns of Henry VIII to James I in Papers from MMS of the Families of Howard, Talbot and Cecil 3rd Volume, 2nd edition, Edmund Lodge 1838
9. State Papers held at the National Archives: 12/239 fo. 93
10. State Papers held at the National Archives: 78/25 fo. 182
11. State Papers held at the National Archives: 78/25 fos 344, 348
12. Correspondence of Sir Henry Unton, Ambassador from Queen Elizabeth to Henry IV of France in years MDXCI and MDXCII, Joseph Stevenson. London 1847

13. The Complete Peerage Volume V. St Catherine's Press 1926

14. Ibid

15. Unnatural Murder – Poison at the Court of James I, Anne Somerset. Weidenfield and Nicolson 1997

16. Devereux, Robert, 3rd Earl of Essex by John Morrill. Oxford Dictionary of National Biography. Oxford University Press

17. Ibid

18. Folger Shakespeare Library: La 269

19. The Double Life of Doctor Lopez: Spies, Shakespeare and the Plot to Poison Elizabeth I, Dominic Green. London 2003

20. Paul E.J. Hammer and Matthew H.C.G. Harrison, Oxford Dictionary of National Biography. Oxford University Press 2004

21. State Papers held at the National Archives: 12/259 f 30

22. British Library: Egerton 2026 f 32

23. Cecil Papers at Hatfield: 65/29

24. Queen Elizabeth I by Sir John Neale. Pelican Books 1960

25. State Papers held at the National Archives: 63/204 ff 178 and 179

26. Historical Manuscripts Commission: De L'Isle ii 395-6.

27. Historical Manuscripts Commission: De L'Isle ii 435, 459

28. Historical Manuscripts Commission: De L'Isle ii 470.

29. States Papers held at the National Archives: 12/275 f 81.

30. A sermon preached at Paules Crosse, on the First Sunday in Lent; Martij 1. 1600 With a short discourse of the late Earle of Essex his confession, and penitence, before and at the time of his death, William Barlow

31. Devereux, Frances (nee Walsingham; other married names Sidney and Burke or Burgh) Countess of Essex and of Clanricarde. Oxford Dictionary of National Biography. Oxford University Press

32. British Library: 74286 fos 13 and 95
33. A Journal, A.H. de Maisse, trans and Eds. G.B. Harrison and R.A. Jones, London 1931

Chapter Six

1. Letters of John Chamberlain Vol 2, Norman Egbert McClure. Philadelphia 1939
2. The Marriage, Baptismal and Burial registers of the collegiate church or Abbey of St Peter Westminster, Joseph Lemuel Chester. Harleian Society 1876
3. Remains, Historical and Literary connected with Palatine Countries of Lancaster and Chester, the Chetham Society 1847
4. Lee, Sidney Dictionary of National Biography by Robert Dunlop. London 1894
5. Ibid
6. Parish history – www.stpetertitchfield.org.uk
7. Burke's Peerage Baronetage and Knightage 107th Ed., Charles Mosley. Wilmington, Delaware 2003
8. The Marriage, Baptismal and Burial registers of the collegiate church or Abbey of St Peter Westminster, Joseph Lemuel Chester. Harleian Society 1876
9. Myheritage.com
10. The Complete Peerage Vol 12 1953
11. Norman Egbert McClure, Letters of John Chamberlain, Volume 2, p.31. Philadelphia 1939
12. The Complete Peerage Vol 12, 1953
13. Somerset, Earls and Dukes of, Encyclopaedia Britannia, Hugh Chisholm. Cambridge University Press 1911
14. William Seymour, 1st Marquess of Hertford and 2nd Duke of Somerset, David L Smith. Oxford DNB 2004
15. Ibid

16. Detailed information about the will of Frances Seymour was given to the author by Graham Bathe, author of 'The Seymour Legacy' chapter in the Book of Bedwyns.
17. Parish records
18. Burlington House: Survey of London Vol 31 and 32, Britishhistory.ac.uk
19. Barry James, 4th Earl of Barrymore (1667–1748), Stephen W. Baskerville. Oxford DNB 2004
20. Queensbury Earls, Marquesses and Dukes of, Hugh Chisholm. Encyclopaedia Britannica, Cambridge Press
21. Wardour, Sir Edward (1578–1646) of Chiswick House, Chiswick and St Martin in the Fields, Westminster, Henry Lancaster. The History of Parliament 2013
22. The Hampshire Hearth Tax Assessment 1665, Elizabeth Hughes. Hampshire County Council 1991
23. The Estate Around Chiswick House, Brentford and Chiswick Local History Society
24. East Riding of Yorkshire Unitary Authority

Chapter Seven

1. Elite Women in Ascendancy Ireland 1690–1745: Imitation and Innovation, Rachel Wilson. Boydell and Brewer, Woodbridge 2015
2. Noel, Hon. Henry (1642–77) of North Luffenham, Rutland, Eveline Cruickshanks, in The House of Commons 1660–1690, Basil Duke Henning. The History of Parliament Trust
3. Ibid
4. Publications of the Catholic Record Society Vol. VII, Bedingfeld Papers. Ballantyne, Hanson and Co. London 1909
5. Bedingfeld Letters, Oxburgh 29 February 1743. British Museum 32 fo2 f115

6. The Structure of Politics at the Accession of George III, Lewis Namier. Macmillan 1957
7. Elite Women in Ascendancy Ireland 1690–1745: Imitation and Innovation, Rachel Wilson. Boydell and Brewer, Woodbridge 2015
8. Handel: A Documentary Biography, O.E. Deutsch. Adam and Charles Black 1955
9. A General History of the Science and Practice of Music Vol. 5, Sir John Hawkins, T. Payne and sons. London 1776
10. The Palladian Revival: Lord Burlington, his Villa and Gardens at Chiswick, John Harris. Royal Academy of Arts 1994
11. The Twickenham Museum Archives
12. The Palladian Revival: Lord Burlington, his Villa and Gardens at Chiswick, John Harris. Royal Academy of Arts 1994
13. Ibid
14. Westminster School Archives
15. Historic England Archives.
16. The Works of Horatio Walpole, Earl of Orford Volume III, Horatio Walpole. Printed for G.G. and J. Robinson Paternoster Row and J. Edwards, Pall Mall London
17. Guide for Chiswick House, English Heritage
18. Westminster Public Records, National Archives
19. The Foundling Hospital archive

Chapter Eight

1. The Duke of Devonshire 1756–1757, G.M.D. Howat in The Prime Ministers Volume the First: Sir Robert Walpole to Sir Robert Peel, Herbert Van Thai. George Allen and Unwin, London
2. The Prime Ministers: From Walpole to Macmillan. Dod's Parliamentary Companion Limited. London
3. Ibid

4. In the story entitled The Final Problem. First published in 1893 in The Strand Magazine

5. Cavendish Georgiana, Duchess of Devonshire, Amanda Foreman. Oxford Dictionary of National Biography. Oxford University Press 2004

6. Memoirs of King George II January 1751–March 1754, Horace Walpole. Yale University Press 1985

7. The House of Commons 1754–1790, Lewis Namier and John Brooke. Boydell and Brewer 1985

8. Burke's Peerage, Baronetage and Knighthood of Commons 1754–1790, Lewis Namier. Boydell and Brewer 1985

9. Cavendish, Lord George Augustus Henry 1754–1834. History of Parliament Online

10. The Strange Laws of Old England, Nigel Cawthorne. Little Brown Book Group 2015

11. Secrets of Burlington Arcade, Eleana Overett in the Gothamist Magazine 2017

12. The Official Baronage of England Volume II, James Edmund Boyle. Longmans, Green and Co. London

13. Church records

14. The Complete Peerage: of a history of the House of Lords and all its members from the earliest times. Second edition, Volume 10. London 1945

15. The Prime Ministers: From Walpole to Macmillan. Dod's Parliamentary Companion Limited. London

16. The Devonshire Diary: William Cavendish, 4th Duke of Devonshire. Memoranda on State Affairs, Peter D. Brown and Karl W Schweizer. Butler and Tanner Ltd London 1982

17. The Duke of Devonshire 1756–1757, G.M.D. Howat in The Prime Ministers Volume the First: Sir Robert Walpole to Sir Robert Peel, Herbert Van Thai. George Allen and Unwin, London

18. Ibid

19. King George III, John Brooke. Panther 1974

20. Cavendish, William the 4h Duke of Devonshire, Karl Wolfgang Schweizer. Oxford Dictionary of National Biography. Oxford University Press. September 2004

21. Portland, William Henry Cavendish Bentinck, 3rd Duke of Devonshire, Ed. Hugh Chisholm. Cambridge University Press 1911

22. Ibid

23. Ibid

24. 'The Death of Duke of Portland'. The Times March 1854

25. Cavendish Bentinck, William Henry MQ of Titchfield (1768–1854). History of Parliament Online 2015

26. 'The Death of Duke of Portland'. The Times March 1854

27. The Conservation History of the Portland Vase. British Museum 2015

28. Cavendish Bentinck, William Henry MQ of Titchfield (1768–1854). History of Parliament Online 2015.

29. 'The Death of Duke of Portland'. The Times March 1854

30. Marylebone pp 242–279, The Environs of London Volume 3, County of Middlesex. T. Cadell and W. Davis, London 1795

31. The Literary Panorama Volume 10, Charles Taylor.

32. 'Imperial India'. Wwwbritishempire.co.uk 2019.

33. The London Gazette 29 January 1791

34. The London Gazette 31 July 1792

35. The London Gazette 2 April 1792

36. The London Gazette 25 March 1794

37. The London Gazette 19 July 1797

38. The London Gazette 6 January 1798

39. The London Gazette 8 January 1805

40. The London Gazette 2 March 1811

41. Press at the Crossroads in India, S.K. Aggarwal. UDH Publishing House 1988
42. Rules of India: Lord William Bentinck, Charles Demetrius Boulger. Oxford Clarendon Press 1897
43. Ibid
44. Ibid
45. The Cleveland Street Scandal, Montgomery H. Hyde. W.H. Allen. London 19763
46. The London Gazette. 7 July 1891
47. The Duke of Portland – Politics and Party in the Age of George III, David Wilkson. Palgrave Macmillan 2003
48. Bentinck, William Henry Cavendish, Henry Morse Stephens. Dictionary of National Biography. Smith, Elder and Co, London 1885
49. The Duke of Portland – Politics and Party in the Age of George III, David Wilkson. Palgrave Macmillan 2003
50. Ibid

Chapter Nine

1. Confessions of Julia Johnstone in Contradiction to the Fables of Harriette Wilson. Benbow 1825
2. An Infamous Mistress: The life, loves and family of the celebrated Grace Dalrymple Elliott, Joanne Major and Sarah Murden. Pen and Sword History 2016
3. Elliott, Grace, Courtesan and writer: Oxford Dictionary of National Biography. Oxford University Press 2004
4. Select Births and Christenings England. 1538–1975
5. Cavendish Bentinck, Lord William Charles Augustus (1780–1826), R.G. Thorne. House of Commons.
6. Survey of London Volume 40 The Grosvenor Estate in Mayfair Part 2
7. The Eldest Brother, Iris Butler. Hodder and Stoughton 1973

8. Scots Magazine. September 1816
9. The Portland (Welbeck) collection. P1 F8/9/8/1. Nottingham University Manuscripts
10. Carver MSS 63/87. Southampton University
11. Morning Chronicle. 11 May 1819
12. The Annual Register of World Events 1820
13. 'Sudden death of Lord Charles Bentinck', Sussex Advertiser. 8 May 1826
14. A Regency Elopement, Hugh Farmar. Letter dated May 1832
15. A Regency Elopement, Hugh Farmar
16. 1841 census
17. Berkshire Notes and Queries Volume, I part 3, 1891
18. Records of the Littleton Family of Teddesley and Hatherton. Staffordshire Archives

Chapter Ten

1. 1871 census
2. The Complete Peerage: Volume xii Part 1, Geoffrey White and G.E. Cokayne. St Catherine Press 1953
3. Ibid
4. The Times, 8 November 1944
5. Ibid
6. Elizabeth, The Queen Mother, Hugo Vickers. Random House 2006
7. The Times. 'Special to the New York Lady Elphinstone'. 9 February 1961
8. The Times. 'Special to New York, Elphinstone Dies'. 29 November 1955
9. The Times. 'Special to New York, Lady Elphinstone'. 9 February 1961
10. The London Gazette. 25 June 1920

11. Theirs is the Kingdom: The Wealth of the British Royal Family, Andrew Morton. Summit Books 1989

12. My Darling Buffy: The Early Life of the Queen Mother, Grania Forbes. Headline Book Publishing 1999

13. The Scotsman, 4 October 1915

14. Elizabeth, The Queen Mother, Hugo Vickers. Random House 2006

15. Burke's Peerage, Baronetage and Knightage 107th Edition

16. Ibid

17. Ibid

18. Elizabeth, The Queen Mother, Hugo Vickers. Random House 2006

19. My Darling Buffy: The Early Life of the Queen Mother, Grania Forbes. Headline Book Publishing 1999

20. Ibid

21. Elizabeth, The Queen Mother, Hugo Vickers. Random House 2006

22. Ibid

23. Ibid

24. Queen Elizabeth, The Queen Mother: The Official Biography, William Shawcross. Macmillan 2009

25. Birth record

26. Elizabeth, The Queen Mother, Hugo Vickers. Random House 2006

27. Ibid

28. The Guardian. 'A Life of Legend, Duty and Devotion' 1 April 2002

29. Queen Elizabeth, The Queen Mother: The Official Biography, William Shawcross. Macmillan 2009

30. The Telegraph. 'Royal Wedding Kate Middleton Bridal Bouquet Placed at Grave of the Unknown Warrior'. 1 May 2011

31. Queen Elizabeth, The Queen Mother: The Official Biography, William Shawcross. Macmillan 2009

32. Ibid

33. Ibid

34. Two Georges: The Making of the Modern Monarchy David Sinclair. Hodder and Stoughton 1988

35. Queen Elizabeth, The Queen Mother: The Official Biography, William Shawcross. Macmillan 2009

36. The Guardian. 'A Wicked Twinkle and a Streak of Steel', 31 March 2000

37. Queen Elizabeth, The Queen Mother: The Official Biography, William Shawcross. Macmillan 2009

38. Ibid

39. Ibid

40. Ibid

Epilogue

1. Young Elizabeth: The Making of Our Queen, Kate Williams. Orion Books. London 2012

2. Ibid

3. Ibid

4. Ibid

5. Ibid

6. Ibid

7. Ibid

8. Ibid

INDEX

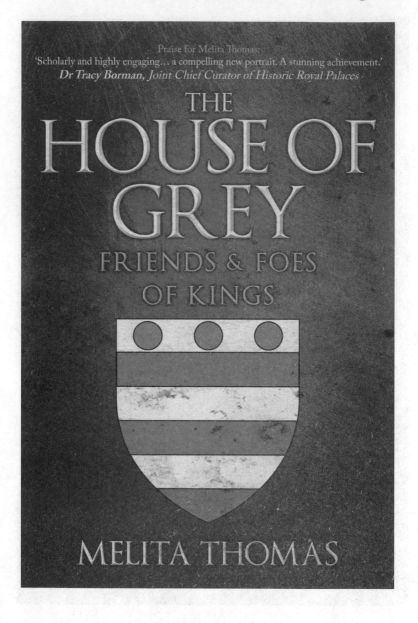